# MORAL FREEDOM

ALSO BY ALAN WOLFE

*One Nation, After All*
*Marginalized in the Middle*
*The Human Difference*
*America at Century's End*
*Whose Keeper?*
*America's Impasse*
*The Rise and Fall of the "Soviet Threat"*
*The Limits of Legitimacy*
*The Politics and Society Reader*
*The Seamy Side of Democracy*
*Political Analysis*
*An End to Political Science*

# MORAL FREEDOM

## The Impossible Idea
## That Defines the Way
## We Live Now

*Alan Wolfe*

W. W. Norton & Company
New York  London

For information about permission to reproduce selections from this book, write to Permissions, W. W. Norton & Company, Inc., 500 Fifth Avenue, New York, NY 10110

The text of this book is composed in Californian Roman with the display set in Hiroshige Book and La Figura
Composition by AW Bennett Inc.
Manufacturing by Maple-Vail Book Manufacturing Group
Book design by Dana Sloan

Library of Congress Cataloging-in-Publication Data
Wolfe, Alan, 1942–
    Moral freedom : the impossible idea that defines the way we live now / Alan Wolfe.
        p. cm.
    Includes bibliographical references and index.
    **ISBN 0-393-04843-8**
    1. Ethics—United States—Public opinion. 2. Public opinion—United States. I. Title.

BJ352.W65 2001
170'.973—dc21                                                           00-051969

W. W. Norton & Company, Inc., 500 Fifth Avenue, New York, N.Y. 10110
www.wwnorton.com

W. W. Norton & Company Ltd., 10 Coptic Street, London WC1A 1PU

1 2 3 4 5 6 7 8 9 0

# Contents

# MORAL FREEDOM

# Introduction

The way we live now is never quite good enough. It certainly was not for Anthony Trollope, whose novel of that title portrayed an 1870s England populated by gambling drunkards, financial swindlers, incompetent lovers, and scheming journalists. "Do you ever read the Bible?" one dissolute character, Lord Nidderdale, says to the novel's most reprehensible figure, Sir Felix Carbury. "Read the Bible!" Felix replies, taken aback. "Well;—yes;—no;—that is, I suppose, I used to do." It's all too much for Felix's cousin Roger, a landed gentleman, through whom Trollope speaks. "The country is changing," he tells his friend Bishop Hepworth. "It's going to the dogs, I think;—about as fast as it can go." "We build churches much faster than we used to," the Bishop replies. "Do we say our prayers in them when we have built them?" responds the squire.

Every generation finds the morality of previous generations better than its own. Trollope's satire of Victorian England may have been savage, but today the Victorians are upheld as models of moral rectitude. "Mid-Victorian England," writes the historian Gertrude Himmelfarb, "was more moral, more proper, more law-abiding than any other society in recent history." Not all Victorians, of course, were so virtuous; the intellectuals among them—Thomas and Jane Carlyle, John Stuart and Harriet Taylor Mill, George Eliot and George Henry Lewes, John and Effie Ruskin—fashioned highly unconventional marriages. That these products of chaotic personal lives nonetheless became public moralists is not so surprising, for, as Himmelfarb points out, their preoccupation with morality could not be divorced from "the irregularities and improprieties of their personal lives."

One thing can be said with some certainty about the way we live now: to find out whether our public and private lives are in accord, we survey opinion. For those who insist on the moral superiority of the good old days, this is proof enough of how low we have stooped, for how can ordinary people presume to know what is best for either their society or themselves? Yet compared to a time when the rules were set by a few and expected to be obeyed by the many, we have become more democratic, and if the voice of the people counts in determining who will fill public offices, it also provides the only acceptable account of how we understand ourselves. With social science methodology, the consumer sovereignty that dominates our economy comes to influence our morality. Instead of reading novelists and philosophers to tell us what we ought to think, we tell them instead what we actually do think.

Suppose that Americans were given the opportunity to speak at length about the issues that are central to the debate over America's moral condition. Would they, like Roger Carbury, insist that there are certain moral and religious truths so essential to the way we live that efforts to violate them can only cause moral chaos? Would they instead be so absorbed with their own needs that they emphasize rights at the cost of responsibility? Or would they be attracted to individual freedom in some areas of their lives yet persuaded of the need for authority in others? We need not, and should not, take the thoughts of ordinary Americans as the final word on our moral condition. But, as the reaction to events ranging from the O. J. Simpson trial to the shootings at Little-ton, Colorado, demonstrate, there is moral talk aplenty in America; if talk about morality were only a measure of morality, we would be hearing about a moral surplus, not a moral deficit.

Once the decision is made to allow the views of Americans themselves into the debate over their moral condition, the important question is not whether to survey but how. I will rely on two different kinds of surveys. The first is a public opinion poll I helped design in cooperation with *The New York Times Magazine*, which was carried out by the firm of Blum and Werpin Associates in March 2000. This poll asked Americans about their views on sex, money, morality, work, children, identity, and God. It tried to probe what made them happy and what caused them anxiety. It asked them to talk about their fantasies as well as their opinions. The results, published in a special issue of *The New York Times Magazine*, give us a sense of how many Americans believe that a more traditional way of life is a better way of life compared with how many understand themselves to be engaged in moral experimentation as they try to find a way to live that works for them. This poll, and others like it, can be relied upon to obtain an overall snapshot of American moral attitudes.

The goal of a public opinion poll is to represent the distribution of opinion throughout any population, including one as large as that of the United States. Polls seek to cluster opinion, to express what is typical. To gain a fuller picture of American attitudes, however, opinion should also be dispersed. Because America is as diverse as it is large, we should seek out Americans whose views, we suspect, gravitate toward the extremes. Their views may not be representative of much of anything—except themselves. But because their views are often deeply and tenaciously felt, they establish the parameters of the proper way to live, within which everyone else makes choices. We may even find that people whose views we presume to be dispersed are actually not all that dissimilar.

To supplement the *New York Times* poll, which was based on a national sample, I therefore conducted in-depth interviews with people chosen from eight distinct communities, each of which was presumed to represent a particular slice of American experience. These communities were the Castro district (and neighboring Noe Valley) in San Francisco, the epicenter of gay America; Atherton, California, home of many Silicon Valley entrepreneurs and the third richest town in America, with an average housing price of more than two million dollars; Lackland Air Force Base and its surrounding neighborhoods in San Antonio, Texas, where much of the population is Mexican-American; the University of North Carolina, Greensboro, attended mostly by first-generation college students seeking better-paying careers than their parents; Oakwood, Ohio, a well-off suburb of Dayton; Tipton, Iowa, a classic American small town of people who, while no longer working on nearby farms, are in one way or another connected to agriculture; Blue Hills, a black neighborhood in northeast Hartford, Connecticut; and Fall River, Massachusetts, a once thriving factory town that has fallen on hard times and is now attractive to recent immigrants.

In each of these communities, twenty-five randomly chosen people were interviewed, except for thirty in San Francisco. (Because these interviews were not meant to be representative of the country as a whole, I added additional respondents in Noe Valley to include lesbians; the Castro is overwhelmingly male.) To help me with the interviewing, I hired eight people—seven graduate students and one faculty member—at colleges and universities near—but, with the exception of Dayton, not in—the communities in which the interviews took place. I visited most of the communities, interviewed the interviewers, and, wherever possible, trained them by sitting in on mock interviews they conducted. Interviews were structured in the sense that a number of basic topics were to be covered, but the order in which the topics were discussed, as well as the emphasis given to them, was up to the interviewers. Most interviews took place in people's homes and lasted about one hour. All interviews were taped and transcribed. My analysis of the interviews relied on both the tapes and the transcriptions. All of those interviewed were promised confidentiality, and in reporting on what people told us, I have changed the names of all those with whom we talked. In a limited number of cases, I also changed other aspects of their identity, such as their workplace or country of origin.

The result of this research is a voluminous, and I hope unique, body of material in which Americans from all walks of life talk about the conditions for leading good and virtuous lives, not only for themselves, but for others. What people say should not be confused with their actual behavior. Especially when it comes to a subject considered as worthy as morality, we can expect that people will emphasize well-intentioned acts and downplay ill-intentioned ones; and clearly, just believing that one is a good person does not make a person good. Any full treatment of the moral condition of the United States must include measures of how people actually act, including all those indicators—from participation in bowling leagues to statistics on crime or out-of-wedlock births—that have dominated the debate over America's moral condition to this point. At the same time, no treatment of our moral state can be considered full unless it also includes data reporting on what morality means to those expected to conform to its understandings.

Moral thinking involves applying concepts derived from sources loftier than human beings—Platonic ideals, God's commandments, natural law, the categorical imperative—to the actual behavior of real people. Neither saints nor devils need ever worry whether the one fits with the other, for saints are expected to do what is right regardless of human weakness and devils can be counted on to do what is wrong despite the existence of a higher law. In its grandest forms, theology and moral philosophy concern themselves primarily with saints, seeking universal truths that appeal to the best to which humans can aspire. In its lowest forms, social science appeals to devils, describing human beings as rational egoists seeking nothing more than the pursuit of self-interest. I work on the assumption that human beings aspire to the good even if they cannot escape the bad. That is why it is important to discover not only how they act, but also the standards they hold. When it comes to moral questions, the "ought" plays as much a role as the "is."

# I. Varieties of Moral Experience

## *The Examined Life*

Sue Simpson can live anywhere she wants and in any way she pleases. An American, she grew up in England, and everything about the place made her uncomfortable. Her parents settled in a quaint village filled with beautiful Tudor homes, but the local residents, suspicious of foreigners, looked down their snobbish noses at her. At first she attended a traditionally male boarding school, where her classmates included around eight hundred boys and only ten girls. Any pleasure she might have taken in being surrounded by members of the opposite sex was quickly quashed, however, not only by the unceasing hazing she faced, but by her discovery that she had no interest in males. Ms. Simpson was delighted when she could finally return to the United States to attend Oberlin, a college that, because it "really allowed you to experiment and try stuff out," made her own coming out as a lesbian relatively painless. Upon graduation, she moved to Boston, but found that city, much like England, too confining.

Then she discovered San Francisco. Thirty-four years old, childless, living with her partner, she believes that self-knowledge is the key to personal growth, and she has devoted much of her life to furthering a yogalike method of reducing stress called the Alexander Technique. What she likes most about San Francisco is that "everything exists here. Things you cannot even imagine exist here." Americans, she believes, devote far too much of their time and attention to shaming others into social conformity, and she will have none of that. Anything goes, she says about San Francisco: "It goes on every level, intellectually, sexually, you name it."

Wendy Samuelson, like Sue Simpson, is a thirtysomething gay woman living in that city's Noe Valley neighborhood. "We put our dysfunctions right out front" is how she describes San Franciscans. "It's like, if we've got people who dress like drag queens, well, that's certainly nothing to be ashamed of." One of her close friends, she goes on, is a drag queen, although, alas for him, "he's not a very pretty girl." Ms. Samuelson cannot understand his obsession, if for no other reason than the money and time involved: "Wigs and hip pads and shoes and all this stuff, it costs. In fact, it's more serious than the Miss America Pageant." Now why, she asks herself, "does he want to go onstage and do that? It's ugly drag. He thinks he's a white black girl, which I find vaguely offensive." Still, she concludes, the whole point of living in San Francisco is to try things out. "He's busting out of his shell and he's not good at it yet, but he might be. And if this is what he wants to do, I should support him in that and just understand."

Kenny Miller also believes he has an obligation to understand and support his friends. A gay man who works as a web designer in San Francisco's Castro district, he resembles Michael Tolliver, one of the main characters in Armistead Maupin's *Tales of the City* series. Mr. Miller believes that most of the men attracted to the Castro are, like himself, "just sort of trying to figure out their lives." A friend of his is really into sadomasochism, and while Kenny at first had his reservations, he has since dropped them. "When he started explaining to me why he was doing this and what it was about and why it was really important to him," he continues, "it sort of made sense." Mr. Miller is wary of imposing limits on the right of a person to engage in explorations that might teach him more about his desires.

San Francisco is the kind of place, and these three individuals are the kind of people, that lead a number of conservatives—from public commentators such as Robert Bork, William Bennett, and Gertrude Himmelfarb to Christian activists like Paul Weyrich and Jerry Falwell—to conclude that something is seriously wrong with the moral character of American life. The most notorious events of the dreaded 1960s—the Free Speech Movement, violent resistance against the military draft, the rise of the Black Panthers, and the drug and music scene with its ground zero at Haight-Ashbury—happened either in San Francisco or across the bay in Berkeley and Oakland. In the next decade Castro Street would become the main street of Gay America, home to not only a direct confrontation with traditional American morality but also, by the end of the 1970s, a disease that seemed to vindicate the wrath of God. With a climate and scenic beauty too good to be true, San Francisco came to represent a repudiation of the self-discipline and delayed gratification that once constituted the core of both capitalist and Christian virtue. Political and theological conservatives therefore find in San Francisco everything that goes wrong when people believe that they can somehow live without obedience to firm rules of moral authority, handed down by tradition, tested by centuries of experience, and inscribed in the great moral and religious texts of the West.

For many religious and political conservatives, gay Americans are a symbol of a sexual revolution that has affected all Americans whatever their sexual orientation. Every inner-city teenager who becomes pregnant, every suburban divorce, every popular sexually saturated soap opera on television is an indication of what happens when America loses its understanding of the importance of sexual restraint and its respect for traditional sexual roles. Were America in general to become more like San Francisco in particular, they believe, its moral condition, already low to begin with, would sink to new depths. To elevate the needs of the self over obedience to God, or any commanding source of moral authority, is to become a slave to the passions and hence radically unfree.

As much as gay men and lesbians focus the attention of American conservatives, those who believe in the power and message of Jesus Christ (especially fundamentalist and born-again Christians) tend to preoccupy American liberals. Mary Masters, a forty-eight-year-old African-American living in Hartford, Connecticut, is one of the devout. When we interviewed her, she came to the door wearing a Christian T-shirt; every question we asked her turned into an illustration of how "my faith in Jesus Christ and in his word is what keeps me on the right path." She holds that the only successful ways to deal with the problems of drugs and prostitution that plague her neighborhood are through programs, such as Team Challenge, that bring Jesus' message to inner-city children. The same could be said for teenage pregnancy, a phenomenon that, in her opinion, could be substantially reduced or even avoided if a Christian sense of shame were still alive in her community. From the large number of babies that are killed each year through abortion to the hypocritical behavior of a president who attends church but also cheats on his wife, Mrs. Masters is convinced that Americans, by failing to bring Jesus into their lives the way she has, are living in an increasingly immoral society.

At the opposite end of the country—and of the economic scale—from Mrs. Masters in Hartford, we talked to Julia Fenton, a high school teacher and mother of three children living in Atherton, California. Mrs. Fenton is also a born-again Christian. "I do believe that Jesus is who he said he was and is, the risen Lord, and he's coming again" is how she began her interview with us. Like Mary Masters, Mrs. Fenton understands the world around her primarily through her faith. Economically successful, she and her husband send their children to secular schools in Silicon Valley, where they learn a certain sophistication and lessons about how to succeed in life. But Mrs. Fenton once taught in a Christian school and loved the experience. What impressed her so much about that school is that "in a culture that is so enamored, falsely so, with the individual and with the rights of the individual," a religious atmosphere "is just so helpful to help deliver people from a self-centeredness that is almost a disease."

Conservative Christians like Mary Masters and Julia Fenton worry those Americans who believe in religious tolerance and pluralism. Fundamentalist Christians, the anthropologist Vincent Crapanzano writes, lack the flexibility of mind essential to democracy. Sectarian in outlook and authoritarian in temperament, according to liberal organizations such as People for the American Way and the American Civil Liberties Union, they want to forbid other Americans from exercising their right to an abortion and to impose on public schools their particular theological orthodoxy. Conservative Christians are not moved by love of God, many leftists argue, but by hatred of those who are different, especially gay men and lesbians. We should not be fooled by their piety but instead recognize that their primary objective is the political one of supporting the most extreme candidates and ideas shaping the Republican Party.

Liberals would not worry so much about conservative Christians if they lived, as they did at previous points in American history, essentially private lives. The problem is that contemporary evangelicals, in their view, are committed to spreading the "good news" of the gospel anyway they can. As a result, the political influence of conservative Christians exceeds their actual numbers, since they tend to operate as stealth candidates, taking advantage of the apathy of others to gain positions of influence. Were more Americans to adhere to the agenda of the religious right, Americans would be in danger of losing their rights, especially their right to be different. To live up to the ideals of diversity and democracy, Americans need to avoid anything smacking of blind obedience and instead celebrate the potential of everyone to become a full human being.

Divided over whether the greatest threat to America comes from moral traditionalists or moral radicals, cultural commentators from both the right and the left find in the growing influence either of homosexuality or of conservative Christianity evidence of something seriously wrong with their country. But the moment we begin to talk to real people who identify themselves as belonging to one or the other of these categories, we begin to realize that how difficult it is to group people in such a way that puts devotion to God over here and the primacy of the self over there. Such a way of thinking assumes that these categories are mutually exclusive. There are reasons to suspect that they are not.

Born-again Christians like Mrs. Masters and Mrs. Fenton strongly affirm their Christian convictions, but both of them also affirm their own participation in the process of discovering them. Because Mrs. Masters's father was a minister who took her to church as a young child, there would be reason to believe that she inherited her faith from him. This, she tells us, is not the case, for the most crucial aspect of her belief in Jesus is that she was born a second time. It happened thirteen years before our interview with her, in 1985. At that time, she was living in sin. Something of a party girl, she stayed out late at night and drank too much. Although she continued to attend church, she now realizes that, at that time, she was not saved. She knew that although she had always read the Bible, the words meant little to her. As a result of being born again, she has changed churches, to one that takes God's word more seriously and now dedicates herself to teaching the Bible to young children on Sundays.

As she talks, it becomes clear that Mrs. Masters's faith has helped her gain control over her life. Her father had abandoned his family, leaving her mother alone with three children. Religion gave her mother the strength to leave Alabama and to find a job up north so that her daughter could go to college. Mary Masters became a nurse, married, and had one child, who is now twenty-eight. But her marriage worked out little better than that of her parents. Now that she is divorced, her faith is more important to her than ever, but it is not something that commands her to abstain from life's pleasures. "I think it's okay to go out and pamper yourself, to do nice things for yourself. I think it's okay for women to go out and get a facial, to get a manicure, to get their hair done." Mrs. Masters does these things because she is lonely and hopes that a little romance will soon enter her life. "My husband left me for another woman," she tells us. "Hey, okay, I've gotten over it. I must go on living. Right now, I'm just waiting on the Lord to send me another man." There is nothing—save, perhaps her divorce—in Mrs. Masters's life even remotely like the lives led by the San Franciscans with whom we spoke. But it would also be wrong to describe a religious believer like Mrs. Masters as a follower of moral traditions handed down to her, for, as the term "born again" so strongly suggests, she has had to make her own way through life and has called on Jesus for assistance.

The same is true of Julia Fenton. More articulate and better educated than Mary Masters, she makes it quite clear that faith is necessary, not for avoiding choices, but for making the right ones. Captivated by Alexander Solzhenitsyn's observation that the line between good and evil runs right down the middle of every human heart, she understands human nature as "a struggle between dignity and depravity." There is, she says, an "enormous, tremendous—beyond what we can imagine—capacity for dignity inherent in human beings," but there is also "an equal capacity for depravity." Since we can go one way or the other, we must direct ourselves in the right direction. "It's a very dramatic arena of choosing" is how she puts it, "and I do very much believe in human freedom of choice." We are not, she believes, prisoners of destiny. "I really, strongly believe that human beings can make a new start," she says, and she feels that she has done so in her own life. That is why she is so inspired by the story of Jean Valjean in *Les Miserables*, for if he can go through "the kinds of incredibly costly choices he made to live a virtuous life," then we who live in better times ought to be able to do so as well.

Born-again Christians emphasizing the need of the individual to choose are met halfway by pleasure-seeking Americans affirming the power of God. Sue Simpson is one of them—if in her own way. Religion was a required subject in her English boarding school, she says, and no one took it seriously, least of all her parents: "The message I got at home was that it wasn't important." Compared to their indifference to religion, she finds herself admiring her grandmother, who converted to Catholicism. Not that she is about to do the same thing, but faith, she understands, gave her grandmother the courage to go on with life after a series of tragedies. Ms. Simpson's own faith is more tied up in personal seeking than it is in organized religion, but, as she sees it, it is faith nonetheless: "Faith is good," she says. "You have to have faith in something in order to carry on." She is skeptical about organized religion because it relies on a sense of social shame to induce conformity to society's norms, but she also believes, very much like Julia Fenton, that people need to make their own choices. There is no choice involved in being gay, she points out, but there is a choice in coming out. Knowing that her sexuality made her different from society's norm, "I had to look at things more, and I had to ask some difficult questions. And in doing so, I'm sure I look at morality differently too because, obviously in some parts of the world they are going to say that I'm immoral for being gay, but I know I'm not. I've had to make an individual morality and see a more general morality in order to make my own functioning seem viable."

At one level, gay men and lesbians are challenging conventional religious and moral ideas, but, at another level, they are redefining them to account for who they are. Wendy Samuelson, the gay woman who understands her friend's need to be a drag queen, announces proudly that within a year of our interview with her she will be getting married. True, she will be marrying a woman, but for her, it is an occasion meant to celebrate the commitment she is making, and she sees no reason that she should not invite all her friends and family to witness the fact that she plans to spend the rest of her life devoted to one person. Kenny Miller, the gay man who believes that sadomasochism made sense for his friend, like a number of the gay men with whom we spoke in San Francisco, and indeed like Maupin's Michael Tolliver, grew up in the South. His Southern Baptist church, which did not allow drinking and dancing, was hardly going to be receptive to a man attracted to other men, and Mr. Miller left his religious environment behind when, at the age of nineteen, he came to terms with his homosexuality. Still, Mr. Miller appreciates the upbringing his parents and congregation gave him. "I mean," he says, "I learned how to be gracious. I learned how to treat people nicely and respect people's wishes." And both his parents and his former church have learned to respect him. When Kenny Miller was nursing his lover, David, who was suffering from brain cancer, his little church back home put his name on their prayer list—and, he adds in amazement, David was not only gay, but Jewish. Kenny's parents, who were only too happy to have him leave home as a teenager, watched the way he took care of his lover and learned to love their son all over again. Too much the typical San Francisco spiritualist to believe in sin and redemption, Kenny Miller, like Sue Simpson and Wendy Samuelson, does not consider himself a Christian, let alone one who was born again, but that does not mean he rejects religion and its ability to make sense out of the world's mysteries.

Society requires a common morality capable of softening and guiding the unchecked desires of its citizens *and* a system of rights capable of protecting minorities and enhancing the self-development of all. Yet neither conservatives nor liberals generally believe that people themselves can be trusted to play much of a role in finding the balance between those two imperatives. For conservative critics of America's moral condition like William Bennett, lessons about the proper way to live can be gleaned from the great stories that make up the Western tradition. Our job is to imbibe those stories, to memorize them and cite them, not to revise and resubmit them. We ought not to substitute for them our own accounts of what is right and wrong, for our accounts will inevitably be subjective, too much the product of a society that emphasizes the sensational on the one hand and the craving for acceptance on the other. America, from the point of view of its conservative critics, is awash in subjectivity as it is: put a camera or a microphone near anyone, and he will immediately begin to talk of his desires and wishes. The last place to turn for an understanding of what is moral and what is not is to Americans' own stories of how they ought to live.

Liberals, in positing the primacy of rights, also look with suspicion upon the views of ordinary people. In their view, majorities so rarely respect the rights of individuals who advocate unpopular views or who lead unpopular lifestyles that courts must restrain democratic exuberance. Public opinion in a democracy cannot be ignored, they believe, but neither can it be the sole criterion of what is permissible and what is forbidden. We ought no more to fashion public policy with respect to abortion or to gay rights by reading polls than we would have done had we allowed slavery to remain legal in the South because the majority of voting Southerners supported it. "The whole point of an independent judiciary," the legal scholar Laurence Tribe has written, "is to be 'anti-democratic.'" If a majority of Americans, upset at the moral condition of their country, were to support laws upholding religion in the public square or punishing disrespect for the flag, we would be correct to ignore them. Liberals, the philosopher Ronald Dworkin has argued, need to identify precisely those civil rights to which political majorities are likely to object and then "to remove those rights from majoritarian political institutions altogether."

Against both of these positions, the views of Sue Simpson on the one hand and Julia Fenton on the other tell us more than what a small number of Americans think; they also help answer the question of whose thoughts should count. There is much to be said for telling and retelling the great moral stories of our tradition, just as there will always be rights that need to be protected against majority scorn. But it is also important that a democracy take into account the stories that people tell about themselves and their own condition. Americans have their own views about human nature, God's power, political authority, virtue and vice, the content of character, and individual responsibility. They will not, we can be fairly sure, express themselves with the brilliance and clarity of Socrates, St. Paul, or Immanuel Kant. But there can also be something dignified about the ways in which people consider the conditions of themselves and their society. If they cannot offer the examined life, they can offer the experienced life. Morality for them is not likely to be based on abstractions but on consequences. Because they live with the choices they make, their views are unlikely to be frivolous—or frivolously adopted.

## Virtue and Vice in American Life

One of the most powerful works of moral philosophy published in recent decades, Alasdair MacIntyre's *After Virtue*, asks us to imagine what it would be like if a catastrophe were to leave us with scientific words like "mass" or "specific gravity" but no one knew to what physical realities they referred. "In the actual world we inhabit," he continued, "the language of morality is in the same state of grave disorder as

17

the language of natural science in the imaginary world I have described." The consequences, adds the theologian Michael Novak, threaten our existence as a nation. "In free societies," Novak writes, "the language of virtue and character is indispensable—so indispensable as to be prosaic, indeed. For how can a people profess to be capable of self-government—of government of, by, and for the people—if they cannot govern their own passions?"

MacIntyre and Novak are right to believe that the way we think and talk about virtue and vice gives us insights into general understandings of morality. Morality defines our duties to self and others. It consists in finding rules to answer such perennial questions as what is right and what is wrong, what it means to lead a good life, whether the vows we take ought to be considered eternally binding, in whom and what we should believe, whether there is justice and how its demands can be satisfied, whether we have a duty to the needy and helpless, about what we should feel a sense of shame, and from what source or sources all rules of right and proper conduct originate. Words like "virtue" and "vice" codify the wisdom found in the best that has been thought and written about morality. When we say that it is right to tell the truth or that sexual promiscuity is a vice, we are translating centuries of moral reflection into ordinary speech.

It is therefore important to discover whether Americans still think and speak in the language of virtue that Novak and MacIntyre consider so essential. We would ask our respondents, What do terms like virtue and vice mean to you? Do you try to live a virtuous life—and how? Are there any vices that are especially attractive to you? What about other people? Do you know anyone who is evil? Would you be comfortable living next door to a saint? What does it mean to say that someone is of good character? Is good character innate or does it have to be learned? If the latter, how? What is your understanding of human nature? Are people inherently sinful but nonetheless capable of doing good? Are people inherently good, even if they occasionally go bad? From what sources do you derive your understanding of the right ways to act?

In the first of the communities in which I began my interviews, Fall River, I immediately discovered that MacIntyre was right: the language of virtue is not on the tip of most Americans' tongues. The first person with whom we talked, when asked what virtue and vice meant, said, "I have no idea. I'm not a literate person." (He meant "literary.") The second person told us that a virtuous person was one who returned library books on time. Another said that being virtuous is doing what you believe in. Yet another said that she would wait until this book came out so that she could figure out the answer. We were about halfway through another interview before it became clear that the respondent did not know what the word "virtue" meant and had been too polite to ask. Not everyone with whom we spoke was made nervous or upset by the question; some, like Marlene Beaulieu, a Fall River homemaker, said that a virtue is "something that comes from within, something deep within" that makes you realize what is right and what is wrong, which is not a bad definition at all. Still, our interviews in Fall River left the impression that, when Americans consider the ways to lead a good and meaningful life, terms like "virtue" and "vice" are simply not part of their everyday vocabulary.

As we moved to other areas of the country, our respondents were a little more willing to speak about the virtues. Most of them emphasized that virtue consisted in being honest, reliable, or trustworthy. They were aware that faith, hope, and charity are considered important Christian virtues. They also insisted on the importance of good character; people can be taught the right way to behave, they generally believe, and people who act out of a sense of virtue can be role models for others. Americans appreciate the selfless quality of a Mother Teresa and certainly think of her as embodying virtuous qualities. They also have views about vice, which they tend to define as lying, cheating, using unfair advantage to get ahead, harming others, committing crimes, or acting with reckless self-indulgence. (In Greensboro, a surprising number of the students we interviewed, when asked what vice meant to them, immediately thought of the television show *Miami Vice*.) On occasion, people would use moving, even eloquent, language to express the idea that virtue consisted in satisfying the needs of others before turning to yourself; as Julia Fenton, the born-again Christian we interviewed in Atherton, put it, you ought "to love your neighbor as yourself, to think of an entire community, to risk your own world, your own security and comfort, for the sake of a higher call." Yet, despite the fact that most Americans appreciate virtue and have an intuitive sense of what the virtues are, they also were reluctant to spend too much time on the question. The concept of virtue was variously described as Victorian or old-fashioned. One of the students in Greensboro said it reminded him of the characters in a Jane Austen novel, "stuffed-up women," as he described them, whose lives he had a difficult time admiring.

There was, it should also be reported, one group of Americans who were quite knowledgeable about the meaning of virtue and vice. These were the very people in San Francisco who celebrate moral diversity in its most extreme forms. For them, terms like "virtue" and "vice" are harmful, at times even dangerous. Virtue, we were told by Sarah Lloyd, a twenty-six-year-old heterosexual business developer, has "been commandeered by people with really conservative or unrealistic agendas." Lee Hayes, a gay businessman, agreed. Gay men and lesbians, he believes, cover the spectrum of humanity from good to bad just like straight people, and those conservative Christians who attack them for lacking morality are, he believes, "hateful." The word "virtue" was variously described by our San Francisco respondents as "heavy," "pretentious," "righteous," "simplistic," "subjective," and "cartoony." One of them, Maxine Bruce, a dental hygienist, invented her own term—"paragonal"—to describe someone "who is put up on a pedestal" and "there's beams of light coming from the heavens onto them," before apologizing for going off on a tangent. After all, as she explained, virtue is "something out of common vernacular," a term that simply was not in her vocabulary. San Franciscans, it becomes clear, are reluctant to discuss virtue because they are afraid of the term "vice": an expression, many of them say, that reminds them of vice squads, thankfully obsolete in their city.

Responses such as these ought to be good news for liberals, who are generally wary of imposing one single standard of right conduct on everyone. But as reluctant as Americans may be to speak about "virtue," they show no hesitation when it comes to discussing the virtues. The virtues have come to America from many different sources: classical Greece and Rome, the Judeo-Christian tradition, aristocratic codes of honor, bourgeois conceptions of duty, and Victorian concepts of propriety. Yet whatever their origin, any list of important virtues relevant to contemporary Americans would no doubt include loyalty, self-discipline, honesty, and forgiveness. These are the living virtues, rife with implications for the complicated and unpredictable worlds in which people actually live. Because they carry such a burden, Americans have given considerable thought to what they mean, when they ought to be taken as commands, whether exceptions to them can be justified, and how people who violate them ought to treated. If Americans still adhere to the virtues, they are likely to do so in the realm of the concrete, not the realm of the abstract.

Is loyalty still appreciated in America? we would ask our respondents. At a time of high divorce rates and intense competition among business firms, are loyal people just suckers to be taken advantage of by others? Can one still be honest in America today? Or does our society preach honesty but reward dishonesty? Can politicians be trusted? Have we become so quick to explain away what used to be called sinful behavior—alcoholism, crime, infidelity—by calling it an addiction that we no longer believe in the virtues of self-control and personal responsibility? Or have we, in our desire to exercise, our tendency to become workaholics, or our concern with diet, become too self-controlled? Is sexual promiscuity a sign of bad character? Is chastity still important? Do we forgive too easily? What kinds of acts and behaviors are unforgivable? Should we shame those who refuse to obey the rules? Once we began to talk to Americans about questions such as these, our conversations with them changed dramatically; they had a great deal to say and they often expressed themselves with passion, imagination, and insight.

Morality at the beginning of the twenty-first century is best approached the way William James treated religion at the beginning of the twentieth century. All religious experience, he showed, contained common elements, yet James could also be struck by and be sensitive to the many ways belief could be expressed and practiced. To treat religion as if it were an objective reality governed by unvarying laws, rather than something people experience in the course of their everyday lives, James believed, "would be something like offering a printed bill of fare as the equivalent for a solid meal." Morality is all too often treated as if its commandments were etched in stone, commanding obedience (if one is conservative) or imposing conformity (if one is liberal). We need to discover whether Americans have an understanding of morality that makes sense to them before we decide whether it can or should make sense to others.

# II. Til Circumstances Do Us Part

## *Loyalty Lost*

Of all the virtues presumed to have been lost in America, loyalty generally takes pride of place. "Thanks to the decline of old money and the old-money ethic of civic responsibility," the historian Christopher Lasch wrote in 1995, "local and regional loyalties are sadly attenuated today." Lasch pointed the finger of blame at upwardly mobile professional elites, whom he portrayed as "turning their backs on the heartland and cultivating ties with the international market in fast-moving money, glamour, fashion, and popular culture." Not only have they contributed to a gap in local loyalties, their lifestyle contributes to a decline in national loyalty. "It is a question," Lasch wrote, "whether they think of themselves as Americans at all. Patriotism, certainly, does not rank very high in their hierarchy of values."

Lasch is not the only critic to accuse Americans of insufficient appreciation of loyalty. William Bennett's *The Book of Virtues*, a blockbuster effort to evoke a world we have presumably lost, includes loyalty as one of the virtues the author hopes we once again can gain. We are, writes the social critic Barbara Dafoe Whitehead, living in a "divorce" culture, in which loyalty to spouse and children is severely tested by the siren calls of personal self-fulfillment and liberation. The problem with our politics, according to the journalist Alan Ehrenhalt, is that we no longer have political machines or even political parties capable of imposing discipline by rewarding loyalty. By focusing too much on the bottom line, American companies, business consultant Frederick Reichheld claims, are not taking advantage of what he calls "the loyalty effect," the benefits to be obtained by being faithful to customers, employees, and investors. The British conservative Roger Scruton writes that "we can understand the Sixties as a collective revolt against loyalty, in behalf of transient and self-interested deals." When people vow to remain committed to each other until death do them part, these critics believe, something is clearly amiss when they part due to circumstances found inconvenient or unpleasant.

In one sense, there can be nothing surprising about this sense of loyalty lost, for critics have been bemoaning the lack of loyalty since America was founded. The philosopher Josiah Royce, a pragmatist (if also one who had his arguments with William James), called loyalty "the central duty amongst all duties." It not hard to understand why that way of thinking would have strong appeal in America, where loyalties have often been severely tested. My country right or wrong cannot serve as a moral injunction if, as during the Civil War, the question is which country is mine. Open societies, as we discovered during the Cold War, are indeed likely to find enemies within. Religious pluralism encourages multiple loyalties: hyphenated Americans have at least two; global capitalists often have none.

America has always had something of a peculiar relationship with loyalty, as manifested in our naïve belief that professing an oath of loyalty, upon which so many institutions insisted in the 1950s, somehow settles the question of whether one is truly loyal. Beneath our concern with loyalty is a persistent feeling that, as a people, we lack it. Loyalty cannot be a guide to right conduct in a society that worships the market in economics and liberty in politics. As virtues go, loyalty is feudal, not capitalist, in origin, evoking images of knightly chivalry on the one hand and codes of *omertà* on the other. Not only was the United States created through a singular act of disloyalty, it has been continually replenished by immigrants willing to break the bonds of family, faith, and community. A population does not expand across and fill up an entire continent if one of its most trusted virtues is loyalty to place and person. The American way of making money is premised on weaning people away from whatever they happen to be loyal to at one moment in order to win their loyalty for something else at the next: the largest mutual fund company in the United States calls itself "Fidelity," but it became so large only by breaking the attraction of its customers to old-fashioned adherence to Christmas Club accounts at local savings banks. Loyalty implies a resignation to fate that is inappropriate to an optimistic society. A loyal person is true to others, but, at least in American culture, rarely true to herself.

Anyone who professes to be shocked by the lack of loyalty Americans display to their friends, neighbors, employers, spouses, and country cannot have been paying much attention to all those other messages that tell Americans to persist by their own effort, move up the social ladder to provide for their children, breathe the free air of the country, worship as they please, exercise their right to speak, and protect themselves as best they can. Despite their professions of loyalty, Americans are adept at designing institutions exceptionally adept at discouraging it. Corporations, professional sports teams, and universities reward those most willing to move elsewhere. Young people are encouraged to serve their country through the benefits to be obtained when their tour of duty is over. Term limits give politicians no reason to be loyal to the electorate—and vice versa. Whatever the theory, the practice could not be clearer: the loyal, when not the losers, are the suckers. Loyalty holds out an ideal of human conduct begging to be violated. No other virtue is so closely associated with mixed signals than one that so stresses obedience to a collectivity in a society so committed to individuality.

### The Disloyal Corporation

Americans share with prophets of moral decline a sense that something is wrong when a society no longer values the importance of loyalty. Loyalty, after all, is not an abstract virtue. It is built into the warp and woof of the things people care about most, especially their families, friendships, and workplaces. Loyalty is a gift, and, like all gifts, it cannot be offered too often or to too many. The absence of loyalty is not some theoretical state of affairs that may cause problems in the future, but an everyday affront—a painful, disappointing, and cynicism-inducing experience against which Americans do their best to protect themselves. Loyalty abused is rarely regained.

No other institution in American life provokes such bittersweet reflections of loyalty lost as the business corporation. Quincy Simmons, who is now forty-seven years old, came to America from one of the Caribbean islands and eventually settled in the Hartford area. A small businessman who makes his living painting and remodeling, Mr. Simmons remembers that "in the old days you got a job and for both the company and the employee it would be different." He is struck by these differences between then and now. Then, "you go back home and at the same time the company will see that you get reasonable pay or whatever for the work you do. But now it goes back to greed, everybody's thinking about the money."

Mr. Simmons's views are surely influenced by the wave of downsizings that took place in his city. Known as the home of the American insurance industry, Hartford was hit hard by managed care, a rationalization of health care costs that, for a time, cut into the profits of such large insurers in the area as Aetna or the Hartford. Given the traumatic effects of economic consolidation on the region, Mr. Simmons's lament was repeated by so many of his neighbors, and in words so close to his, as to constitute a kind of folk truth. Since the big companies started merging, as Kellie Moss, a retired bank clerk, puts it, "there's no heart. It takes the heart and soul out of a company. They make more money—and it all comes down to money—but they don't take care of it. Everything is merging, merging, merging. Push this one out, buy this one out, get him out." Laverne Eaton, a fifty-five-year-old grandmother, could see the changes in her own life. She worked for the same company for thirty-two years before retiring. "They cared about us; we cared about them; we would work ourselves silly because it was important to the company, and the company always showed in kind that they cared about us," she recalls. Her son now works for the same firm, and his experiences are entirely different. For him, "there's no loyalty and people don't care about doing the job that they're hired to do."

Those who write about the declining importance of loyalty in American life generally chastise individuals for no longer believing in such old-fashioned virtues, downplaying in the process any role that powerful institutions like business corporations might play in its loss. By contrast, many of those in a community like Hartford see themselves as virtuous people trying to live by old-fashioned rules, yet unable to do so given the reward system of contemporary capitalism. Few of those with whom we spoke felt this way with quite the passion of Caroline Bowen, a thirty-seven-year-old buyer for a chemical company in nearby Fall River, Massachusetts, once a thriving mill town, but now better known for the factories sitting empty near the waterfront. Mrs. Bowen, who grew up in Fall River, is a fierce loyalist to her friends, her family, and the coparishioners of her Catholic church. Reflecting the characteristics of what sociologists call "urban villagers," she believes that corporations need to be loyal to workers, while workers have no particular obligation to be loyal to companies. That is because "companies are here, they're institutions. They're going to be around a long time." Employees, by contrast, "are living lives. Companies don't live lives." Because people have lives to lead, things happen to them: childbirth and sickness, to take just two examples. "I think that the company has to learn to adjust and be loyal to and help their employees get through those periods and in turn make them a loyal employee as well."

Mrs. Bowen's thoughts on this question were in one sense atypical; most of the others with whom we spoke think that loyalty ought to be reciprocal between the company and its workers. Still, the emphasis she placed on individuals and their experiences was in line with the views of others. For what is a company but a collection of individuals, all of whom make decisions that will have an impact on those around them? As Mrs. Bowen sees it, of course companies have to make money. Yet, "everybody from the person on the production line to the president of the company has things happening in their lives." When problems arise, which they surely will, people from all levels of the corporation ought to be able to sit down and make things work. Employees will be more productive if they feel more secure, which means that a smart company will tailor its institutional needs to the requirement of individuals, not ask the individuals who work for it to shape their lives to fit the company's agenda.

On matters involving loyalty, Americans retain a nostalgic longing for the old days; according to the *New York Times* survey on "The Way We Live Now," when presented with the proposition that their country was better off when people had a stronger attachment to where they lived, twice as many agreed than disagreed. Tipton, Iowa, a rural community in a state that has lost large numbers of people to big cities, symbolizes that lost world, and many of those with whom we spoke there were considerably more upbeat about the value of loyalty than people in Hartford and Fall River. Philip Beaty, a young archaeologist just starting his career, is, like many of his neighbors in Tipton, a strong believer in the importance of loyalty. "I feel very loyal to my employer and I know he is loyal to me," he says. "Just from the things that other people have told me that he said about me when I am not around, I can tell that he really respects me as a person and as an employee. And I respect him as an employer as well." It is not just personal experience that persuades Mr. Beaty that loyalty is alive and well in contemporary America. "Microsoft is incredibly loyal to their employees and they're doing quite well," he notes.

Yet even Philip Beaty recognizes that not all companies take the "balanced approach" to corporate loyalty he admires. With his boss, Mr. Beaty often debates the ideas of Adam Smith. "My boss makes the point that morality has nothing to do with capitalism and I think it has to exist in a moral framework. Maybe," he adds, "if you treat your employees well, you're not going to have as large a profit margin as if you only work him 39½ hours so they don't qualify for benefits, like some employers that I've worked for." Philip Beaty would define disloyalty as when a company lays off "eight thousand workers and the CEO gets a bonus because the stock jumped." Pausing for a moment, he retracts his choice of words. That's not disloyalty, he adds, "I think that's being immoral."

While people in Tipton are more optimistic about the prospects of loyalty than people in Hartford or Fall River, they nonetheless share with Mrs. Bowen the sense that loyalty matters because people matter. It is not as if loyalty were some kind of virtue standing on a pedestal before which we ought to bow in homage. Loyalty, in their view, is not just a good thing in itself, it is also good business practice, the kind of thing smart employers and employees will work out among themselves. Jason Benning, sixty years old and active in local lodges and the Methodist Church, had previously lived in a big city, Minneapolis, where he worked on the railroad. In that context, loyalty meant that he received his paycheck, no more, no less. Sure, he tells us, the company paid decent benefits, and he was glad for them. "But they really didn't give a darn." In Tipton, by contrast, Mr. Benning is an employer, not an employee. He has a small landscaping business, which employs four full-time workers and one part-time. "I mow cemeteries, and I can send them any place I need to mow and that job gets done and there's a darn good reason for it. They're honest with me and I'm honest with them." His views were similar to those of Gina Loftus, a legal secretary. Asked whether loyalty is an important ingredient of business success, she responds: "Oh yeah. I think the better you treat the employees and the better the employees treat their employer . . . that's when it does prosper. Just myself, I've worked in this law firm I'm in for ten years, and we've all grown in the business together. I guess the better I do, the better they do, and it all just kind of rolls around." For someone like Mrs. Loftus, the cutthroat world of a New York law firm, in which potential partners compete with one another furiously for billing hours, is as far away as China or Japan.

This emphasis that so many Americans place on the personal side of business practice runs up against the way most economists and defenders of business treat the issue of corporate loyalty. Institutions are not, in the view of the latter, like people, subject to emotions, possessing a potential for empathy, and capable of dialogue. Rather, corporations, to be efficient, must act rationally, dedicated to doing whatever is best for stockholders, irrespective of the impact of those decisions on those, like employees, who have a personal stake in the company's future. Indeed, from this perspective, the only issue raised by downsizing is why companies allowed themselves the luxury of taking on so much "fat" (in the form of unproductive workers) in the first place. As free market economists see the world, a company forced to let employees go, no matter how loyal those employees may have been in the past, is just responding to the impersonal logic of the market. Market discipline leaves companies no choice but to act efficiently, whatever the spill-over effects may be with respect to loyalty.

This way of thinking rubs many Americans the wrong way. It did not escape the notice of Donna Teele, an assistant attorney general for the state of Connecticut and the very epitome of African-American middle-class success, that the Hartford Insurance Company cited efficiency as its justification for laying off workers, only to hire them back a few years later when the economy of the region once again picked up. Clearly, she felt, the company was doing the easy thing rather than the right thing when it made its initial decision. Had it been just a bit more thoughtful, it could have avoided adding to its already considerable reputation for disloyalty. Even when companies have to take actions that hurt, people will often retain their faith in loyalty so long as they think the company acted fairly and with due regard for the people involved. It is not downsizing that bothers them. It is the aloof, and often imperious, ways in which companies carry it out. Henry Muller, an engineering professor who once worked in the private sector in Dayton, Ohio, recalls the time his company froze the salaries of its middle-level employees for two years. But during that time the company's president, who had engineered the sale of some of the firm's divisions, saw his salary more than triple from one year to the next as incentive clauses in his contract were activated. Before that happened, Mr. Muller sided with management on most issues when discussing the firm's business with his friends and co-workers. These days, he is not so sure. As he sees it, the problem is not that Americans no longer believe in a virtue like loyalty. They sometimes believe in it so much that they go into a state of shock when the firms for which they work no longer seem to practice it.

"How can an individual be loyal to an institution," asks Judy Wasserman, an administrator at a local campus of the state university near Fall River, "if an institution isn't loyal to them?" It is a good question. Many observers of the new corporate realities dominating American society are persuaded that there is no easy answer to it. Among them is the sociologist Richard Sennett. Analyzing the short-term perspective of many American corporations, he writes that "'no long term' is a principle which corrodes trust, loyalty, and mutual commitment." Sennett's comment was prompted by an encounter with a man he calls Rico, the son of a janitor he had interviewed for a book a quarter of a century previously. But the actual story told by Rico suggests that even as loyalty is being corroded by American business practice, people want to make the best of the situation facing them. Rather than blame the company for downsizing him out of a job, he instead emphasized his own autonomy: "I make my own choices," Rico told Sennett. "I take full responsibility for moving around so much."

Sennett interprets Rico's comments as reflecting "a somewhat fatalistic, old-world sense of people being born into a particular class or condition of life and making the very best of what is possible within those constraints." But Rico's comments can also be understood as anything but fatalistic. When a firm justifies its decision to lay off loyal employees on the grounds that market competition leaves it no choice, it is essentially saying that business activity, usually justified in the name of market freedom, is outside the control of real people. But when someone like Rico insists that he is making his own choices, irrespective of what his company may be doing, he is claiming for himself the very freedom to choose that the companies insist they no longer have.

There is, therefore, a surprising benefit that emerges out of what Gary Radzikowski, a retired chemist in Dayton, calls "the hard, cruel world of business." No longer willing or able to put into practice what so many of our respondents despairingly call "blind loyalty," they decide for themselves how and what the requirements of loyalty are. That is the moral axiom followed by Betty Mann, an actress and acting teacher in San Francisco: "I always felt I did the best job for my employer no matter what, because I was raised to have a fairly high degree of personal integrity about work. So the loyalty was still to myself and my own belief system, but the benefits still accrued to the employer. I'm not sure they knew the difference." The golden rule of the old days—whatever else, be loyal—now comes with an upgrade: give to others, but never so much that you leave nothing for yourself.

Hartford's Daryl Sims, a computer programmer, is one of those who feels that under current workplace conditions he can no longer follow the rule of being loyal at all times. At first, Mr. Sims sounds like a pessimist about the state of loyalty in America these days. "As we've gotten into bigger and bigger companies and corporations and the almighty dollar is the king," he says in ways so similar to his neighbors, "loyalty is eroded because the idea of an employee staying with an employer for a lifetime has dwindled." The results are clear. "I think that in a person's lifetime, you're going to have anywhere from five to eight different employers. Knowing that, you've got to look out for yourself." The more he speaks, however, the more clear it becomes that Mr. Sims does not view this as all bad. In contrast to those who might view this lack of loyalty as a vice—looking out for yourself certainly suggests being disloyal to others—he views it as an opportunity, and not just for himself, but also for his company. Mr. Sims knows that companies lay off workers, even just before their retirement, in order to cut down costs, but, he feels, that is just the way it is. And if the company puts its self-interest first, so can he. Mr. Sims worked at a firm in a job that increasingly grew sour to him, and he was glad that he could move elsewhere. "It wasn't like I was being disloyal to them," says this forty-three-year-old divorced man. "I was just looking out for my future." These days, workers and companies both want more flexibility to find what's right for themselves, and on the whole, he believes, that might be the best way to organize the economy.

Working for a big company has become a little like serial

monogamy: you are faithful for a while, and in your own fashion, until another opportunity comes along. Fall River's Charles Placon works for a linen rental service. He feels that "a person has to become accustomed to feeling like a bouncing ball" in the present economic environment. Asked about his own approach to loyalty, he put his philosophy this way: "I'm loyal, but I still send out résumés." His neighbor Patrick Lonergan, a counselor for a smoking cessation program, adds: "I think what a person should do in an employer-employee relationship is their job, and nothing more. If they can get a better opportunity, they should grab it and not stay with the company because they've been there for a number of years. I just don't think that works at all." San Francisco's Carl Lamb, who works in one of the many Internet start-up companies in his region, says that "one owes zero loyalty to one's employer," before amending his comment to the proposition that "one owes loyalty to one's employer as one is treated." Even when people are not looking over their shoulder for other jobs, they ought to put up boundaries around themselves, argues Fall River's Kelly Houston. Her volunteer work in a hospice emphasizes teamwork and cooperation, and as much as she believes in those ideals, she also feels that they can be used to exploit her willingness to give to others. Under such circumstances, keeping your distance does not mean you are disloyal. It means instead protecting yourself so that when you offer your loyalty, it is offered sincerely.

No matter how attractive the idea of serial monogamy may seem to those faithful in marriage, it is not always easy to practice, and much the same could be said for the new rules of corporate loyalty. To follow them well, you have to engage in a kind of fine-tuned moral accounting designed to help you recognize when loyalty to the company is and is not appropriate. Matthew Moore, a Hartford aircraft mechanic, thought it was all about making distinctions. You can be more loyal in a small company than a big one, he told us. Loyalty to a privately owned company is more important than loyalty to a publicly owned one.

Younger workers have less reason to be loyal, given the uncertainties of the future, than older ones. On this last point, Mr. Moore has much to say. He asks us to imagine two groups of workers. For those in Group A, the younger workers, "the definition of success now is that my retirement plan is secured before age thirty-six." The only proper kind of faith for them, he believes, is faith in themselves. Mr. Moore defines Group B as the Social Security generation. People in this group still have faith in others, especially their company and the government. Which group is better off? Mr. Moore—who is fifty-six years old—clearly prefers the greater appreciation for loyalty among his own generation. Still, he is enough of a realist to recognize that there are advantages either way and he is keeping an open mind: "I've been watching, and I haven't come to a conclusion."

Not only are people put in the position of deciding when loyalty to the company takes precedence over loyalty to the self, they also have to balance workplace loyalties with their loyalties to other people. Suppose you are in the situation faced by Fall River's Margaret Adams, the very model of the high school English teacher she is. Her union considered going out on strike, which she thought was a bad idea. The strike vote was public, forcing her to stand up in front of her co-workers and vote with management. When the strike took place, she had to decide whether she should cross the picket line. Mrs. Adams considers herself a very loyal person; the problem was that there were too many people to whom she was being asked to be loyal. (She eventually decided to honor the picket line, although, as she puts it, "I still don't know what the right thing was to have done.") A similar conflict of loyalties was faced by a San Antonio engineer named Lou Lamkin. He hates the fact that his company, an old-fashioned, paternalistic one that emphasizes loyalty, makes so many demands on his time. After all, he has obligations to his wife and children as well as those to his job. Because of the company's insistence on loyalty, "we can't make any plans because you never know when I'm going to have to hit the road." Mr. Lamkin sent his boss an e-mail in which he said that he owed the firm his loyalty, but only in a limited way. "I will do my job to the best of my ability," he told them, "but I was not going to sacrifice my family life for the good of the company." He knows that this will get him in some trouble, and in fact, his message was not well received. Hopefully he will be able to negotiate a job in a different division in which his wishes will be respected. If not, he may have to find another job.

Nowhere in the United States is the principle of being in charge of your own loyalty more firmly enshrined than in those areas of Northern California that are home to Internet start-up companies. To be sure, start-up companies "succeed because they have an intense amount of loyalty," we were told by Atherton's John Howard, a mortgage banker who has started two companies. "The company is small, they're very relaxed, there's not a lot of management structure, they don't wear coats and ties," and "they sit around in a garage or places where they let dogs come to work." Under those conditions, employees tend to be fiercely loyal, working long hours for little money, in the hopes of a future payoff. But there is also a process of natural attrition that sets in, Mr. Howard continues. "Unfortunately, as these companies grow, the focus on management, materialism, getting back the stock options—all that comes to the fore," and that is when loyalty begins to disappear. Mr. Howard is not pleased by the emergence of what he calls "temporary loyalty." Yet he also recognizes that the days of lifetime loyalty with one company are gone for good, and that is probably as it should be.

Other successful businessmen in Atherton had few, if any, of Mr. Howard's regrets about the loss of loyalty in the workplace. The atmosphere in Silicon Valley, many of its residents told us, is the direct opposite of what they take to be the Japanese model of working for one company for one's entire life. Young, talented, in demand, entrepreneurial, the successful engineers and businessmen with whom we spoke in

Atherton live in a postloyalty world. In the past, says Jim Crowley, the chairman of a money management company, firms tended to be paternalistic; he doesn't think those kinds of companies were "mature" because they treated employees in a "parent-child relationship" that did not welcome individual growth on the part of those who worked for them. Henry Lo, the son of immigrants from China who came to the United States in 1943, is an unabashed enthusiast for the new world he sees being created in Silicon Valley. "There is no more loyalty," he says, "and there probably shouldn't be." Mr. Lo thinks that the free agency system developed in professional sports is the right model for this new industry. Employees with a skill ought to sell their services to the highest bidder, putting enough money away so that they can be free to take the risks of grasping new opportunities when they arise. His extended time horizon is about two decades long. People ought to work as hard as they can for that amount of time and then devote their lives to whatever interests they develop along the way.

As Mr. Lo talks, and as we compare his remarks with others around the country, it becomes clear that while some people fear change, others enthusiastically welcome it. Atherton entrepreneurs, as one might expect, are in the latter category. "The world is incredibly dynamic. Nothing stays the same," as Mr. Crowley puts it. Atherton's Timothy Johnson, who has been very successful as an economic consultant, says that he and his wife are people who "embrace change. We think change is good." There cannot be a rule insisting on the importance of loyalty because, in this dynamic world of constant change, there are no rules—or at least no fixed rules.

Still, a lack of fixed rules does not mean the absence of any rules. Loyalty in Silicon Valley needs to be understood as an evolving practice, something that emerges out of the experiences of people engaged in finding their own avenues of cooperation. As problematic as such a concept might be for old-fashioned conceptions of loyalty, it does have its advantages. One is that it rewards those individuals who deserve to be rewarded. Calvin Lister, an Atherton software executive, believes that "we really run our company as a meritocracy." As such, loyalty ought to be thought of as a quid pro quo arrangement: good workers who are efficient earn loyalty from his company, and hence his company is obligated to extend loyalty to them in return. That's why he believes that even in Silicon Valley, it would be wrong to conclude that everyone is a free agent looking out for himself. On the contrary, earned loyalty is better than blind loyalty, because it allows employers and employees, all of whom know that they owe their jobs to their own abilities, to treat one another with respect. Like many executives in the region, Mr. Lister has trouble finding employees who can afford to live near his firm. Recently, his secretary approached him and said that it had become impossible for her to continue her commute and she wanted to relocate to a more convenient office in the company. Although not wanting to lose her services, he recognizes that her past loyalty has earned her this favor and he plans to help her with her transfer.

One of the oldest ideas involving loyalty is the nepotistic notion of putting members of one's own family first. Nepotism stands in sharp contrast to the principle of merit emphasized by Mr. Lister, for loyalty to blood was considered a higher loyalty than reward for accomplishment. That way of thinking has little place in Silicon Valley, even among those who came there from more traditional environments. David Wong, an immigrant from China, recalls the time he was able to use his connections to get one of his cousins out of China and into Canada. Putting family first, Mr. Wong set him up in business and give him 30 percent of a company. "I mean you can't ask for anything more," he continues, "and then the next thing I found is that he wasn't loyal to me. He's been working with other people and trying to dismantle my things, siphoning off funds and all that. Well, the first thing I did was to fire him." Mr. Wong's message was clear: if loyalty is earned by good people, it can also be lost by bad ones.

The redefinitions of loyalty taking place in Silicon Valley are especially interesting because this is a region where loyalty takes on tremendous practical importance. The path to riches among Internet companies can be found inside the brains of the individuals who develop the ideas that make money. Intellectual copyright law gives firms some protection against the prospect of disloyal employees' taking their ideas to other companies, but because there is no foolproof way to prevent individuals from leaving one firm for another, there are limits to reliance on the threat of litigation to discourage disloyalty. Companies and employees are better off treating individuals as free agents in charge of their own fate and assuming that such individuals will make loyalty a personal priority, many of our California respondents insisted. The kind of massive downsizing experienced in a place like Hartford would be quite counterproductive in Silicon Valley, since the last thing competitive firms want is to manifest a lack of trust in their employees for fear that the latter will return the favor. In return, employees, free to move anywhere they want, also need to put limits on how disloyal they will be. Timothy Johnson is well aware of these new realities. On the one hand, there are always opportunities beckoning. On the other hand, he believes that so long as a company offers "a fair day's work for a fair day's pay," then its employees know that "you don't sabotage things, you don't steal secrets."

Whether or not Silicon Valley constitutes the future of the American workplace, it suggests where America may be headed on the loyalty question. We can see this reflected in the comments of the students with whom we spoke in Greensboro. Almost none of them believe that they will wind up working for the same company for most of their lives. Are employers loyal to their employees? we asked Curtis Jackson. "Shit no, hell no, that's ludicrous" is his prompt response. "When you can't produce, you're toast." Not everyone is quite as blunt as Mr. Jackson, but almost all of them believe that, as Joseph Anderson, a student majoring in business, puts it, "we have a market economy these days, it's very competitive, and I guess you either eat somebody or get eaten." As much as this may be a fact of life, it also just does not seem right to him. Echoing, whether consciously or not, biblical language, he adds, "If you buy a company and they have fifty thousand employees and you lay off thirty thousand, then what exactly have you gained?"

Obviously, if America returned to the days when monopolistic firms could offer lifetime employment, Americans would no longer need to think of themselves as responsible for figuring out the conundrums of loyalty. But a highly competitive economy cannot make do with a highly old-fashioned sense of loyalty. When firms need the flexibility to adjust to changing market conditions, employees will insist on the need to adjust to changing moral conditions. "It's difficult to stay loyal," we were told by Ben Farrell, a loan officer in Fall River, "when you displace workers and open factories abroad." But, like so many of those with whom we spoke, Mr. Farrell believes that workers should turn this around to their own advantage. "I don't consider that really a form of selfishness," he adds. "You know, it's not necessarily something that's wrong." What cultural critics bemoan as the loss of this one particular virtue is also lamented by many Americans. But it is not in their character to sit around and cry over their losses. As much as they might prefer to live in a world in which loyalty between employers and employees could be taken for granted, they will do their best, as Ben Farrell puts it, to "make whatever situation is best for them."

### The Divorce Option

Families are not societies. Formed by a union of two adults unrelated by blood but united in love, they stand in sharp contrast to the impersonal ties that link together strangers for the purpose of facilitating social cooperation. Small in size, families look inward toward self-protection, while societies, huge in scope, have foreign policies and, on occasion, venture into outer space. Still, for all the differences between them, it is something of a truism that the fates of family and society will be interconnected. Products of strong and loving families, we believe, make better citizens. Unstable, disruptive, and unhealthy families cannot be good, neither for their members nor for others around them.

The fate of families, always at the center of our concerns, is particularly of concern when loyalty is viewed more as practice than as prescription. Americans have learned from their experiences in the workplace that old-fashioned ideas of unquestioned loyalty no longer are encouraged by their employers and are no longer valued by themselves. This discovery intensifies the difficulties of being loyal in a society that places little value on the "death do us part" variety. For if loyalty is learned, most of the learning will take place in families. And of all social institutions, families are the most strengthened or weakened by the everyday behaviors and decisions of their members. Labor unions and business corporations experience the problem of the free rider—the individual who receives the benefits offered by the institution without making a commitment to its practices—but not families, or at least not healthy and mutually satisfying ones. Will people who have learned lessons of disloyalty in the workplace apply what they have learned to their family life? If they do, can an institution as fragile as the family possibly survive?

In theory, Americans expect to be loyal to their spouses; according to the *New York Times* poll on "The Way We Live Now," 86 percent said that, if they got married today, they would expect to be married for the rest of their lives. Yet in practice, divorce rates increased dramatically from 1960 to 1980, before leveling off at a relatively high rate. One therefore has to wonder if the lessons taught at the workplace—where most Americans spend most of their days and earn the income that determines how they shall live—have an impact on the lessons learned at home. Some of our respondents were indeed quick to point out ways that the rules which structure interaction in the former arena can be applied in the latter. San Francisco's Sarah Lloyd has what she describes as a "blissful" relationship with a man. At the same time, she rejects the notion of a marriage vow and the commitments of loyalty it entails. In the world in which she travels, there simply are not very many married couples—and that's the way she likes it. Adultery, in her view, is not a good thing, for if it takes place, something is probably wrong with the relationship. But it's not necessarily a bad thing either, if two people have a way of trusting in each other so that the nonsexual aspects of their relationship are preserved. Ideals of marital loyalty convey to her a picture of a "bigger figure who is more powerful and charismatic, and the little faithful lapdog" following him around. That is just too passive an ideal for her. Searching for a better way of thinking about the problem of commitment, she invokes the typical Silicon Valley workplace with which she has become familiar: "Loyalty is about teams . . . that's reciprocal loyalty. It's not a hierarchical power structure." The top-down organization is a thing of the past, and, if Ms. Lloyd could have her way, so would the top-down marriage.

Drawing upon experience in the business world as a way of explaining what happens in family life was especially common among the Silicon Valley entrepreneurs with whom we spoke. Henry Lo offers one example. When asked about marital loyalty, he approaches the question with the same kind of systems mentality he applies at the workplace: "I guess I am sort of an engineer at this thing" is how he puts it. "Is it irretrievably broken or can you patch it up? Was there a basis for the marriage in the first place? Is there a basis for working together as part of a team to move ahead from where you are and ignore the past?" Jim Crowley offers another. A man with a well-developed philosophy that explains success in business based not on the organizational character of the firm but on the personal attributes of the people who work for it, he applies the same lessons to marriage. "I'm much more interested in the internally driven responses to things than those are done externally," he says. When people come to him for investment advice, he tells them to pursue their passion. He has succeeded in business, he believes, because of his genuine love for taking risks. For much the same reason, a marriage will work when people find that sense of mission inside themselves. His own divorce was the result of what he calls "a starter marriage," a venture into family life that did not succeed because he lacked the passion for it. Older and wiser now, he feels he has made the commitments to his present marriage that will enable it to last. The point is that there is no one-size-fits-all model for marriages. Some people will discover that "the cost-benefit doesn't seem to work anymore" and will seek a divorce. Others will grow internally because they are able to resist the temptations and to stick with what they have.

Silicon Valley has made a religion out of opportunity, and it is this same belief in opportunity that shapes how Americans view marital commitments in other places. Dayton's Krystina Romanowski, one of the most energetic and passionate of our respondents, describes herself as a "DNA coded" Republican, a firm believer in fiscal responsibility, small government, and low taxes. She traces her deeply conservative politics to the fact that she, like many Polish-Americans, had firsthand experience with a Communist regime. An attorney, Ms. Romanowski represents undocumented aliens anxious to remain in the United States. It's not always work that teaches loyalty to the law. If she knows, for example, that a charge of drunk driving against one of her clients could result in a deportation, she will appeal to the judge to exercise discretion, even if such an exception might step "outside the boundaries of the specified statute that the legislature of Ohio put up." Ms. Romanowski has been married three times and has two daughters. "Culturally, I had nothing to relate to with those husbands," she says of her first two. "Nothing. One, he tried to have me as a trophy wife, the other one was a shotgun wedding because we got pregnant." As she speaks, Ms. Romanowski recognizes that her ability to operate in what she calls the "gray areas" of her law practice influences how she treats the question of marital commitments. A libertarian in business, she is something of a libertarian in marriage. "I don't look at the divorce rate as necessarily a bad thing or as a demoralizing thing," she says. Her girls are beautiful, she gets along with their fathers, and her quest for the right man has taken her "back to my roots," since now "I have a man I can speak Polish to." Marriage, she admits, "is scary as hell." But, then again, "I don't like anybody to tell me what to do."

Politically speaking, Kenny Miller, the gay man in San Francisco who understands why one of his friends would be into sadomasochism, lives in a different universe than Krystina Romanowski. Mr. Miller worked for one of the country's leading drug companies before taking a job in a media firm. He does not know what loyalty in the workplace means, especially when he worked in the pharmaceutical industry. His firm was a "huge company. You don't know anyone, so how can you feel loyalty? Do you feel loyalty to this big granite building? Do you feel loyalty to a product line?" When David, his lover, developed a brain tumor that destroyed his body's ability to manufacture testosterone, the disease created havoc in their sex life. Was he faithful to David during this period? No, he was not. Nor did he feel all that bad about it. "I'm not totally sold on the idea of monogamy," Mr. Miller tells us. "If one of us strays, is that a bad thing? I mean, we live in San Francisco. We're gay men. A lot of the stereotypes about gay men are true, you know? Eyes wander." Krystina Romanowski may be a Republican conservative and Kenny Miller a typical San Francisco left-winger, but their attitudes toward loyalty in relationships are remarkably similar. Both understand themselves as thoroughly modern Americans. Living in a society in which loyalty is not generally respected, they have not made a vow of loyalty to one sexual partner central to the way they lead their lives.

Critics of America's divorce culture worry about the widespread breakdown of marital loyalty. Barbara Dafoe Whitehead believes that our willingness to contemplate marital breakup is due to a sense that Americans "became more acutely conscious of their responsibility to attend to their own individual needs and interests." The views of Sarah Lloyd, Krystina Romanowski, Henry Lo, Jim Crowley, and Kenny Miller confirm her way of discussing the issue. And they were by no means alone. "Why should you eat oatmeal when you want cake?" Hartford's Harold White, who is divorced, asks us rhetorically. "Why should you stay in that marriage if you know that it's not going to work and your kids are going to be miserable?" Hugh Heston, who works in a quarry near Tipton, Iowa, is also divorced—and anything but miserable about it. Not only is he happier in his new marriage, he is sure that his former wife, who lives in a nearby town, is also much happier in hers. Even his two children from his first marriage, he believes, benefited from their decision. Mr. Heston listens to Dr. Laura Schlessinger, the radio therapist who emphasizes the need for firm rules in life, but he is unwilling to follow her advice: "Sometimes I don't believe that it is right to keep two unhappy people together if it's going to be damaging to the kids."

Should we, then, worry that family life is indeed an arena in which a less than strict approach to loyalty can have pernicious consequences? Before we begin to do so, it is important to remember that not all Americans have become libertarian with respect to the marriage vow. Lou Anne Mobley, a homemaker in San Antonio, believes that she and her husband, who married young, were too self-absorbed to be really aware of what their marital commitment meant. The first five years of their marriage were painful to both of them. Mrs. Mobley was helped by a visit to a pastor who told her that God was aware of her difficulties and would help her find a way past them. That gave her the confidence to try to work things out. "We have such a joy now," she says, "that sometimes I wake up and say: 'God, I must be one of the happiest people on earth.' We laugh, we have friendship, I give to him, he gives to me, but it all comes from working past that point of selfishness, which is what people won't do. They won't go through the fire to get to the other side." Not only has her marriage worked out, Mrs. Mobley believes, so has her life in general. "We're striving to live the same moral standards," she says of her family, "the same goals in what we're doing with our life, to raise our kids well and to impact the community for good." Without that common bond, she knows that her life would not be as rich as it is.

Even people whose lives have not been as blessed as that of Mrs. Mobley share this traditional sense of marital loyalty. One of them is Mary Masters, the born-again Christian working as a nurse in Hartford who hopes that the Lord will someday bring her a man. Loyalty, Mrs. Masters believes, is a gift from God. Men who do not act as good husbands or good fathers are doing more than harming their families, although they are doing that. They are also rejecting God's gift. Good men, by contrast, "realize that the woman is part of them. They're part of the woman. When you marry, the Bible says that you are no longer two. You come together and are one." To separate from your wife, in that sense, is to separate from yourself. In Mrs. Masters's view, women are also under an obligation to remain loyal. This does not mean that they have to give up on careers. "I don't mean being subservient," she says, describing the model of a good wife. "But they are willing to be obedient Christian women. They're willing to work with their men, support their men, take care of their men, you know." Mrs. Masters's strong feelings on loyalty are no doubt due to the hurt of having been abandoned by her husband. "I think trust and loyalty between a man and a woman are more important than even the best sex could ever be because when you can trust your husband and he's your friend, he's your lover, he listens to you, he supports you"—those are the things that really matter.

It has become something of a cliché among sociobiologists that women are more likely to be committed to old-fashioned ideals of loyalty, while men are driven by some deep evolutionary programming to sleep around. Lest the reader come away thinking that the comments of our respondents prove the point, a number of the men with whom we spoke made clear their sense of marital commitment. Henry Muller, the Dayton professor of mechanical engineering, thinks he would have to be "off his rocker" ever to act like Bill Clinton or O. J. Simpson. He tells a story that, he insists, did not happen to him but to someone he knows. This man was on a business trip, traveling with a woman from the same company. Put in rooms next to each other at a Holiday Inn, she invited him in for a drink. As soon as she made an advance, the man pulled out his wallet and showed pictures of his kids and then got out as fast as he could. "He was just not going to be in that situation," Mr. Muller concludes. "The temptation was there. And he could have acted on it. But he certainly chose the right way to go simply because of ethical standards—and that the long-term consequences would have been disastrous."

Others among our male respondents see a connection between loyalty at work and loyalty in personal relationships. In contrast to Kenny Miller, the gay man who believes that stereotypes of gay lifestyles contain a ring of truth, Lee Hayes, who owns a successful manufacturing company that employs a number of lesbians and gay men, tells us that "loyalty is very important to me." Most of those who work in his company have been there over ten years, he says proudly, and, because of the culture of solidarity he believes has grown up around AIDS, he goes out of his way to give them latitude and to treat them with respect. He follows the same rule in his emotional life. Recently separated from his lover, he made it a point never to cheat on him. And if his lover had had an affair, he could have forgiven him, but not if he had been dishonest about it. So many of his friends have died that he feels a passionate connection with those, like him, lucky enough to survive. "We're in this together and it makes you want to support each other," he says of both being gay and being at risk for AIDS. "We know we're a minority, so yeah, I think it bonds you."

Despite the fact that ideals of marital loyalty still flourish in America, even among some of those prohibited by law because of their sexual orientation from being married, there is also good reason to think that those who worry about a culture of divorce have just cause. Of all social institutions, families are closest to the individuals who form them. So basic, so seemingly natural, is the family that we often think it constitutes a building block upon which all other social institutions rely. But as ubiquitous as families are, they are also, as social institutions, far more fragile than other institutions like business corporations. As such, families are quite vulnerable to the economy in which they strive to flourish; in Iowa, for example, one of the regions in which we conducted interviews, a thorough study of the farm crisis of the 1980s demonstrated that "economic stress may exact a heavy toll in marriage." That stress, moreover, was not just economic but emotional; difficult times make it difficult for families to sustain the interpersonal solidarities that enable them to function properly. We like to believe that the loyalty taught in families will carry over everywhere else. More likely, the emphasis on putting one's own interest first taught in the economy will carry over into the family.

When business firms treat workers as disposable commodities, the last thing on their minds is that their actions could have an effect on the divorce rate. Americans started divorcing one another long before the current wave of corporate downsizing, but there is nonetheless a relationship between workplace disloyalty and marital disloyalty that runs throughout the comments of our respondents. The moral maxim learned in the world of business comes down to the proposition that if you can no longer trust your company, you have no choice but to trust yourself. Because America is a business civilization, one in which every institution finds itself conforming to the logic of profit even when it has another ostensible purpose, it is an easy temptation for people to apply the same moral maxim to the family. The American divorce rate is high for a reason.

An instinct toward self-protection may make a good deal of sense in the firm because corporations, as so many of our respondents insisted, are so impersonal and unfeeling in their approach to loyalty that one would be a fool to put one's trust in their word. But precisely because they make a distinction between institutions and people, Americans cannot easily apply the same way of thinking to the family. One can admire Americans for their ingrained skepticism about the larger world, but that same attitude in the intimate world conveys a striking failure of nerve. Loyalty can indeed be a reserved seat for suckers, but critics of America's divorce culture are right to point out that it can also be a ticket to a world of fulfillment and purpose. Understanding this, Americans recognize that divorce symbolizes a society in which loyalty is no longer taken as seriously as it might be. At the same time, they also recognize that family life has become too complicated to be organized by the principle that divorce is always wrong.

The real story about America's divorce culture, therefore, is not that people no longer believe in marital commitments. It is instead that they take the marriage vow seriously, but that they also take seriously other vows that may come into conflict with it. The way this takes place can be illustrated by examining the accounts of two groups of Americans whose commitments to marriage as an institution are strong and sincere. One such group is composed of those who think that divorce should be considered only in the most extreme cases. The other can be found among those young people in our sample who, themselves the product of divorced homes, are determined to avoid divorce in their own lives. Despite their commitments to marriage, both groups find themselves arguing that the divorce option must be kept open in some form or another.

Many of those with whom we talked made it quite clear that they were anything but frivolous in the way they thought about divorce. Consider Warren Johnson, a Tipton plumber. His parents once split up, and he spent a lot of time with his grandmother. "That was a really hard time in my life," he now recalls. "I hated life in general when that happened because there was nothing I could do about it. It was all so negative. There was always someone crying, someone arguing, someone fighting." When Mr. Johnson's parents finally got back together, not only did his childhood improve, he found himself with a new brother. The experience was such a powerful one in his life that when he and his wife began to have marital problems, his first instinct was to do everything in his power to protect his young son. He and his wife called in their pastor for help and went to church frequently, but none of it seemed to matter. Finally, his marriage broke up. "I remember driving down late," he tells us, "and my son had left with my wife, who had packed her stuff. It was a very sad moment in my life and I cried for a long time, because I was doing to him exactly what I promised never to do to him." None of this makes Mr. Johnson feel proud. His son turned out to do okay in life, but, he says of both incidents, "it was as evil a thing that has ever happened to me or that I had to do to somebody. It's a very evil thing to make somebody feel something you don't want them to feel."

Mr. Johnson's words remind us the American commitment to divorce is not a sign of hedonism run amok. Americans think hard about the conditions under which divorce is or is not justified. Antonia Gomez, a San Antonio homemaker, remembers the time her parents began to hurt each other—and their children. When she was in the ninth grade, her father, an alcoholic, hurt her mother once too often; unable to take the abuse, she left him. "I remember telling my mother and my father that I didn't care what their problems were, and I didn't care how they solved them, but they had to solve them because they had me and my little sister," she says. Get divorced later, when your kids are grown, she told them. It seemed to work, for her parents did find a way to reconcile—and her father did stop drinking. The lesson of commitment is one that has stayed with her to this day. "I think that when you have children, you have to stop thinking about yourself." Marriage, in her view, is training for responsibility for others, and the least you can do for your children is to put their happiness before your own until they are grown.

Divorce is a hurtful business, and because our respondents tend not to want to see people hurt, some of them, like Antonia Gomez, will continue to believe that divorce is wrong. Yet this desire not to see people suffer could just as easily become an argument in favor of divorce, for others might conclude that divorce has to be held open as an option of last resort when abuse and violence spin out of control. As it turns out, one of those others is Maria Gomez Romero, Antonia's sister-in-law. She, too, grew up in a family marked by an abusive and alcoholic father. But her reaction to the problems facing her parents were completely different than Antonia's. Ever loyal, her mother, as Maria tells the story, would excuse her father's behavior, to Maria's great annoyance and frustration. "I remember countless times telling my mom to divorce Dad. You know, he drinks too much. You know, we're terrified." And her mother would respond that it was important for her to remain married for the sake of her children. Antonia believes that the fact that her parents never divorced gives the story a happy ending. Not Maria. Just as Antonia learned from her experiences the importance of commitment, Maria learned about distrust. "It makes you very hesitant about having a relationship with other people, because you feel like you're going to go through something like that." She loves her husband and her child, which is why she is committed to her marriage. But if the love were ever to disappear, so, presumably, would the commitment.

The potential for abusive families poses a moral dilemma for some in our sample. So long as such a potential exists, the difficulty is not deciding to be virtuous but instead deciding which of competing virtues to honor. Remaining in an abusive marriage can be taken as an expression of loyalty, but it can also be viewed as a violation of the principle never to condone cruelty. Breaking up such a marriage puts a commitment against cruelty first, but at the cost of a certain disloyalty. Confronted with such a dilemma, very few Americans would insist that divorce be made impossible. They are more likely to hold that, like abortion, it should be legal but rare. It is not that they view divorce as a good thing so much as that they conclude that the absence of any grounds for divorce is a bad thing. In an individualist culture, only the individual can make the determination of whether the abuse is such that the family ought to stay together or has gotten so out of hand that it must perforce break apart. Antonia Gomez may choose one way and her sister-in-law the other, but both are making choices.

The presence of children complicates the question of divorce even further. Even when cruelty to children is not an issue, the principle of remaining loyal to a married partner can come into conflict with the pursuit of other virtues. Our respondents from Tipton indicate how this can happen. Parents who stay together for the sake of the children may think they are being loyal to each other, but they can also be viewed as disloyal to their children. Jason Benning, who insists upon loyalty in his lawn-mowing business, is one who thinks this way. Unhappy parents can use their children as an excuse to stay together, he says, "and I hate to see kids used as an excuse." In a similar way, Grant Lowell, who runs a small machine shop, thinks that the pursuit of one virtue, loyalty, can contradict another, honesty: if the parents "are not truly in love with one another, they're going to show it to their children and they're going to live under false pretenses, so to speak, and that is not going to be beneficial to anyone." Nearly everyone with whom we spoke agreed on the moral principle involved: do no harm. But they disagreed on what following that rule actually means. Under conditions in which not being cruel can lead either to divorce or to a marital recommitment, one has to approach the question, as Philip Beaty, the archaeologist, puts it, "on a case-by-case basis." He is no longer sure what loyalty even meant. "If you're in a bad marriage," he says, "you're being loyal to yourself if you take steps to get out of it, and maybe that's loyalty too."

The second group of Americans who instinctively react against divorce and in favor of marriage are those who experienced at first hand the pain of divorce as they watched their parents' marriage fall apart. Claudia Campbell, a twenty-eight-year-old marketing manager in San Francisco, is as strong a believer in loyalty as one is likely to find. "I am loyal to the company I work for," she tells us, "and this goes for every company I've ever worked for." She feels the same way about personal loyalty. About her husband of seven years, she says, "I trust him one hundred percent, and I know he trusts me too, and I couldn't even imagine him doing anything behind my back or being distrustful or harmful." There is little doubt in her own mind that Ms. Campbell's beliefs about loyalty were shaped by the ugliness of her parent's divorce. "How can you leave my mother with three children?" she asks rhetorically of her father's decision to split from his family. How could he "pick up and go and start a new life, with a new home, and with no kids, no responsibilities in the family? That was not a loyal act, no." In her view, you simply do not do such things to your children.

Since young people are by definition either unmarried or recently married, we cannot yet know whether younger Americans will divorce at lower rates in the future. But we do know that the divorce rate peaked in the early 1980s, suggesting that the frequency of divorce can reach a point when it no longer contributes to even greater frequency of divorce. There is also evidence from surveys that indicates a statistically significant upswing in the number of teenagers who say that they believe in the importance of long-term marriages. Younger people tend to be more idealistic about the potential for goodness in the world, which ought to lead them to a willingness to stick things out with others. Yet our interviews with a group of young people—students at the University of North Carolina in Greensboro—found mixed support for the proposition that the younger someone is, the more likely he or she is to value marital loyalty.

Sue Lydon was one student who emphasized loyalty in marriage. Her parents are divorced and her mother, with whom she is in close contact, lives in what she calls a "weird" relationship with her stepfather. "It's not really a marriage at all," she tells us. "They don't sleep together in the same bedroom," and, when she is at home, no one eats a meal together. Ms. Lydon hopes that her generation can do better. "If you are going to cheat on somebody, you shouldn't be in the relationship in the first place," she says. Because her parents never took into consideration the fact that they had her—"It was strange. Got shipped back and forth a lot" is how she puts it—she believes that people ought to be older and more mature before they make a commitment. Her views resemble those of Glenn Nordstrom, a nineteen-year-old marketing major, who, when he thought of marriage in the future, says, "You wouldn't want your child to be in that kind of environment where the mother would be going out and maybe sleeping with another man" because of the pain that would cause.

Trends in American life send two contradictory messages to these students in North Carolina. On the one hand, having grown up in a world far removed from traditional society and its ties across generations and having witnessed frequent divorce among their own parents and those of their friends, they have begun to appreciate the importance of long-term, stable marriages. On the other hand they are convinced, from the tales they hear from corporate America, that loyalty is an underappreciated virtue in American life. Existing in a world in which loyalty is upheld as an ideal in one arena of life but treated as a disposable commodity in another, these students can best be described as "conventional libertarians." Their language indicates a yearning for the conventional morality of yesterday; but, determined to protect their options for tomorrow, their behavior is as libertarian as that of their parents' generation. Sue Lydon, who complained about being shipped back and forth between her parents, finally concluded that she could not blame them for what they did and that, in the long run, their divorce may have "worked to my advantage." Whether or not it did, she herself is a single mother with a preschool child. Glenn Nordstrom believes that marital vows should be forever, but if he got married and his wife had an affair, he does not see how the marriage could survive "if the trust were gone." If there are signs that a younger generation is more likely to stick by marriage vows, they have not shown up to any significant degree among the Greensboro students we interviewed.

Not only do even those Americans most strongly committed to the marriage culture hold out for themselves the possibility of divorce, they also recognize that traditional conceptions of loyalty cannot necessarily be legislated for everyone. Asked about marital loyalty, Sharon Rice, a pharmacy technician in Tipton, laughingly responded by telling us that we were making her "think, like, Catholic stuff." Still, that "stuff" was important to her: "I think that when you get married, you should be married for life." But Mrs. Rice was unwilling to say that everyone ought to rule divorce out of order at all times. Eventually, people have to consider their own situation and decide what works best for them, she believes. "How loyal can you be if somebody's wronged you?" we were asked by Grace Floro, a Dayton housewife. "When is loyalty appropriate and when isn't it? You can be loyal to a fault just like you can be honest to a fault. That's what makes life so difficult. Nothing is black and white and every circumstance merits its own judgment."

## Loyalty Tests

Despite what sometimes seems as an overwhelming deluge of messages to the effect that loyalty is a thing of the past, one hears echoes of an earlier, more loyal, time in the responses of some of those with whom we spoke. Paul Richard—pronounced, he tells us, in the French way with the emphasis on the last syllable—works in an industry as remote from modern America as one can find: he is a commercial fisherman. "When you work on a boat," he tells us, "you're dependent on all your comrades. That's how you make a boat work. I mean, it's not a piece of machinery that you can push buttons on and stuff like that. A boat is like a physical thing. Everything's got to work in sequence, and people have to do certain things. That's where you rely on your shipmates. And when you're at the end of the trip, you feel great and you want to let your hair down, you know." Mr. Richard lets his hair down in a Fall River fisherman's lodge, and he insisted that we meet him there for our interview. Because there is a long period of time between fishing seasons, he spends a lot of time there, as do his shipmates. Here one can find America before it ever thought about a loyalty deficit. "It's like a man thing, I guess you could say," he adds, a place where buddies can get together and not feel guilty about it.

Americans who talk this way about loyalty sound remarkably similar to those academics who pay attention to the declining quality of civil society in America. Such is the case with Tipton's Warren Johnson, the man who told of the pain involved in his own divorce. He recalls the time "when loyalty was really good." For a resident of a community like his, that was when "family lodges offered things, when they would have potlucks and they offered entertainment in rural areas to be able to eat together and enjoy belonging to this organization." His thoughts were seconded by Warren Wilson, a former military officer and substitute teacher in Dayton. Unlike many of our respondents, Mr. Wilson was unabashedly forthright in asserting the importance of traditional virtues. For one thing, he believes that a person is under a strong obligation to judge others when they sin. For another, he holds that even when you disagree with a person—indeed even when you disagree with a norm or a rule—you ought to be loyal anyway. These attitudes, he readily acknowledges, are the products of a twenty-four-year career in the military, where "I had the good fortune to be associated with people I considered virtuous enough to give them my loyalty." For him the military is one of the few places left in America where loyalty still means something. The same is true for Curtis Jackson, the Greensboro student who is strongly suspicious of corporations for the lack of loyalty they demonstrate. Curtis, who is thirty-five and married for the third time, clearly has loyalty problems of his own. But he remembers the military as one of the few places in America still committed to the ideal. "The guys I served with in the service," as Mr. Jackson puts it, "were loyal to each other no matter what. When I say no matter what, I mean no matter what."

Americans who set a premium on loyalty have become odd men out in a society in which things move so fast that loyalty cannot stand still. They are, for that reason, at the opposite end of the spectrum from those trying to redefine what loyalty means in the context of a society in which fishing crews, or even military units, are increasingly exotic. Attempts to redefine loyalty are most likely to be found among our Californians, not only because their state is one long associated with new beginnings, but because so many of them work in an industry that challenges traditional ways of doing business. Atherton's Theresa Lombardi is a fifty-two-year-old who has worked in investments and acquisitions but now describes herself as a homemaker. She lives in an area surrounded by successful people like herself, people who are used to working long hours for high pay, and she has seen lots of occasions in which people will be disloyal to others because money was on the line. Stabbing people in the back is a way of life for many of the people in her circle, yet at the same time she also recognizes that a person has to create some relationships of loyalty somewhere. Like many of her friends, Mrs. Lombardi married late, and because she did, she feels far better prepared to stick with her husband. The friendships she now makes she also considers more solid precisely because they reflect common interests. "I had a bunch of my women friends over and one of my friends said that with our generation—now this is people between forty-five and fifty-two—one of the reasons everyone is still together is because they kind of grew up together, they worked together, they were successful together, they were each other's friends and they still are." Jay Boylen is an Atherton headhunter, and therefore someone who, as he puts it, has a vested interest in disloyalty. Atherton does not have much of a sense of community, he tells us, because so many of the older elite San Francisco families that once made it their home have moved out, to be replaced by people who are complete strangers to one another. But maybe there is an advantage in that, he believes. After all, in the older, more exclusive communities, "if you're not one of them, then you're not automatically welcomed into the neighborhood." In communities in which people are strangers, by contrast, "all move there too, so you kind of all start from the same place."

Another Californian who finds himself engaged in the business of redefining the meaning of loyalty to suit changing times is Tom Ullman. Raised as a Mennonite by deeply religious parents—he continues to be active in an organization called the Brethren/Mennonite Council for Gay and Lesbian Concerns—Mr. Ullman has learned from his life as a gay man in San Francisco "that people now have a whole new way of measuring what's good." For him, loyalty does not imply commitment to following "nineteen rules" or whatever else any particular religion prescribes, but instead is measured by what you do. "Just because you are a card-carrying member of a church doesn't really count for much other than you get your name in the membership book," he says. As for loyalty, "I think it speaks more where you show up, if I can use that phrase. Do you show up when people are in trouble, when somebody needs help, when someone's building is damaged during a storm? Are you there? Do you agree to serve on the committees? Are you part of the community? Those are the things that I think are much more true measuring sticks of a good person, a person with integrity, with values, with a strong moral center."

Americans can be placed along a continuum, ranging from loyalists at one end who believe in staying with one company or marriage no matter what to postloyalists at the other end who believe that individuals ought to grab new opportunities when they arise. When they talk, loyalists in our sample start with the importance of rules developed by institutions of moral authority and from them eventually make exceptions, under unusual circumstances, for individuals. Postloyalists, on the other hand, distrustful of institutions, discuss loyalty by beginning with people and what they do, moving ever so slowly to institutions like churches and what they ought to do. One should not minimize the differences between these approaches, for they involve quite contrasting conceptions of how one ought to lead a good life. Yet it is also true that however disparate the places in which they begin, each way of thinking is forced by contemporary circumstances to move closer to the other.

Loyalists would almost never find attractive the notion of a Japanese soldier falling on his sword because ordered to do so by a military superior; that is simply not the way things are done in the United States. Just as those Americans who believe in strong marital commitments also believe in keeping alive the divorce option, strong believers in loyalty know that their beliefs are impossible to maintain in anything resembling their pure form. Warren Johnson, for example, laments the passing of social clubs in Tipton, but when he cites as one of the reasons the fact that "there's just too darn much stuff to do," he also reminds us how the decline of loyalty can create more personal opportunities. Nor is the military, so admired by Warren Wilson and Curtis Jackson, always an advertisement for loyalty. Maureen Irvine, a neighbor of Mr. Wilson who had her career in the National Guard, thinks that cutbacks in the military budget represent a form of disloyalty to the ordinary enlisted person no different than downsizing in the corporate sector. Nor would Mr. Wilson elevate loyalty above all else: "If the general says, get in the car, we're going to storm the White House, well, you call the police and they lock up the general. Unchecked loyalty is just stupid."

From the other direction, postloyalists generally find a kind of emptiness at the heart of a culture that too often pays more attention to the needs of the self than to commitments to others. Many of the friends Theresa Lombardi has made decided to join the same Catholic social club. Because Atherton is a wealthy suburb, because many of those who belong are older parents, and because so many of the women work, this is not a club that resembles the Knights of Columbus and other Catholic organizations once so prominent in Boston or Chicago. For all of the decline of one kind of loyalty, new kinds are always emerging, for Mrs. Lombardi's club clearly serves the needs of its particular members just as earlier versions did for theirs. In a similar way, San Francisco's Tom Ullman is quite aware of the fact that fidelity in sexual relationships is not a high priority in the Castro district where he lives. "Gay social culture," as he puts it, "doesn't support it very well at all." Still, there is, in his view, no doubting what loyalty means. "It means telling the truth and it means keeping your commitments." Maintaining those commitments remain vitally important to him, even when—especially when—we can no longer count on religious institutions to instruct us in the art of keeping our promises.

The decline of a conception of loyalty in which people pledge to remain together until death do them part can be keenly felt, but it is not clear whether it can or should survive the onset of new ways in which loyalty is redefined to accommodate itself to how we actually live. Not even the critics of America's loyalty deficit, when all is said and done, go as far as to say that the ties of loyalty ought to be bound quite so tightly. For instance, Barbara Dafoe Whitehead writes in her account of our divorce culture, "We must assume that divorce is necessary as a remedy for irretrievably broken marriages." Aware that adherents to competitive market capitalism will dismiss loyalty as idealistic and impractical, Frederick Reichheld stresses that "loyalty provides the unifying framework that enables an executive team to modify and integrate corporate strategy and operating practices in ways that will better serve the long-term interests of customers, employees, and investors." Even William Bennett writes that loyalty "is very different from being a rubber stamp. Loyalty operates on a higher plane than that." There is simply no escaping the fact that, whatever loyalty means these days, it does not mean blind acceptance of moral authority.

Once this is understood, we can begin to recognize that loyalty has not disappeared in America. Instead, Americans are called upon to determine for themselves what loyalty means—and to do so precisely at the time when some of their major institutions act as if loyalty means nothing much at all. It is not just at the workplace and within the family where one can find excruciating loyalty tests, not all of which are passed. One ought to be loyal to one's own religion, but, as Greg and Ally Sauvage, Catholics from Fall River, put it, that becomes harder to do when you hear so many stories about kids being sexually abused by priests. Dorothy Meyer, who is retired from the University of Dayton, notes that people in academia were once loyal to the college they worked for, but now "profs are much more loyal to their professional associations." A national psychodrama involving the President of the United States led many of our respondents to wonder whether Linda Tripp's betrayal of Monica Lewinsky was a sign of too little loyalty, whether Hillary Clinton's decision to stand by her man revealed too much, and whether Bill Clinton's willingness to carry out an affair and to lie about it to everyone around him revealed a man with no idea of loyalty whatsoever.

Not only were our respondents acutely aware of the moral messages contained in the downsizing decisions of major corporations, two of the cities in which we conducted interviews were involved with questions of professional sports that seem to demonstrate an absence of loyalty in American life. People living in Dayton watched with disbelief as the long-term owner of the Cleveland Browns moved his team out of the city despite the intense loyalty of the local fans, while those living in Hartford thought they had gained a professional football team only to see the owner go back on his word and keep the team in a Boston suburb. One need not look past the newspapers and the television to find lessons about the degree to which loyalty rarely seems to pay.

Josiah Royce, America's philosopher of loyalty, believed that we needed to be loyal to the idea of loyalty, by which he meant that acts of particular disloyalty could be justified if they resulted in promoting larger loyalties to others. That way of thinking, argues the legal philosopher George Fletcher, "harbors an insouciant faith that one can simply choose the cause of one's 'willing and thoroughgoing devotion.'" Fletcher does not believe one can, for we do not choose in any direct way those historical circumstances into which we are born and which establish our obligations to others. No doubt Fletcher is right to criticize the lack of a "sense of tragedy" inherent in the idea of creating and re-creating one's loyalties as one goes along. Yet Josiah Royce, although writing as the twentieth century got under way, understood the problems Americans would have with loyalty a century later: "We can win back something of what we have lost," he wrote, "only if we in this country can get before ourselves and our public a new, a transformed conception of what loyalty is." That, to the best of their ability, is what the Americans with whom we spoke are trying to do.

# III. Eat Dessert First

## A Life-and-Death Struggle

Lou Anne Mobley is a homemaker who lives with her husband in a small ranch-style house near Lackland Air Force Base in San Antonio. Dressed casually in a T-shirt and khaki shorts for our interview, she nonetheless gives the impression of a person who carefully chooses what she wears. In fact, everything about Mrs. Mobley suggests a passion for order. Her political views are quite conservative. She organizes her life around her husband, her children, and her church. In our interview, Mrs. Mobley insists on the importance of self-control and self-discipline. Giving into pleasure is not the way to lead a good life, she insists; as she puts her own moral maxim, "you give into pleasure, you become miserable."

Mrs. Mobley was not always so virtuous. By the time she was a senior in high school, she felt that there was something missing in her life. Whatever it was, she chose to fill the void with alcohol, drugs, and sex. Her college years were a desperate quest for some kind of bearing: flirting with New Age religion, thinking of herself as a Buddhist, then as a Muslim, meditating, hanging out with people who were into witchcraft. After college, Mrs. Mobley joined the military, hoping to find some direction, but that didn't work either. She describes the military environment around San Antonio as one big party scene, and most of what she remembers from those years is sleeping around with lots of men, usually in a haze induced by alcohol and marijuana. She knew that she was destroying herself, but no one seemed to care.

Then she found herself among people who really did care. At first, when some new friends began to talk about Jesus, she was skeptical: "Oh, I know. Jesus. Christmas. Easter. All that." But they persisted, and she began to hear their message. One day, as they continued to pray for her, everything fell into place. "I just got down on my knee," she tells the story, "and said, 'God, if you really are there, I want you in my life. I know I've sinned and I'm asking you to change me.'" From then on, Mrs. Mobley was set on a new course. "The next morning I woke up and I felt something fresh and new. I felt like my mind had been washed clean and I began to read the Bible and it speaks of how the blood of Jesus washes from our sins." It has been thirteen years since she was born again, and Mrs. Mobley continues to thank God every day. "Jesus Christ has transformed me," she says. "He is pure love, he's honest, he's good, but he is righteous and he judges sin." Now she offers help to others in the same way her friends once helped her. One of the reasons she wanted to meet with us was to get Jesus' word out. "I hope this is recorded," she said at the end of her interview. We assured her that it was.

Dayton's Warren Wilson is a fifty-three-year-old bachelor. He spent twenty-four years in the United States Air Force, many of them piloting transport planes, and retired as a colonel. Working as a substitute teacher (when the phone rings), he is trying to develop a career as an inspirational public speaker. In his speeches, Mr. Wilson talks a great deal about virtue and vice. He is often invited to high schools in the area, and when he speaks at them, he emphasizes the importance of extreme situations, such as war, in forming personal character. A fan of

Steven Spielberg, Mr. Wilson believes that both *Schindler's List* and *Saving Private Ryan* make clear, even to young students, that adversity can bring out the best in people. That's true of his own family, he tells them. His grandfather survived World War I and the even deadlier Spanish flu epidemic that followed it, only to witness three more wars in his lifetime. His parents, born in 1918 and 1920, led a more morally serious life than the generation that followed them because they too had "suffered the tragedies of the first half of this century." Mr. Wilson is himself part of that latter generation. Compared with those who came before, he worries that his own life has been too easy. He was a mediocre student, not very happy doing his homework. When he was drafted to serve in Vietnam, he fought the process kicking and screaming.

Lou Anne Mobley was not saved by the military, but Warren Wilson was. He describes his Vietnam experience in ways similar to her religious conversion. "It turned my life around," he tells us. "There's nothing like loading a few coffins," an experience he found himself confronting a number of times, and one that had an instantly sobering effect. Now when he looks at the generations younger than he is, he finds people expecting good things without doing the hard work necessary to make them possible. "The wonderful thing about democracy and capitalism," he says, "is that it leads to the good life, as Aristotle would want us to have it. But the bad news is that we tend to lose focus on the virtues," the most important of which he then proceeds to enumerate: "hard work, dedication, sacrifice." Like Lou Anne Mobley, Warren Wilson is a conservative and a Republican, "in that order." He believes that while most younger people are soft, not everyone need be. "You have to have the right family structure and a hard-ass mom, or an aunt that makes you hit the books, and you can make something of yourself."

The stories of Lou Anne Mobley and Warren Wilson would have sounded quite familiar to Americans whose ideas about vice and virtue were formed in earlier periods of American life. Following the historian

Peter N. Stearns, we can call those ideas Victorian, so closely were they associated with the self-help manuals, sermons, and popular literature of nineteenth-century Great Britain and the United States. There was no agreement on the sources of good and virtuous lives a century ago, for Protestants spoke in different tones than Catholics and what made sense to rural America made little sense to the world of industry and large-scale organizations coming into being. Still, contemporary writers, perhaps with a touch of nostalgia, look back on that time and discover broad agreement over the principles by which people ought to live. Sounding very much like Warren Wilson, the historian Gertrude Himmelfarb has enumerated them: "Work, thrift, temperance, fidelity, self-reliance, self-discipline, cleanliness, godliness—these were the preeminent Victorian virtues, almost universally accepted as such even when they were violated in practice."

Americans inherited their Victorianism from Great Britain, barely changing it along the way; as Himmelfarb puts it, "the Victorian ethos of the new country had much in common with that of the old." Both versions held that human beings are by nature shortsighted and egoistic. Predisposed toward sin, especially the sin of pride, they will, if left to their own devices, choose self-indulgence over obligations to others. It is therefore never easy to be put on the straight and narrow path. The work was so hard—"To repress a harsh answer, to confess a fault, and to stop (right or wrong) in the midst of self-defense, in gentle submission, sometimes requires a struggle like life and death," one nineteenth-century Southern matron wrote—that no one could do it by her efforts alone. That is why strong character required the existence of strong institutions. The commands of God, the duties of family life, the teaching of character in schools—these were necessary to point the way toward the right path, so that people would not be led down the wrong ones.

In many of their forms—warnings against masturbation, Sylvester

Graham's combination of sexual restraint and wholesome eating, McGuffey readers, Catholic worries about the corruptions of liberalism—Victorian ideas about self-control have long been subject to ridicule. Yet they nonetheless possessed a coherence that made them attractive to people in search of ways of leading a meaningful life. One continues to see that coherence in the reflections of Lou Anne Mobley and Warren Wilson. No one can doubt the dramatic improvement in their lives that followed their willingness to give up short-term gratification for long-term reward. It is clear from talking with them that this willingness is itself dependent on the comprehensiveness of the Victorian theory of self-control. Those ideas offer a credible link between private conduct and public life. A sense that the larger world is out of control made it essential for both of them to assert control over themselves. Mrs. Mobley knows that there is little she can do to move the United States in the conservative direction she favors, but she also knows that it is within her power to assume responsibility for the education of her children, which she tries to do by refusing to own a television set. At some point she will have to release her children to that larger world and all its temptations, but so long as they are young, she can protect their purity and give them a chance to be the children they are. She feels that her faith in Jesus has empowered her, which it clearly has. Through their experiences with life, both she and Warren Wilson learned what the Victorians knew: strong institutions, whether rooted in the demands of faith or the commands of order, open possibilities as much as they close them.

Lou Anne Mobley and Warren Wilson think of themselves as exceptions in America. As they look at others around them (especially, in Mr. Wilson's opinion, at those living amid inner-city poverty), they see little of the self-discipline they have learned to practice in their own lives. In this, they would find themselves in full agreement with those social critics who believe that self-discipline is no longer a virtue in which Americans have much faith. Institutions once designed to instill respect for moral authority—schools, churches, marriage manuals—now preach permissiveness and self-indulgence, we are frequently told. Once we worried about the ill effects of alcohol; now we face the temptations of drugs too numerous to count. Consumerism is rampant, never more than during holidays once considered sacred. A therapeutic mentality dominates all our institutions, even, in one recent account, governmental ones, and such a mentality puts a premium on feeling good over the sterner stuff of traditional morality. Take all the major institutions of American life, and add up the sum total of the moral messages they convey, and the result, these critics are convinced, will be the exact opposite of the maxim expressed by Lou Anne Mobley: seek pleasure, lest you be miserable.

Yet as much as we may have left Victorianism behind, we have not abandoned it completely, for at least some of the institutions of American life, as well as the professionals and intellectuals who write on behalf of them, have rediscovered the virtue of the virtues. When it comes to drugs, "zero tolerance"—today's term for prohibitionism—is the operating principle in one school district after another. Alcoholism is more likely to be regulated by twelve-step recovery groups than by state legislatures and city councils, but it is being regulated nonetheless. Every day at sunup, significant numbers of Americans rouse themselves out of bed to run around their neighborhoods, and in this they are urged on by a large industry devoted to this particular kind of self-discipline. Lou Anne Mobley and Warren Wilson do not associate with liberals and feminists, but if they did, they would find among a number of them a shared concern with controlling the instincts. Nineteenth-century crusades against pornography define the outlook of a number of theorists who consider themselves at the cutting edge of feminist ideology. Universities across the United States, anxious to police any possible incidents of sexual harassment, find themselves regulating sexual activity in ways that Victorians would find quite familiar. As much as Americans are instructed to put pleasure first, they are also being reminded, actually quite frequently, about the necessity of repression.

Nowhere are the contradictions of self-control in America clearer than among those who stand in polar opposition to the worldviews of Mrs. Mobley and Mr. Wilson: those younger Americans, both hetero-sexual and homosexual, who have made San Francisco their home, determined to enjoy life's pleasures in whatever form they take. Melissa Pritchett, a cocktail waitress, is one of them. "You have to self-indulge," she tells us. "It makes you feel good sometimes. It's good to be naughty like that." Louise Sullivan, a gay graduate student, spoke of her "wild side," in which she will go out on binges of self-indulgence. "One of the problems I have with Christianity is the denial of pleasure," adds Sarah Lloyd. Carole Yamada, an unemployed nurse, is a Japanese-American who thinks that the strongly instilled sense of shame she associates with her family's culture is destructive because, in enforcing a group's sense of right and wrong, it leaves little room for people to live as they like— especially those who want to live in a way different from the norms established by the group.

Yet not even the denizens of America's pleasure palaces are com-pletely immune from a kind of lingering Victorianism. After attacking pleasure deniers, Ms. Lloyd went on to point out how unsatisfying behavior like adultery, for all the thrill of transgression, can be. And in ways similar to feminists against pornography, both Carole Yamada and Melissa Pritchett, despite their moral libertarianism, proved to be moral regulators. Ms. Yamada, who believes that it is important for individuals to resist being shamed, is also a big supporter of hate crimes legislation—the purpose of which, one could argue, is to use legal deterrents to shame people into not using their freedom of speech to utter nasty words about another person's sexual or racial makeup. Ms.

Pritchett works in a bar and acknowledges that she is bothered by all the smoke. When asked the obvious followup question—is she in favor of banning smoking in the city's bars and restaurants?—she quickly responds yes. Smoking, after all, is a vice that hurts other people, she says, before pausing in wonder to exclaim: "'Vice': I just used that word!" In the heart of both of these advocates for self-indulgence lies a barely recognized sense that people ought to be able to control themselves better than they generally do.

Self-indulgence and self-restraint are oddly mixed together in the American mind, in ways that play havoc with Max Weber's theory about the Protestant ethic. Capitalism, in Weber's view, was dependent upon a type of personality associated with Protestant asceticism; the person who denies himself pleasure accumulates wealth for the purpose of plowing it back into investment. In more recent years, Weber's thesis has been convincingly modified by the sociologist Daniel Bell, who has argued that capitalist society no longer posits a sharp dichotomy between self-discipline and self-indulgence. It is true, Bell points out, that capitalism requires self-restraint in order to produce its panoply of goods, but, then again, it also requires hedonism to encourage people to buy them. Bell called the resulting tensions the "cultural contradictions" of capitalism. Modern societies are torn between their sense that earlier Protestant notions of self-denial ought to be as relevant as ever and their attraction to more contemporary ideas of self-indulgence.

Americans from all walks of life find themselves living with those contradictions every day. Churches pray for the souls of their parishioners while setting up bingo tables. Schools teach character but inflate grades. Cigarettes are both a sin and a tax-generating industry. Education, presumably a good thing, is financed by gambling, presumably a bad thing. Sex causes disease and sells everything else. The social critic David Brooks has written that America's upper class is Victorian and anti-Victorian simultaneously, affecting a bohemian lifestyle while practicing the bourgeois virtues of hard work and personal ambition. He is correct, even if what he says is true of most Americans, not only the successful among them. All the more reason, then, to find out how Americans try to obtain the benefits of self-discipline while achieving the rewards of self-indulgence at the same time.

## The Not So Lonely Crowd

How we think about character in contemporary America continues to be shaped by the way David Riesman and his colleagues engaged in their own reflections about the Protestant ethic in their 1950 book *The Lonely Crowd*. Riesman wrote about a society that was in transition from people who were primarily "inner-directed"—guided by strong convictions about character inculcated by the traditions to which they belonged—to those who could be described as "other-directed," motivated by a "psychological radar set," which Riesman and his co-authors described as "a device not tuned to control movement in any particular direction while guiding and steadying the person from within but rather tuned to detect the action, and especially the symbolic action, of others." Although the distinction between these two ways of being was meant to be descriptive and clinical, the book's authors left the clear impression that the transition from inner-direction to other-direction came with great cost. Inner-direction looked backward to the days of pioneers and self-made men—entrepreneurial people guided by convictions of duty and responsibility—while other-direction suggested a world in which people, eager to obtain clues about how to act from others, were in danger of losing their capacity to think and act on their own.

In preparation for their analysis of American culture, Riesman and his colleagues conducted interviews with Americans from all walks of life. Half a century later, when we talked to Americans around the country, we found that they get their moral cues in ways strikingly similar to those out-lined in *The Lonely Crowd*: they consult the media, read self-help manuals, and talk with others in their workplaces and neighborhoods. Yet there is little overlap between what people told Riesman then and what our respondents told us now. Of course the references are different; Riesman's respon-dents listened to the radio, whereas ours watch television, and they talked about programs, personalities, and events that only trivia buffs today can recall: "Milkman's Matinee," Jimmy Stewart in *Harvey*, and Raymond Gram Swing. More important, we did not find much evidence suggesting that Americans take their cues from others. To be sure, they no longer adhere to the Protestant ethic as enthusiastically as their forebears; but their will-ingness to indulge themselves in pleasure from time to time hardly marks a failure to think for themselves. On the contrary, Americans are actively redefining the Protestant ethic to bring it into accord with the way they believe life should be led.

It is a good thing, many Americans told us, to have a plan for life. And it is a bad thing to be swayed by all those temptations that come along to deter someone from fulfilling his or her plan. But not all plans are good, and not all temptations are bad. Self-disciplined people pay a price. When San Francisco's Richard Banks thinks of self-disciplined people, what comes to mind are not capitalist entrepreneurs or God-fearing preachers, but people who go in for vegetarianism or who commit themselves to herbal medicines. He calls them "subtractionists—these are the people that know how to subtract something from their life." Self-discipline, in his view, is a form of self-punishment. Against them, Mr. Banks prefers what he calls "self-directedness," the ability to add things to your life to make it richer, rather than subtracting things that make it poorer.

Highly successful Americans are not as ascetic in their self-denial as the herbalists Mr. Banks has in mind, but they too can be viewed as paying a personal price for their self-discipline. David Wong, one of the Atherton residents in our sample, thinks that his wife, a nationally ranked athlete, is self-disciplined—to a fault. "She sees a goal and she goes for it," he tells us, while he himself is quite indulgent. Comparing their contrasting approaches to life, he does not believe that hers is somehow better than his. He is a pragmatist. If one thing doesn't work, he will try another, and at some point, hopefully, he will reach his goal. There is, in the way Mr. Wong thinks about goal attainment, a respect for experimentation and flexibility that resonates with the catch-as-catch-can entrepreneurial spirit driving the "new" economy of Silicon Valley. His wife's more direct way of achieving her goals can result in frustration, leaving her filled with stress, (including the stress she puts upon herself), which is something the more circuitous Mr. Wong would rather avoid.

Athertonians like Mr. Wong know something about that particular kind of self-discipline called workaholism. Tim Crowe, an MIT-trained venture capitalist in Atherton, is also an entrepreneur, a man willing to take risks that the more weak-minded are likely to avoid in the hopes that his aggressive approach to business will reward him (it has, with substantial wealth). "I think that as a businessperson, I'm Type A," he says, pointing out his tendency to work extremely hard and for long hours. For Mr. Crowe, the opposite of drive is resignation to fate, of which he will have none: "I have a hard time giving myself to God, and saying that things are just going to happen. I have a hard time going with the flow." Mr. Crowe spoke in terms nearly identical to those used by another resident of Atherton, Lisa Becker, a retired musician. Mrs. Becker thinks that self-discipline is a "real virtue" because without the dedication of her musical training, she never would have developed the skills to be a successful performer. When she later obtained her license as a stockbroker, her discipline paid dividends once again. Now in retirement, she has taken up painting with the same dedication. The lesson, she believes, is simple: "If you want to achieve and work toward things, you've got to be self-disciplined."

Yet there is more to both these individuals than single-minded dedication. For Mr. Crowe, unlike the capitalists described by Max Weber, the whole point of depriving yourself of something now is so you can better enjoy it later. As much as he appreciates self-discipline, he thinks that "straying from time to time is probably a good thing." Sure, nonfat ice cream is good for you, "but once in a while having a great meal or a really good bottle of wine or a good cigar or not getting the exercise you need" can also be good for you. Because he does not stray often, Mr. Crowe enjoys straying all the more. He loves to get together with his equally busy friends, whenever they can find the time, and let loose a bit. Nor does he disparage others for their occasional fun. Even his own children do not necessarily benefit from strict discipline: unlike Riesman's inner-directed individual, who sets firm goals for his children, Mr. Crowe would rather let his enjoy childhood, because, he believes, that's what childhood should be about. Mrs. Becker feels the same way. Self-discipline is more important than self-indulgence, but it is also true that "you have to reward yourself once in while. The reward of getting to this goal is self-indulgence." For all their love of capitalism, Americans do not see themselves as workaholics; 79 percent of them, according to the "Way We Live Now" poll, do not measure their success in terms of how much money they make and 75 percent believe that their roles at home define who they are much better than their roles at work. It is sobering to learn that this disinclination to make the workplace the centerpiece of life applies just as much in an area so seemingly dedicated to the work ethic as Silicon Valley.

Many of our respondents insisted that, when taken to extremes, even good things, like self-discipline, become bad things. "I think people can be virtuous and overdo it," said Dayton's Michael McBeal. "They can be self-destructively virtuous." The person who sets a goal and then tries to carry it out, refusing to be swayed by whatever sirens sing along the way, can be successful, but such behavior, many of those with whom we spoke also believe, can be addictive—an ironic conclusion given the fact that other addictions, such as drinking and drugs, are seen as reflecting a lack of self-discipline. Like an addict, moreover, the self-disciplined person can wind up hurting not only herself, but others as well. People too focused on achieving their goals can be ruthless, rigid, cold, even sadistic, and Americans think that self-discipline ought to stop when it begins to hurt someone else. Mortgage banker John Howard, one of our Atherton respondents, sums up this whole point of view when he says, "If you're self-disciplined and you work hard to become successful at something, I think that can be very positive. If you become so self-disciplined that you shut out everything else in your life, you can become an obsessive-compulsive, and I think that can affect the quality of your life and those around you."

Mr. Howard's view was repeated by people all around the country. "You can be disciplined in a bad way," Tipton's Sharon Rice tells us. "You work seventy, eighty hours a week, ignoring your family. I don't think that is a good self-discipline." What is good self-discipline, we ask? That would exist, she responds, when "you can make it through your day doing mostly right and little wrong." Donna Teele is a very successful lawyer and public official in Connecticut, proud of what she has accomplished with her life. But she would agree with Sharon Rice that workaholics who ignore their own family ought not to become role models. In fact, she goes on, there is no reason to accept the idea that high achievement is a sign of virtue, for people who accomplish a great deal sometimes stab others in the back along the way, which is also not conduct we ought to admire. Similar thoughts were expressed by one of our Greensboro students, Nan Washington, who works as a nurse. She describes her sister as a self-disciplined person because she is never late for an appointment and fully in charge of her life. Still, there is something "regimented" about the way she lives that disturbs Ms. Washington. Not only that, her sister's five-year-old daughter is self-indulgent to a fault, probably because her superorganized mother does everything for her. As these individuals talk, it becomes clear that for them self-discipline can paradoxically also be a form of self-indulgence, because the highly disciplined person gets that way only by putting his or her needs ahead of others.

Influenced by ideas about the Protestant ethic, both Victorian and contemporary moralists tend to think that self-discipline is a virtue and self-indulgence is a vice. Yet over and over again, Americans told us that they agreed with the first half of that sentiment—but not the second. One reason they feel this way is that a little bit of self-indulgence can go a long way toward humanizing people and in that sense making them better individuals. "People need certain releases" is the way Fall River's Ben Farrell puts it, and things like smoking, drinking, and eating too much "are probably more of the tamer ones in our society." Self-indulgence, like self-discipline, comes in good and bad versions, and so long as one indulges the right way—"Take some time out for yourself. Take a nice warm bath," as Hartford's Margaret Bates advises—one can become a better person.

There is another, more important, reason to encourage a moderate form of self-indulgence. Its logic runs like this: Self-discipline is a virtue. By its very nature, however, it has to come from within. It is more likely to come from within if a person feels good about himself. A person is more likely to feel good about himself if he occasionally indulges himself. Ergo, self-indulgence is not a vice because it promotes the virtue of self-discipline. Dayton's Allan Powell, an orthodontist, is one who thinks this way. He holds that governing the self first requires appreciating the self: "If you don't have a good concept of self-worth, then you're really no good to yourself or anybody else, because you can't really achieve anything." Another similarly minded person is San Francisco's Gina Grossman, who works as a therapist. Just as many in our sample believe that the self-driven person can ignore or even step on others, she argues that the self-indulgent person can be good to others: "When you feel good about yourself, I think it just sort of overflows. You can be nicer to other people and make better choices and take other people into account."

Unlike the people Riesman interviewed halfway through the century, those we interviewed at its end experienced, directly or through the stories of others, the 1970s and its aftermath. However they felt about those years, and however they feel about them now, the Me Decade is alive and well in their insistence that one cannot ignore one's own needs. "Have you read the book *Life Is Uncertain … Eat Dessert First?*" Atherton's Nancy Watkins asked. Intrigued by its title, I did. Not surprisingly, its authors advocate the Protestant ethic in reverse: if you wait until you have lost weight or gotten your act together before you find the right mate or land the right job, you never will. "Don't be too quick to knock hedonists," its authors write, "you may be surprised to learn that you're a hedonist yourself. On the other hand, if you believe you should seek pain and avoid the pleasure of the moment, you could be a masochist. If you believe it's sinful to pleasure yourself, perhaps you're a religious fanatic. If you pursue intellectual pleasures but turn up your nose at physical delights, you could be a prude."

This is the kind of popular self-help book that critics love to satirize. It is easy to do so, given the book's breezy language and superficial philosophy. But I doubt that the simplistic message of books like this ought to be confused with what readers take from them. Mrs. Watkins's life story is that of Lou Anne Mobley in reverse: she grew in a heavily Christian environment, one in which dancing and trips to the movies were forbidden, and she has now grown to believe that constantly making people feel guilty for their moral failings does no one any good. Reading *Life Is Uncertain …* taught her that "self-discipline can be taken too far," from which she concludes that "there is a place for self-indulgence." The key word here is "place." Mrs. Watkins is not saying that self-indulgence is preferable to self-discipline. She is saying instead that each has its place. It is up to the individual to determine how to reconcile the cultural contradictions of capitalism, how to find the right balance between the self-discipline that keeps society humming along and the self-indulgence it offers as its rewards.

Social mobility on an individual level is widely understood in America: the people of one generation sacrifice so that their children can succeed. We are now witnessing that kind of mobility on a societal level. Americans know that people like Warren Wilson's grandparents and parents suppressed whatever longings they had for self-indulgence in order to overcome the twin experiences of the Depression and war. It would be wrong, they believe, to ignore the sacrifices of those who made their own prosperity and security possible. But it is not wrong, so long as it is done moderately and judiciously, to take advantage of the opportunities created by the self-denial of previous generations. The judgment that we can afford to relax a bit where self-discipline is concerned is a considered, not a rash, one. Self-discipline, even in its strictest incarnations, has always been a means to another end, not an end in itself. Americans today do not disagree with that. They just want the ends to include an opportunity for people to enjoy some of the fruits of their country's great success.

### *Moral Equality*

Victorian morality did more than tell us how to live well. It also constituted a lesson on how others might live badly. The whole point of insisting on the importance of good character was to isolate and contain bad character. Victorian morality was a public morality. It was designed to establish standards of right conduct applicable to all. For that reason, it was perfectly justified—indeed, it was a duty—to point the finger of shame at those who failed to live up to its requirements. The criminal and the prostitute were as central to Victorian morality as the sober workingman or the industrious capitalist. If the latter proved the benefits of forgoing short-term pleasure for the sake of long-term reward, the former demonstrated the consequences of the failure to regulate one's desires. These judgmental aspects of Victorian morality exercise a powerful appeal on contemporary writers persuaded of America's moral decline. It should not surprise us that Gertrude Himmelfarb, one of the sternest of those writers, is by profession a historian of Victorianism. Echoing the Victorian outlook on life, she writes that we enforce laws against criminal conduct not only so that we can be free of crime, "but also because it signifies a reaffirmation of the law itself, a relegitimation, as it were, of the law."

Contemporary critics find flaws with both our private and our public morality, and it is not always clear which is worse. On the one hand, Americans are viewed as self-indulgent, too willing to cut corners and to find the easy way out. Even worse than their unwillingness to place demands on themselves, however, is their reluctance to place demands on others. No longer do we believe, as the Victorians did, in public standards whose violation constitutes an opportunity for shaming, if not legal punishment. We comfort ourselves with the thought that, in refusing to judge others, we are practicing the virtue of tolerance when, in reality, we lack the courage to insist that some ways of life are better than others. In defining deviancy down, we elevate the symbols of Victorian depravity up, celebrating the hustler, coddling the criminal, and seeking out the libertine in all of us. If self-discipline is something we can safely ignore, the costs will be born not only by ourselves, but by others. Failing to pass judgment on those determined to seek immediate gratification, we encourage them to live in ways that will harm them in the long run.

Reporting on the state of middle-class morality in my book *One Nation, After All*, I wrote that, with the exception of homosexuality, Americans had become reluctant to tell other people how to live. I found this tendency both surprising and disturbing. It surprised me because, before I conducted my research, I had thought that many Americans, especially those who lived in the heartlands of the Midwest and South, still adhered to strongly judgmental standards of proper Christian conduct. And it disturbed me because Americans seemed to be copping out of their obligations to others by adopting a version of moral laissez-faire in which seeming tolerance became an excuse for not taking others seriously.

Those Americans with whom we spoke about virtue and vice are just as nonjudgmental as those I interviewed about middle-class morality. One of the clearest indications of their nonjudgmentalism is the readiness with which some of them rely on genetic or medical factors to explain why people sometimes do harmful things, both to themselves and to others. Fall River's Cheryl Broca, for example, believes that people who lack willpower are not bad people, just bad role models whose weakness of will can be attributed to a medical or genetic condition over which people have no control. Caryn O'Toole, also of Fall River, believes this to be the case. She has a friend who is wildly overweight, but she would not turn that into a character issue. "There's other reasons behind why people do the things they do," she says. "It doesn't mean that they have bad character because they do them. It could be a number of reasons. They might not feel good about themselves. They might not be happy about a certain situation in their life. Maybe they have no companion. It could be because they are depressed." People who spend too much on themselves or chase after people of the opposite sex have bad habits, according to San Antonio's Orlando Pradera, but they are not bad people. It all depends on what you do. "If you indulge in something that's not right, it's bad, but then if you indulge in something that's good for you, that's okay." And even when you do something bad, it depends on whether you are a bad person or just a person with bad habits. "There's a difference," he insists. San Antonio's Christina Rios, a nurse, offers an intriguing take on the issue. Maybe a person who indulges herself is not a bad person but merely lacking in one quality while being superior in another. "Just like any other type of physical defect," she adds. "You know, the blind, they can hear better." No one knows for sure the degree to which such conditions as being overweight are determined by the genes or are a consequence of self-indulgence, but more Americans lean toward the former explanation than the latter. While one can find a few people in our sample who said flat out that people who cannot control themselves are bad people, nearly everyone else did not want to make a judgment about the inner state of another person based on that person's outer forms of behavior.

So strong is the culture of nonjudgment in America that even those who believe that they ought to make the self-destructive behavior of others their business generally do so defensively. Grant Lowell, the self-employed machinist in Tipton, expresses the old-fashioned idea that in a small community people ought to take responsibility for others. He believes that "we are all obligated, to a small degree, without being obnoxious about certain things, to help another person." When he was a heavy smoker, other people would remind him of how bad the habit was, an interference in his life that he greatly resented. When he finally did quit smoking, he realized that he was grateful to them for their concern, "as long as they presented it in such a matter that got me thinking about it." People like Mr. Lowell, who do believe that they ought to step in and point out to others the errors of their ways, speak as if they have to apologize for having such oddball views in the first place. Despite talk of how it takes a village to raise a child or, by extension, to care for an adult, contemporary Americans shy away from interfering with others and what they do.

Why do so many Americans think this way? Those who believe that America could use a bit more of Victorian morality have a ready answer. If any one aspect of Victorian morality stands out today, it is its self-confidence. The Victorians believed that some things are just right, and others are just wrong; and life consists in doing as much of the former, and avoiding as much of the latter, as possible. It would be easy to conclude that America's nonjudgmentalism reflects a lack of such confidence: uncertain about what is best for them, Americans are also uncertain about what is best for others. Paul Richard, the fisherman in Fall River, expresses his nonjudgmentalism this way: "You want to do drugs," he says, "you want to be a drug addict, you want to be a boozer . . . if that's what you want to be, if you've paved in your own way and nobody's living in your shoes and you're not hurting anybody but yourself, then I don't think it's anybody's business but your own." One can easily imagine the way contemporary Victorian moralists would respond to what he says. "Have more faith in yourself," they would tell him. "You are a law-abiding citizen. You ought to appreciate your own virtuous behavior more and tolerate those who lack your good moral sense less."

Yet something more than a lack of self-confidence is going on as Mr.

Richard shares his views. (Even the Victorians were not as confident as they sometimes appear; running throughout their moral strictures, as the historian Karen Halttunen has shown, was a crisis of social identity brought on by the hustle and bustle of urban and industrial life.) The non-judgmentalism of Americans has its own form of philosophical undergirding. When our respondents expressed a reluctance to pass judgment, they were, in their own way, indicating commitments to two important political ideals: respect for others and equality.

Some of them believe that we run the risk of not showing sufficient appreciation of other people and the choices they make if we think we know what is best for them better than they do. They hold that as responsible individuals, people ought to remain accountable for the decisions they make, a principle that can be violated if we insist that they should have made other decisions. San Antonio's Lucy Martin, a substitute teacher, has a friend whose deep Christian convictions lead her to tell other people that they should not wear earrings, dance, or drink, not even at a wedding. "That's too much," Ms. Martin thinks. People are adults, in her view. If they want to enjoy themselves, her friend has no right to interfere. Tipton's Lilia Swenson believes that for a person to change, the motivation has to come from within. Gina Loftus, whose husband was an alcoholic, was upset with his lack of self-control and tried her best to change him, but found he was able to deal with his problem only when he himself decided to do so. The word "maturity" came up fairly frequently in our interviews. People who do the wrong thing are not so much immoral as immature. Most people eventually do mature. They can be helped, for maturity is a process that has to be guided. But no one can just order another person to grow up. When all is said and done, individuals have to be the ones to take charge of their own lives.

The more interesting commitment Americans make when they talk in the language of nonjudgmentalism is to moral equality. Explaining his own reluctance to pass judgment, Paul Richard says, "I don't think anybody is better than anyone else. I really don't." His comment would have sounded strange to a Victorian. When the rules were fixed, known to all, and followable by all so long as one showed the proper dedication and self-discipline, those who failed to live up to them could not be considered the moral equals of those who did—because their failure was due to their inherent flaws. Today's Americans, by contrast, believe that, morally speaking, people are equal until proven otherwise. There are so many ways of being human, many of our respondents believe, that one cannot assume the automatic moral superiority of one over another. Their unwillingness to point the finger of shame at others, which to a certain kind of moral temperament represents the vice of cowardice, can also signify the virtue of humility. If we judge too much and too often, we turn harsh and hypocritical, not unlike the self-disciplined person whose overriding commitment to success leaves others harmed in his wake. This does not mean that no acts are outside the pale; Mr. Richard, for example, is a supporter of capital punishment for crimes like murder. But so long as the harms are minor—or, as Paul Richard's comments make clear, destructive of oneself rather than others—we should be reluctant to step in and police them. Just because another person may live by different standards does not make him inferior.

We are most likely to find this kind of commitment to moral equality among our San Francisco respondents, since they are the ones whose lifestyle encourages them to think constantly about the judgments made about them. Lee Hayes was cut out of his parents' will after he told them he was gay. As it turns out, one of Mr. Hayes's brothers, who had taken over the family's construction business, was indicted by a federal grand jury for rigging bids on government highway contracts. He served two years in federal prison, his relatively light sentence and "country club" style incarceration due to his close friendships with high-ranking Republican politicians. Six months after his brother was released, he was included in the parents' will, despite being a convicted felon, while Mr. Hayes was not.

Reflecting on the lesson in moral inequality he learned, Mr. Hayes now says, "You can steal millions from the government, like he did, and you're forgiven by everybody. That's okay. He's a businessman, you know. But it's wrong to love another man. That's bad, and I should be thrown out of the family for that."

Gay men and lesbians see examples of such moral double standards frequently. Although Kenny Miller has become reconciled with his family and the Southern Baptist congregation of his youth, he still remembers how he felt when, at the age of nineteen, his church kicked him out. What was he supposed to say to their insistence that he was less than fully human? he asks us. "I'm not good in these people's eyes, but I know that I am a worthy human being." A few years after his expulsion, a friend of Mr. Miller's sister found herself pregnant, but because she was able to get married, her behavior was considered acceptable. "If they can accept her for that," Mr. Miller asks, "why can't they accept me for my homosexuality?" As a result of what he sees as a double standard, "I started reprocessing everything." He goes on: "I consider myself to be someone who is conscious of treating other people the way I want to be treated." Such moral equality compels nonjudgmentalism because "I don't make assumptions about other people's lives. I try not to judge anyone for decisions they make, appropriate to their circumstances."

The issues with which our respondents are wrestling are also issues with which moral philosophers deal. The legal theorist Ronald Dworkin takes a position that adds philosophical rigor to the egalitarian instincts of Lee Hayes and Kenny Miller. Dworkin argues strongly in favor of preserving and protecting a woman's right to an abortion or a dying person's right to end his life with the dignity he sees fit. But he also does more. He suggests that laws that prohibit abortion or euthanasia violate equality as well as liberty. People who believe in individual rights express one moral position and people who believe that abortion ought to be outlawed express another. When government endorses the moral outlook of one—say, by regulating or banning abortion or euthanasia—it condemns those who adhere to the other to second-class moral status. Robert George, a political philosopher of a far more conservative bent than Dworkin, disagrees with him—and, implicitly, with many of our respondents. The people with whom we spoke believe that you show respect for another person by staying out of his business, whereas George argues that treating people with dignity and respect means that we have an obligation to prevent them from harming themselves through wrongful acts. "Where demeaning, degrading, or destructive self-regarding conduct is involved," he holds, "there certainly need be nothing inegalitarian in legislative action aimed at preventing it."

Robert George makes an important point: There is no greater respect you can show to people than to demonstrate your willingness to criticize them when you believe they are wrong. We do not fulfill a commitment to equality by holding those we believe victimized or oppressed to a different—which means lower—standard of what ought to be expected of them. If anything, we instead reveal inegalitarian sentiments in so doing, as if, down deep, we really think of such people as too inferior to us to be able to meet the standards we set for ourselves. Still, Americans who would disagree with George's position have given the matter considerable thought. Their nonjudgmentalism, however thin it often seems, is not (or at least not always) a form of moral laissez-faire. One can argue with them about whether such principles as respect for others and equality are best served by a stance of nonjudgmentalism, but one cannot deny the importance of those principles to them.

## Addicted to Addiction

When it comes to self-discipline, Americans are often viewed as addicted to addiction. What the Victorians considered self-destructive behavior requiring punishment we consider self-destructive behavior requiring treatment. It all began innocently enough with the success of organizations like Alcoholics Anonymous, which really did seem to be effective in getting its members to stop drinking. But before anyone seemed to know it, the language of addiction had spread to all aspects of life. People were said to be addicted to food, sex, violence, work, the Internet, God, and, according to codependency theorists, other people. Encouraged by authors seeking best-seller status and popularized by daytime television, the language of self-abuse and step-by-step recovery seemed to offer both the solace and the grace once associated with traditional religions.

Almost as widespread as the language of addiction in America has been full-throttle criticism of the negative consequences for American society that follow from its premises. The most common complaint is that addiction is an excuse individuals use to avoid taking responsibility for their own actions. Despite the fact that Americans believe that alcoholism is a disease, some experts claim that there is no medical evidence supporting that proposition. And while cravings for alcohol and other drugs may have a neurological, chemical, or hereditary basis, critics of the addiction culture insist that no hard science can explain why people take up drugs in the first place. The popular language in which addictions are discussed on television, they claim, is not based on hard science but on the most dubious of the sciences: psychology. The concept of an addiction assumes that people have no self-discipline at all, that their indulgences are not the product of an unregulated appetite but the consequences of abuse, abandonment, misunderstanding, jealousy, or any other condition the therapist chooses to find. In the view of its critics, addiction language is the logical end-result of a society that no longer believes in the virtue of self-discipline. Not only does it offer an excuse for the failure of the individual to control his instincts, it also offers seemingly scientific reasons for our failure to judge others. A society of addicts has no need for either virtue or vice, since what is good about us and what is bad are both beyond our control.

Critics of the culture of addiction are right on one point: Scientific concepts have a way of entering mainstream discourse very quickly, and before long Americans find themselves using words like "genetic predisposition" or "obsessive-compulsive syndrome" that would have been foreign to their grandparents. One of our Fall River respondents, Kelly Houston, thought that being heavy was caused by a defective thyroid, before extending her analysis beyond problems of weight control. Talking about gamblers, alcoholics, and drug addicts, she says, "I think there's an internal something within them that's drawing them to it. I don't think that a person's character is weak or anything. There is some sort of weakness there, but it doesn't make them any less of a human being." This is a strongly held point of view, repeated in one form or another by a number of her neighbors. The reason some people behave better than others, as Caroline Bowen understands it, is that "some people are more prone to physical addictions than other people. They become physically addicted maybe to overcome things in their lives, to alter their state of mind, or something like that. I've known some people who I thought had pretty strong characters that were prone to addictive behavior." Rosalyn Esposito, a kindergarten teacher, accepts the widespread view in America that alcoholism is a disease: "If you have ten people that are exposed at age twenty-one to drinking, a certain number of them will become alcoholics because it was already part of their system." These residents of Fall River reflect the extent to which scientific discourse has replaced moral reasoning in America, hardly surprising in a society in which the benefits of scientific knowledge are so obvious.

So widespread is the medicalization of social problems in the United States that it applies not only to those viewed as self-indulgent, but also to those who pay for the consequences of that indulgence. Smoking provides an illustration. Some of our respondents believe that really strong-willed people can give up smoking; some of them even say that they did so themselves. The more common view, however, is that smokers are driven by biological cravings over which they have little control. Yet smoking is also widely unpopular in America, forbidden in airplanes, regulated in restaurants, and increasingly subject to the kind of "politically correct" approach to moral regulation that uses shame to deter people from indulging their vice in public. This opposition to smoking is itself interesting, for it seems an obvious exception to the reigning nonjudgmentalism; when it comes to cigarettes Americans seem to have no problem at all telling others how to live. Richard Klein, a French professor at Cornell, believes that opposition to smoking is one way in which an old-fashioned Victorian morality is kept alive in America, for all the negative images we attach to smoking—it is unhealthy, selfish, clandestine—were once applied to other frowned-upon vices as well.

When nonjudgmental people make judgments, they often defer to the scientific and medical authorities whom they cite in avoiding making judgments in other situations. If some people are understood to be chemically addicted to smoking, others explain their aversion to smoking on the basis of an allergic reaction against it. An aversion is a preference, and as such cannot be given any more weight than any other preference. But if a friend, family member, or co-worker has an allergic reaction to smoking, then the smoker's taste cannot count as much as the inhaler's asthma. We asked Tipton's Chuck Macready whether there was a difference between a religious leader's telling a person not to smoke and a doctor's doing the same thing. Yes, he replied, there is. "The surgeon general has science to back him up. I guess the clergy is just an opinion."

When smoking is considered to be an addiction rather than a vice, the smoker is absolved from responsibility for her sin. The same logic works in the other direction: when opposition to smoking is grounded in the ill health it produces, the antismoker's concern for other people is no longer a virtue but a necessary step in a public health campaign. Many of our San Franciscans did not like the word "virtue" because of its association with the idea of vice. Yet they also believed that smoking is something that people ought not to do. Scientific authority helps them resolve the dilemma of instructing others how to live without seeming to impose a morality on them. Carole Yamada believes that the Christian Coalition has no business preaching abstinence, because people ought to be able to lead healthy sex lives without guilt, so long as they practice safe sex. (She adds that people attracted to conservative Christian causes are religion addicts, desperately in need of a codependent relationship with God). As a nurse, however, Ms. Yamada supports efforts to limit people's behavior when such efforts have a scientific justification. "So if research has shown that smoking is bad for you, I tend to appreciate the public service campaigns to decrease or increase people's awareness of the health hazards of smoking, drinking, and unsafe sex." Listening to San Franciscans talk, one gets the impression that science can be a substitute for conscience. Unable to find an acceptable way to regulate behavior they know can be dangerous, they leap on science to give them reasons to practice the self-restraint they are reluctant to admit is necessary. That is why Melissa Pritchett, the cocktail waitress who thinks that there is nothing wrong with a little naughtiness, also believes that it is necessary to warn kids about the dangers that sex can pose in the age of AIDS.

Sex involves more than one person, and so, at least since the discovery of secondhand smoke, do cigarettes. Few Americans have read John Stuart Mill's *On Liberty*, but just about everyone understands Mills's harm principle. We ought to allow people the freedom to live as they like, Americans insist, but that freedom stops where harm to others begins. A 1997 Gallup Poll indicated that 55 percent of Americans—including 64 percent of non-smokers—believed that secondhand smoke is harmful; if smoking hurts others, a justification is provided for fairly broad regulations about what people ought to be allowed to do. Describing himself as a "classic eighteenth-century liberal," San Francisco's Carl Lamb says, "I don't have a philosophical problem with someone wanting to smoke." But he also finds smoking nauseating, believes that smokers are rude, and wonders how people could ever get themselves addicted to something so disgusting. It is as if two of his strongest held beliefs—personal enjoyment and the importance of a healthy lifestyle—have come into a conflict he is unable to resolve.

Quick to apply medical concepts as explanations for behaviors that would once have been held up as examples of virtue or vice, have Americans become increasingly uncomfortable with the concept of individual responsibility? In Fall River, where the language of addiction was resorted to more often than any other place in our study, addictive behavior is not necessarily seen as outside people's control. Lauren Druze, a lawyer, believes that "there are plenty of disorders that are maybe partly chemical or partly psychological." People who have those conditions, she continues, are less likely to resist the temptations around them, but if they do not learn to control themselves, they will, in harming other people, manifest a flawed character. Her views were far from atypical. Greg and Ally Sauvage hold that people who eat or drink too much have a fault in their genetic inheritance, but one still has to do everything one can to help them straighten themselves out. As they understand these issues, people ought to be held responsible for their acts—even when they have a medical condition that predisposes them to act in a particular way.

Of all our respondents in Fall River—indeed, of all our respondents across the whole country—no one had as much experience with the problem of addiction as Marlene Beaulieu. One of seven children, she watched two of her brothers die from drugs. One of them served in Vietnam, came back with an addiction, and, in her words, "never got completely away from it." Her other brother was born with a genetic disorder and developed a drug addiction as a result of his treatment; he too died very young. Mrs. Beaulieu is one of those Americans convinced that addiction is rampant in American life. She believes that, when it comes to drugs, "there's an inborn tendency toward some of these problems."

In comparison with Victorian times, America has most definitely entered a new era in which virtue and vice are redefined in terms of public health and addiction. Still, Marlene Beaulieu's story reminds us why Americans might not wish to emphasize issues of willpower and personal responsibility too emphatically. Neither of her brothers was fully responsible for the conditions that started their addictions; one had a serious disease and the other was exposed to the horrors of the Vietnam experience. A widow, Mrs. Beaulieu might be excused if she were to conclude that her life has been driven by factors over which she has no control. But the fact is that she is not so resigned. In a way that might make little sense to those who deride Americans for their insistence on addictive syndromes, Mrs. Beaulieu believes that resisting temptation "helps us take control of our lives more. We will always have a tendency toward weakness in different ways, but if we let that take over, we become less of who we are." For her, the notion of addiction explains enough about the world to give her the confidence to try to influence those aspects of her life that are subject to her influence.

In her attempts to explain away self-destructive behavior by attributing it to addiction, Mrs. Beaulieu clearly lacks the stern moral backbone that today's moralists attribute to the Victorians. But she also has something they lacked. For all the difficulties life has sent her way, Mrs. Beaulieu is an optimist about life with kind and good words for everyone. In that, she is fairly typical of our respondents. Many of those Fall River residents who insist on the addictive nature of bad behavior do so because they think of themselves as caring people just trying to be good to others. In ascribing bad behavior to addiction, they are asking how much good it really does to others to lecture them for their weakness of will. If people have a problem, they need help, and Americans generally want to be helpful. This ethic of care can be naïve, and real addicts are likely to take advantage of it. Yet the language of addiction, for all its problems, nonetheless testifies to a deeply held belief in the inherent goodness of everyone.

### When Temptation Calls

About a mile from where San Francisco's Carl Lamb lives, there is a store which advertises that it has forty thousand different videos on hand. Always curious about such claims, Mr. Lamb one day ran the numbers and realized that he would have to watch three films a day for the next forty years in order to see everything they stocked, "provided that not another movie is made." The lesson he takes from this is that, when it comes to temptation, he has to be selective. He sees aspects of the Protestant ethic in himself, but he also views himself as a procrastinator, putting off or avoiding whatever unpleasantness comes his way. He knows that he should be living on a tighter budget, for he does not make much money, but he enjoys pampering himself on occasional consumer binges. Married, he has an unabashed appreciation for sex; it is, he tells us, "a healthy part of my life and that's something I feel good about." The more he talks, the clearer it is that Mr. Lamb enjoys the good things in life too much to be all that selective when it comes to temptation. It is as if he really wants to see all those videos before he dies.

Americans will respond to the temptations around them in different ways, but all of them will have to determine for themselves how selective they will be. A surprising number of Americans are very selective indeed. For all the talk of a sexual revolution in America, public attitudes toward sex, as the *New York Times* poll on "The Way We Live Now" revealed, remain stubbornly conventional; 62 percent, for example, said that sex was over-rated when compared with satisfying work or friendship and 63 percent agreed that people who have children lead richer lives than those who do not. Reflecting this sexual conservatism, we found more than a few students at the University of North Carolina determined to hold on to their virginity. One of them, Kirsten Glenn, twenty years old, confessed to feeling ashamed about her determination. Eighty-five percent of the campus is sexually active, she claims, and a good deal of the difficulty involved in resisting the temptation to join them is not pressure from male students but the preening of female ones. When they finally go to bed with a man, she says, "they felt more like a woman. They just glowed, and they thought they crossed this threshold into womanhood that made them more female, because a man loved them enough that they could share their body with them." Ultimately, though, they often came to regret their actions, feeling cheapened and exploited by their experiences. When that happens, Ms.

Glenn believes, they simply ought to say no. "It's not like they have to continue. They have the choice. They can stop if they want to." Although she sometimes feels as the odd person out, Kirsten Glenn takes great pride in having the self-discipline to wait.

Whether they resist or give into the temptations, sexual or otherwise, that so surround them, Americans rely on themselves to make the appropriate decisions. Most individuals will make different decisions at different points in their lives. That is true of Betty Mann, the actress living in San Francisco. Her mother taught her that God's greatest gift "was free choice and free will," and that people who just follow "a set of rules, without ever really choosing for themselves," constitute "a kind of sheepdom." Her father also had a similar outlook on the world, but one day, when Betty was sixteen, he gave it all up in favor of Jesus and became a fundamentalist Christian. Looking back on those days, Ms. Mann feels that while her father was trying to be sincere, he was also very self-absorbed and made little time for his family. She responded by becoming sexually active in high school, provoking a crisis in the family. This was all too much for their father. "He would sit down in the kitchen," Ms. Mann continues, and "he would go to the drawer and pick out the biggest knife in the drawer and put it on the table in front of us and say, 'Why don't you just stick this in your mother's heart?'" It was a shattering thing to do, one that left deep scars on family members. As for Betty herself, she says, "It's not surprising why I went into drama."

Betty Mann did manage to get control over her life. She has no trouble conceiving of self-discipline as a virtue and tries to live according to its demands. Divorced but soon to be remarried, she holds to very old-fashioned views about child rearing. Describing herself as "harsh and judgmental" toward others, she will have no truck with the language of addiction; people who give in to temptation too easily, she says, have "a lack of willpower, a lack of moral fortitude. It's stupid. It's indefensible." It's not that Betty Mann is a pure Victorian in these matters. Self-denial, she believes, is a little too "Jonestowny" for her tastes. Her father, she tells us, would view the kind of behavior in which she engaged as "evil and bad," whereas to her it was "self-destructive." Brought up as a Methodist, but with roots in her family that reach back to the Puritans, Ms. Mann retains enough of the ideas of the Protestant ethic to believe that an individual is put on this earth to lead a good and worthwhile life. But she is enough of a modern person to realize that she ought to do this for her own reasons as well as for God's: "I want to lead a good life because I will be a better person if I lead a good life."

In whatever form it took—Calvinistic pietism, Victorian morality, or Riesman's inner-direction—the Protestant ethic upheld the ideal of an inner calling. One did right by doing good and one did good by finding within oneself the imperatives of duty. It is not difficult to understand the nostalgia for such conceptions of morality among contemporary social critics. Ideas associated with the Protestant ethic convey a sense of moral seriousness, a resonance with a tragic sense of life, and an insistence on rectitude, all of which stand in sharp, and sometimes positive, contrast to the non-judgmentalism of contemporary America. And stoic conceptions of self-discipline often work; especially for those at the bottom of the economic ladder, self-discipline is a requirement for overcoming the debilitating effects of poor schooling, avoiding the temptations of a criminal life, and succeeding in the workplace. A society that turns its back on self-discipline will be more likely to punish those who need it than those who have already obtained its benefits.

The movement away from strict conceptions of self-discipline demonstrated by many of our respondents does not necessarily make life easier to live. For all its heroic character, the Protestant ethic did not call upon the individual to decide where his duty lay; it was up to the individual to resist temptation, not to redefine it. Contemporary Americans clearly live in more relaxed moral times than their Puritan, Victorian, and inner-directed ancestors. They prefer a psychological language to a religious language, at least as religion was understood in the eighteenth and nineteenth century. When they talk of self-discipline and self-indulgence, they think of consumer goods, not God and Satan. But if choices have less dramatic consequences, there are also more choices. There may not be forty thousand temptations out there, but there are enough to cause a certain moral vertigo. That is why so many of those with whom we spoke, rather than chastising people who give into temptation for their weaknesses, are more likely to emphasize the strength it takes to resist any temptations at all.

Dominique Mottau, a cancer prevention specialist in Tipton, Iowa, once lived in India, where she got to meet some cloistered monks. She would describe them as self-disciplined. "But they seclude themselves from the world," she points out. "It's a lot easier to seclude themselves from worldly temptations." For people who live in America at this time, it is much harder to be self-disciplined, she believes, because the temptations of self-gratification are so much more ubiquitous. Randy Craig, a research psychologist in Dayton, is one who thinks he has managed well enough. He is aware of how much self-absorption one finds in the United States these days. "There's a lot more of this yuppie mentality," he says, "and I guess I'm part of it too." But he also understands that giving in to the constant demands made on him to consume would not make him happy, and he has learned to set his own limits. "I don't bother trying to be fashionable or up-to-date. I don't want a BMW. The fact is that I earn enough money to live in a bubble, but I don't have a lot of stuff." He is just going to figure out what works for him and to try to make the best of it.

Mrs. Mottau underestimates how hard it is to live a monastic lifestyle, and Mr. Craig reduces questions of character to questions of consumption. Yet they both remind us that the morality of the Protestant ethic was narrow but deep; the individual had few choices to make, but all those choices were serious. Our morality is shallow but broad; we have many more moral issues to consider, even if few of them will result in eternal damnation, social ostracism, or the poorhouse. Americans are not going to lead twenty-first-century lives based on eighteenth- and nineteenth-century moral ideals. They will not subject themselves to the severe and demanding tests of character imposed on individuals governed by one version or another of the Protestant ethic. But that does not mean that the morality by which people live now makes them soft. It means only that the new morality is different, making up in the bewildering array of temptations it must face what it lacks in rigor and unswerving self-confidence.

# IV. Honesty, to a Point

## *The Ignoble Lie*

Honesty is one of the cardinal virtues of not only our own way of life, but also of most other ones. The Bible warns against bearing false witness. The great St. Augustine could not imagine any justification for lying; speech, he believed, like all other human capacities, was a gift from God, one we abuse if we then engage in the sin of falsehood. The equally great Enlightenment philosopher Immanuel Kant wrote that "to be truthful in all declarations is . . . a sacred and unconditionally commanding law of reason that admits of no expediency whatsoever." Generations of American children were raised to believe that the first president of their country could not tell a lie and that the sixteenth was too plainspoken to suffer fools. In the 1960s, leftist radicals interpreted honesty to mean personal authenticity, while in the 1990s religious conservatives thought of it as fidelity to the literal truth of God's words. Honesty, we tell one another frequently, is the best policy. We want to believe, even as we sometimes know better, that people mean what they say and say what they mean.

To create the conditions of a truly good life, we must find means of cooperation with others, and dishonesty seems to destroy that possibility. Why would anyone else be willing to share with me the fruits of their labor, the pleasures of their imagination, the joy of their love, or the gift of their understanding if I were to make a persistent habit of lying? And why would I ever trust them if they were to return the favor? A society of liars, whatever else it is, cannot be much of a society. Enemies lie—and are supposed to lie. Friends we trust to tell the truth.

The sheer complexity of modern society—the fact that our interactions take place neither with friends nor with enemies but with anonymous strangers we do not know yet whose behavior nonetheless influences everything we do—makes it even that much more essential that we value honesty. Every time we take medicine, fly in a plane, drive to work, eat in a restaurant, or send our children to school, we presume the honesty of those to whom we consign our fate. We think of some virtues—chivalry is one and honor, to the regret of some, may be another—as belonging to a time long past. No one could say the same about honesty. The more we are exposed to others, the greater our need to take what they say on faith. No wonder that so many contemporary thinkers, while not quite as absolutist as Augustine and Kant, nonetheless write in their tradition. The philosopher Sissela Bok recognizes that injunctions always to tell the truth are too strict, but concludes that we need not resort to the lies to which we have grown accustomed, including those little white lies we generally believe do not harm. Even economists and sociobiologists, who often go out of their way to emphasize the self-interested nature of human behavior, have taken to arguing that honesty is a rational strategy for businesspeople to pursue or that human beings (as well as other animal species) gain evolutionary advantages when the signals they give out can be taken to be truthful.

Yet as essential as honesty may be to the smooth functioning of society, people have always told lies—and society has always managed to survive. Not all philosophers treated honesty with the solemnity of

Augustine and Kant. Plato thought it perfectly acceptable for a just soci-ety to perpetuate itself through a lie—so long as it were sufficiently noble. Machiavelli urged leaders to tell falsehoods when demanded by reasons of state. Augustine's view of lying as invariably sinful soon led to the efforts by Thomas Aquinas to distinguish between mischievous lies, the telling of which did constitute a mortal sin, and other kinds of lies, such as those meant to be helpful and those told in jest, the telling of which were not sinful (thereby launching a veritable growth indus-try of casuistic reasoning with respect to this one particular virtue). Kant's severe and unbending stricture against lying was prompted by the criticism of another philosopher, Benjamin Constant, who believed, as most other philosophers do, that there is no duty to be truthful to someone bent on murdering a person we are hiding in our house. Truth telling is one virtue among many, and it may not always be the proper choice. As the political philosopher Ruth Grant reminds us, the anti-hypocrite, suffocating us with self-righteous certainty, can sometimes seem as problematic as the hypocrite.

No one has written in defense of lying as passionately as Augustine and Kant wrote in favor of honesty, since those like Machiavelli who jus-tified the telling of untruths were concerned primarily with politics, not all aspects of society. Yet one can detect an indirect defense of something akin to less than complete honesty in an important tradition in twenti-eth-century American sociology. As if to repudiate any notion that dis-honesty, in destroying trust, makes society impossible, the sociologist Erving Goffman explored the many ways in which social interaction is premised upon our capacity to manage impressions of who we are that might, or might not, have much to do with who we actually might be. Borrowing metaphors from the world of the theater—a place in which, prepared for illusion, we would rightly feel cheated if performers opted to be Kantians—Goffman's morality consisted not in being true to one-self and others, but in one's willingness to accept the claims of others about themselves. No wonder that the moral philosopher Alasdair MacIntyre, who is convinced that Americans are "unwilling to influence another except by reasons which that other he or she judges to be good," finds the sociology of Erving Goffman descriptive of the condition he deplores.

Sociologists like Goffman implicitly argue that the pursuit of pure honesty is not only impossible, but also undesirable. Yet while dishonesty may be impossible to avoid, we would hardly want to celebrate it as a code of good conduct. One does not have to be a nostalgic conservative longing for a return to a more wholesome time to recognize that America has had a problem with honesty since at least the late 1950s. It all seemed to begin with President Eisenhower's lying about U-2 flights over the Soviet Union. Then, in rapid succession, the public discovered that quiz shows failed to reveal the fact that contestants were given answers in advance; that radio disc jockeys secretly accepted payments to push particular records; that amateur athletes were professionals in everything but name; and that preachers pilfered from their flocks. Now we know that presidents lie about their sex lives, their foreign policies, and their plans to cripple opposition parties. We know that scientists sometimes cook their data and that tobacco companies have suppressed research exposing the carcinogenic properties of their product. It is not always possible to know whether the skeptical—some would say nihilistic—views of sociologists like Goffman were a cause or effect of events in real time. Yet the period in which their writings flourished seems to be a time in which Americans discovered that one respected institution after another was betraying its stated purpose. Duplicity, some critics charge, has become a built-in feature of the American way of life.

When the religious traditions, philosophers, and sociologists cannot quite figure out when honesty is required and when it is not, how do people walk the fine line between the honesty that makes them virtuous and the dishonesty that enables them to function? Everyone, to live in this world, has to become something of a moral philosopher. Is honesty always the best policy? we asked our respondents. Many of them replied the way Kerry Cross, an ultrasound technician of Fall River, did when she pointed out that "everyone lies—to a point." Where that point lies for her and the others with whom we spoke might provide a clue as to how anyone maintains any form of honesty in what is increasingly perceived as a dishonest world.

## Managing the Truth

No matter how we phrased questions about actual virtues and vices in our interviews, people invariably responded by citing honesty as one of the defining qualities of a good and virtuous person. Other virtues are important. None of them was brought up as spontaneously, and as frequently, as honesty.

It is, however, a far cry from believing in the importance of honesty to believing that being honest constitutes a categorical imperative. Some Americans take strong positions against dishonesty of any sort; Lewis Watts, the owner of a commercial cleaning business in Hartford, believes that, because "right and wrong is according to the Bible, not what I think," he would follow the advice of his elders, who told him that "a lie is a lie." But far more Americans find the truth-telling ideals of an Augustine or a Kant, however admirable, unrealistic. (One of them brought up the example in dispute between Benjamin Constant and Immanuel Kant and took Constant's side; you have a duty, he believes, to lie to someone who knocks on your door hoping to kill your wife.) Blanket statements, most Americans insist, are not always to be trusted, including such statements as always putting truth first. As our respondents spoke, it became clear that they followed three guiding principles in deciding when the rule always to tell the truth ought to be upheld or relaxed:

- Be more honest with those in your immediate circles.
- Do not be honest if doing so causes harm.
- Honesty must be earned.

Residents of Tipton, Iowa, a small town worlds away from cheating scandals and inside-the-Beltway positioning, speak about honesty in terms that would have been understood by Parson Weems, the late-eighteenth-century clergyman and author to whom we owe the legend that George Washington could not tell a lie. However many examples its residents may had heard of people lying to get ahead, Tiptonites are doing their best to live by their word. Elaine York, a retired secretary who is active in a large number of clubs and lodges, spoke for many of her neighbors when she told us of the time when her small children inadvertently walked out of a restaurant with two candy bars. The next morning on her way to work, she stopped in and paid the owner for them; he in turn then gave her coffee and donuts, the cost of which, she quickly noted, was more than the candy bars would have cost. That's the way people ought to live, she believes, and, fortunately for her, that's the way people in a place like Tipton can live.

Tiptonites know one another personally, and personal relationships reinforce the virtues, a point illustrated through the remarks of Colin Thomas, who sells livestock feed. Farmers are not like other businessmen, he tells us. Other businessmen "can do business anyplace, but the farmer stays there. His family is there. His friends are there." Drawing on a historical analogy, Mr. Thomas talks about the Civil War. Courage is a difficult virtue to practice, but because the Civil War was fought close to home, many young men, knowing that their actions would be reported back to their loved ones, found it impossible to let cowardice overtake them, a condition that "helped make them better people." Honesty, as Tiptonites talk about it, is a matter of reputation, and nothing can be more important in their town than having a good one. "We have to depend on repeat sales in this part of the country," we were told by Daniel Bletzer, who washes cars and cleans apartments. "People catch on right away if you're a straight shooter." Philip Beaty makes the point this way: "When you look someone in the face, it's harder to lie."

But what happens if you do not have to look someone in the face? Philip Beaty's comment was prompted by the question of whether people can get away with things like lying. "If they're lying to individuals, I think they are less likely," he responds. "But they are more likely to lie to entities like corporations." Here we hear echoes of the way Americans approach the question of loyalty; those who trust people are not necessarily going to trust institutions. By emphasizing the role that personal connections play in reinforcing honesty, they are, implicitly or explicitly, criticizing large-scale institutions for reinforcing dishonesty. We do things differently in Iowa, is what many of them believe, for as Dennis Fletcher, an at-home dad who describes himself as an Ayn Rand libertarian, puts it, "you lose virtue when you move to a larger community." His neighbors agreed. Sharon Rice, who is thirty with two small children, is related by marriage to a multimillionaire who heads a large insurance company in the state. But, she says, he drives an old car, wears flannel shirts, and doesn't like to have his picture taken. She leaves no doubt that he is an honest businessman because he grew up on a farm and was taught to be a virtuous person. Hugh Heston, the general superintendent of a local quarry, talks in a similar way about his company. His firm sells stone to contractors in Des Moines, and while the company could increase its profits, and even employ more locals, if it cut back on quality, were it to do so, word would quickly spread to the state capital and undercut its reputation.

As much as Tiptonites value honesty, in short, their comments leave open the possibility that under circumstances quite different from their own—for example, in the larger and more anonymous world of impersonal organizations—dishonesty may sometimes be permissible. Tucker Newman, a retired accountant, is as skeptical about honesty as any urban sophisticate. The idea that there ought to be one standard for lying "strikes me as absurd to begin with," he says. Stealing bubble gum when you are a kid—a situation not unlike the youthful theft of a neighbor's pears which left St. Augustine persuaded that he was a sinner—is not the same as "if you killed somebody and lied about it." Mr. Newman simply does not believe in absolutes.

His neighbors too find that they cannot be faithful to the rule that one must always tell the truth—even if only to those you know personally. Consider Philip Beaty, the man who believes that you cannot lie to someone you are looking in the face. Like some of our other respondents, he recalls seeing the movie *Liar, Liar,* in which the lead character is unable to speak anything but the truth, and it reminds him that the pursuit of truth can be taken to an extreme in which it becomes nonsensical. So how can one be committed to being truthful if one cannot be truthful all the time? In the tradition of Aquinas, he responds by saying that "maybe you can be honest about everything you say, but there should always be things you do not say." Even though the point of a rule is to give objective moral guidance as a substitute for subjective judgment, Mr. Beaty still finds that he has to use his own judgment in determining whether silence or speech is the more appropriate response.

To complicate matters further, most Americans would rather be kind than honest; according to the *New York Times* poll on "The Way We Live Now," 60 percent of Americans agree with the statement that "lying is sometimes necessary, especially to protect someone's feelings," compared with 37 percent who do not. Throughout our interviews, people said, in one way or another, that brutal honesty, like blind loyalty, is a virtue transformed into a vice, more characteristic of a sadist than a person of good character. The moral instinct of Tiptonites is to value honesty more when the recipient of one's honesty is a close neighbor or friend than when it is a stranger. But the injunction to avoid the truth when the truth hurts means that one inevitably tells justifiable falsehoods to friends that one need not tell to strangers. This is why, as Fall River's Judy Wasserman puts it, "you've got to be well skilled in being honest."

The question of when to be truthful has to be handled with the tact of a diplomat. When you are convinced that someone has made a mistake, you ought to let them know, says Greensboro's Will Thurber, a twenty-one-year-old student, but "you can't just blindly go in there and bum-rush somebody into this or that" because that would be intimidating. His fellow student Joseph Anderson agrees; you shouldn't "go after somebody with a hammer," as he puts it, but you can "approach somebody under the cover of friendship and say we need to talk about this." Preaching from a position of holier-than-thou virtue, according to Dayton's Maureen Irvine, might make you feel better, but if you are not tactful with other people, "you're not doing anyone any good." Warren Wilson of Dayton, who learned the meaning of loyalty in the military, is among the most morally traditional of our respondents, but that does not mean he thinks that we can be honest all the time. It is bad, he thinks, to lie for reasons of personal advantage but it is not bad to shade the truth to make someone else feel better. There is, he says, "a definite distinction to be made. There's plenty of gray areas out there for maneuvering."

Truth, it would seem, is not something we tell but instead something we manage. As important as telling the truth may be, other matters, like friendship, can be important as well. Judy Wasserman wants both to be honest and to have good friends, but it is not clear to her how to maintain both. She says, "We don't have the same level of friendship with everybody we come into contact with. If you have one or two people that you really feel that kind of friendship and closeness to, that's great." If she were to follow the moral command to be honest with everyone, Mrs. Wasserman thinks that her capacity to decide that friends are more worthy of her honesty than strangers would be taken from her. On the other hand, if she follows the command so popular among Tiptonites to reserve honesty just for her friends, she might find herself with fewer of them. That has happened, she tells us. Mrs. Wasserman recalls experiences in which, persuaded of her friendship with another person, she chose to be honest, only to discover that the friendship could not survive the honesty. There are, then, limits to honesty. "You can't open up your closet and pull all your skeletons out and survive," says Fall River's Julie Blanc, a forty-year-old single woman.

Sometimes people find themselves believing that there is such a thing as too much honesty. Like so many of those we interviewed, San Francisco's Gina Grossman, the therapist, who is also a community activist, says that we ought not to say unkind things in the interests of truth. But she went much further than most of our respondents: "I think the whole idea about honesty got a little bit skewed after the 1960s. Honesty got defined as just like spilling your guts in whatever way moved you." That wasn't really honesty, she suggests, but a form of self-indulgence. Honesty can become an excuse for not doing the hard work of considering the feelings of other people: "You know, people say shitty things and then they go, 'Well, I was just being honest.'" Classical conceptions of the virtues believe that a person of good character will be honest. Ms. Grossman, by contrast, would place "being of good character above honesty." Character means knowing what is right, which means knowing when not to be fully honest. "There are lots of different ways to be honest," she says, and a good person will figure out which one is the most appropriate for which situation.

Finally, our respondents believe that honesty must be earned. If we were always honest to everyone, we would be giving the gift of honesty both to those who deserve it and to those who do not. Maddy Riessman, a student in Greensboro, tells us about the time she set her alarm for the wrong time, thereby missing a test. Needing a doctor's note, she tried to get one, only to discover that she could not fool the authorities. She finally confessed her lie to the teacher, and the teacher, in turn, excused her. Although she questioned the school's policy toward unexcused absences—each one requires a reduction in a student's letter grade— she understands that there are legitimate reasons for the college's rules. But not all rules are considered legitimate by our respondents, especially when they are formulated by bureaucratic agencies that are viewed as inflexible. Another student, Stewart Helen, told of a friend who signed up to join the navy. On the bus, Stewart's friend talked to someone who was rejected because he admitted that, five or six years ago, he had taken drugs. Were Stewart in that situation, he believes that lying might have been justified. The navy's rules were not legitimate because they did not take into account a person's "potential for change." One reason Americans believe that they are justified in being less than truthful to bureaucratic institutions is a persistent feeling that such institutions have not done all they could to win people's trust.

Of all the bureaucracies with which Americans come in contact, none is viewed as having earned honesty less than the Internal Revenue Service. One of our retired Tiptonites believes that companies would be wrong to cheat their customers. His reasoning is straightforward. People who do business with you expect you to be honest. If you then lie to them, you not only gain advantages for yourself, but upset their expectations of how you are supposed to act. Is there a difference between that and cheating on a tax return? we asked. Yes, he immediately replied, there was, for the IRS expects to be cheated. People who lie to the tax authorities—he is not one of them—therefore do not violate the expectations that IRS authorities have. Many of our respondents made it a point of insisting that they were honest on their taxes, a finding reinforced by the "Way We Live Now" poll in which 84 percent claimed never to have cheated on their taxes. People may or may not be quite that honest in reality; if they are not, distrust of the IRS, widely shared among our respondents, may be the reason. One of our Hartford respondents would immediately return money to a helpless person—say, an elderly lady on the street—if she dropped it, but he believes that there are circumstances in which cheating on taxes can be justified. A respondent from Fall River sums up this whole way of thinking. "I consider myself to be really honest," he says. "However, there are times when I keep my mouth shut." Without prompting, he then went on to say that "I will cheat the IRS if I have a chance. And insurance companies, I would cheat them too."

The IRS, moreover, is not the only governmental agency widely perceived as being unresponsive and not always deserving of honest treatment. An immigrant from an Eastern European country living in San Francisco tells how he once tried to deal honestly with the Immigration and Naturalization Service (INS) and was instead treated with arrogance and contempt. That arrogance may constitute one reason that the INS is often considered fair game for less than honest treatment. Whether or not governmental agencies deserve their reputation for dishonesty is not an issue on which our respondents spend much intellectual energy. This kind of thing is just assumed, often surrounded by a deeply entrenched folk wisdom to the effect that such agencies are always cutting corners with the truth. One of our Hartford residents is convinced that the police of his town ignore the drug dealers and go after the law abiding for speeding, especially when they have quotas to fill. This does not lead him to advocate breaking the law, but it does persuade him that honest people pay a price for their honesty.

Perhaps the most extreme example of a situation in which honesty is viewed as an unearned response came from one of our respondents in San Francisco. She works for an organization providing medical marijuana for people dying in hospitals, an activity that is quite illegal, but one that is nonetheless tolerated by the authorities on the grounds that the relief of suffering is a good thing. Her employment, furthermore, is as illegal as her work. She once suffered an injury, thereby acquiring disability status that made her eligible for insurance—on condition that she is incapable of working. Does she feel guilty about cheating the insurance company? Not really, she says. They try to play games with her and she plays games with them. Under such circumstances, "you feel a little more lenient with honesty, as it were."

Neither St. Augustine nor Immanuel Kant would find much to admire in the way modern Americans think about honesty. Whether they live in local communities or big cities, Americans do not believe that telling the truth constitutes a moral command they ought always to obey. Few of them would work in an illegal capacity for an illegal organization. But whether to be silent or to tell the truth, whether to be more truthful to friends because you value their friendship or less truthful because you want to keep their friendship, whether to hurt another's feelings, whether to be honest with those who are less than honest or fair with you—these are the kinds of issues they have to answer themselves in the course of daily life. Being less than honest in every circumstance may be a vice, but it is something they cannot seem to live without. Moral commands help them with the black-and-white questions, but their daily lives are dominated by the gray ones, where such commands can only be suggestive, not definitive.

### Unexpected Realpolitik

Once relatively trustful toward government, Americans, according to nearly all polls, now look with suspicion upon it. Survey researchers use the term "optimism gap" to express the difference between the prospects most Americans envision for themselves and their family, which are usually positive, and those envisioned for their country, which are negative. That gap is as high as it has ever been. Generally suspicious of most forms of authority, Americans have become especially suspicious of political authority. For those who believe that we need government to bind us together as a people and to express our common sense of purpose, this withering away of public confidence in our political institutions ranks as one of the most serious problems we face.

The lack of confidence Americans have in politicians cannot be overemphasized. Can we trust politicians to speak honesty? we asked our respondents. The near universal answer was that we cannot. "Politicians, they never talk straight," says Fall River's Karim Abdullah, an Egyptian-born small businessman. "They always find an excuse for everything. They make up things." Grant Lowell of Tipton thinks that the political arena has become "infected." San Francisco's Doug Reed, who manages a medical library, considers himself an idealist who believes that politicians ought to be truthful, but, he also feels, it's all "elaborate pretend and deceit." We were told by Sarah Lloyd, also of San Francisco, "I'm really disgusted with our political system." "It's extremely difficult to get elected without twisting the truth," adds Richard Banks, a systems group manager. As far as politics is concerned, "there's inherent dishonesty there."

Attitudes toward politics and politicians were no different among the younger respondents with whom we talked, such as the students at the University of North Carolina in Greensboro. The rewards of following politics get "smaller and smaller every year," according to Maddy Riessman. Theresa Howard believes that politicians ought to be as honest as anyone else, but, because they are not, she cannot find a way to trust what they say. A lot of them are outright liars, adds Derrik Brown, and even when what they say is nonetheless based on fact, they will find a way to twist the facts around to suit their own purposes. In theory, politics unites people around common values. In practice, at least in America, what people hold in common are negative views about politicians.

One reason Americans believe that politicians will lie to them is that so many of them have. Bob Woodward, the best-selling *Washington Post* journalist, easily found enough material to fill a fairly thick book devoted to examining the untruths of the last five presidents of the United States. The philosopher Hannah Arendt is one of many thinkers who have wondered whether democracy can survive such pervasive disregard for the truth. She once posed the issue through the following thought experiment: Would it be worse to live in a society without truth than a society without justice or freedom? Her answer was that we could still imagine an unjust or unfree society, but no society would even be imaginable without truth. For society remains alive even when those who live within it at any particular point in time do not. "No permanence, no perseverance in existence, can even be conceived of without men willing to testify to what is and appears to them because it is," she wrote. Arendt looked out on America in the years after World War II and did not like what she saw. In earlier times, statesmen, sometimes following the advice of a Machiavelli or Hobbes, would lie, but what Arendt called the traditional lie "was never meant to deceive everybody; it was directed at the enemy and was meant to deceive only him." In contemporary society, by contrast, given over to image making, lies are offered even on matters known by everyone to be true, which means that we all become participants in a world of mutual self-deception. "Under fully democratic conditions," she wrote, "deception without self-deception is well-nigh impossible."

Arendt penned her thoughts, one hastens to add, *before* President Lyndon Johnson started lying systematically about America's role in Vietnam and Richard Nixon deliberately lied about his role in Watergate. If the evidence compiled by surveys—and by my interviews—is linked to the recent history of presidential shenanigans, citizens and their elected officials find themselves in a vicious cycle in which each assumes the worst of the other. The results, many believe, can hardly be encouraging for democracy. Cynicism, the sociologist Jeffrey Goldfarb has written, is something we associate with mass society—"the underside of democracy," he called it—and with authoritarian states. Because "cynicism promotes acceptance of the existing order of things," it operates invariably as a conservative force, turning away the eyes of Americans from the task of energizing their democracy to make it better.

Nonetheless, just because Americans believe that politicians do not tell the truth does not mean that they think politicians should tell the truth. Some lies, they might conclude, are justifiable, perhaps even required. If so, their outlook is neither cynical nor suspicious but reflects an understanding of, and perhaps even an appreciation for, traditions of realpolitik that require leaders to be less than straightforward. No one can doubt that the great majority of those with whom we spoke do not trust politicians to speak honestly. The surprise is how many of them nonetheless trust politicians to lead.

A number of our older respondents recall that Franklin Roosevelt insisted on his isolationism even as he prepared to lead the country into World War II, that the Allies intentionally confused the Germans about the location of their invasion of Europe, and that Harry Truman kept secret the use of the atomic bomb that ended that same war. These, they believe, were fully justified actions; indeed, reflecting on Truman's decision, Tipton's Tucker Newman insisted that dishonesty, not truthfulness, was the more virtuous way for him to act. Although he expressed much stronger commitments than Mr. Newman to the principle of putting honesty first, Tipton's Philip Beaty also understood that matters of state require very different kinds of actions. He tells us that he would not want to go to a doctor or lawyer who was not trained, so he understands that politicians also need a certain amount of professional autonomy. So long as national security is really at stake—Mr. Beaty worries that dishonest politicians will cover their actions by invoking national security concerns when they are not appropriate—politicians would be justified in lying.

Yet as they talked about the relationship between truth and politics, the thoughts of our respondents went well beyond matters of national security. Some of them believe that because politics is a different realm than ordinary life, the rules of ordinary life do not, and perhaps ought not, apply. When Fall River's Barbara Brown, who supervises a state child-care facility, thinks about politics, she recognizes that standards of honesty might have to be lowered. "I guess if they have their eye on the right star and on the right goal that is a laudable goal," she says, "I could overlook a few things along the way." It is not that Mrs. Brown thinks the end always justifies the means. But she does think that if politicians might have to bend a few rules here and there, nothing is really wrong if they do so in pursuit of worthwhile causes. In a similar way, San Antonio's Enrique Lopez, an auto mechanic, sees nothing wrong if a politician lies—so long as she does so for the purpose of doing good. Hartford's Donna Teele agrees: "If there is a bigger good," she says, "I guess maybe a little dishonesty is okay if the ultimate goal you're willing to achieve is going to be better for a larger group."

Randy Craig, the Dayton research psychologist, is politically knowledgeable enough to know that Michael Harrington was a socialist writer and that Martin Luther King Jr. held positions on issues other than race. When he speaks about politics, he makes a sharp distinction between the private qualities of politicians and their public jobs. "I think there are conservatives and liberals who are terrible role models for young people, but they have a legitimate policy or political viewpoint to advance." Then, he continues, one has to consider the different kinds of tasks they set for themselves. "Many politicians are honorable people struggling with difficult choices in a democratic society," he points out, and he would include in that category former Speaker of the House Newt Gingrich, whom he otherwise does not like. Sure, he says, a lot of politicians are not honest. They take bribes and look out only for themselves. But a democracy can survive such petty corruption. "I'm not saying it's good, but I wouldn't put it on the same plane as organizing the destruction of the Jewish population of my country."

People who respond this way understand at some instinctual level that politics, because it contains the potential for violence, has consequences that require a special kind of temperament. Jim Crowley, the Atherton money manager, has given extensive advice to clients concerning their investment portfolios in the course of his career. "I've had to make some tough decisions in my life," he ruminates, "but they never involved the loss of life of other people." All he can say about politicians is "I'm glad I don't have to make those kinds of decisions."

In theory, cynicism toward politics ought to have its greatest effect on the young, since their entire private lives have been lived in the shadow of one public scandal after another. While it is true that many of the students with whom we spoke in Greensboro believe, like everyone else in their society, that politicians lie, they too understood that politics is not like ordinary life. Cory Hanson, a twenty-two year old, has no illusions about politics; politicians will say anything to get elected, frequently making promises they have no intention of keeping. But is that so bad? he wonders. It may be deception, but "that's how you get into office." If a person cannot win by running on his convictions, but nonetheless has such convictions and wants to influence the country based on them, of course he will hide those convictions. In politics it is important to keep things moving and a little dishonesty can help that along. So there is always going to be some dishonesty and, the more Mr. Hanson thinks about it, the more he reaches the conclusion that maybe there ought to be some dishonesty. "I know that's kind of the wrong answer," he adds, sounding as if he were trying to be a dutiful student. But shifting tone to sound like a realist, he concludes that "it's also important to understand that it's there." Ordinary people can afford to be moral, Will Thurber believes, because the decisions they make are not all that complicated. Politicians, by contrast, "have more variables to look at than the rest of us." If what they do will help the greater good of the society, and if there is no other way to obtain that good than by telling falsehoods, then it is better that they should lie.

There is yet another reason to question whether negative attitudes toward politicians properly can be considered cynicism. The cynic speaks from the position of an ideal corrupted: I have high standards for our politicians, she would say, but because they fail to live up to them, I have been forced, against my inclination, to lower those standards. But suppose our politicians lie because we essentially ask them to do so? Jon Hunter, an eighteen year old, reasoned along these lines. A political science major, he has come to realize that people often have unrealistic expectations of what they want from government. Somewhat naïve, they vote for people who offer them easy solutions, even when there are no easy solutions. "The public wants the easy answer. That forces a politician to be dishonest" is how he puts it. He recalls the time that one candidate for the presidency, Walter Mondale, told the truth: if you want the services that government provides, you will have to be pay for them in the form of higher taxes. His opponent—"I think it was Reagan"—when asked if he would raise taxes, "said no and sat down. That was his answer. Nothing followed." If people vote for the man who makes promises that can never be kept, Jon won't blame the politicians but the public. Another Greensboro student, Tracy Lachance, an education major active in religious activities, has high hopes for a recently elected congressman from her district. If he eventually goes bad, she thinks, the voters will have only themselves to blame for not rewarding him for trying to be good. One can hardly call views like these cynical. They instead reflect the fact that democracy encourages, not the mutual self-deception emphasized by Hannah Arendt, but the mutual responsibility that citizens and leaders have toward one another.

If it is true that Americans can and do understand the need for occasional dishonesty in politics, it follows that, for all the talk of how cynical they have become, they can nonetheless appreciate good leadership when they see it. Our respondents distrust politics in general, but they do not necessarily distrust all politicians. Reflecting the distinction between personal and impersonal authority so characteristic of their outlook on life, many of them are wary of their national politicians, although they are more likely to admire the local variety—up to and including their representatives in Congress. But there are also national politicians who meet their test of approval, even if some of them—Colin Powell's name is mentioned with some frequency—did not make their career in politics. It may reflect a kind of nostalgia, but they look back on previous presidents like Harry Truman, John F. Kennedy, and Ronald Reagan and find them worthy of admiration. When those with whom we spoke do not necessarily admire a politician, they are also capable of making distinctions between those aspects of his character they may not trust and those policies he pursues that they like. (The bulk of our interviews took place during the period in which President Clinton was under the threat of impeachment and removal from office. Just as the polls taken during that time indicated, most of our respondents thought Bill Clinton a man of bad character because of his tendency to lie, but many also thought the country was doing well under his leadership.)

There has long existed a distinguished tradition of political reform in America preoccupied with the failure of people to live up to high standards. Once persuaded that citizens drank too much, were too boisterous, or tended to vote for political machines for no other reason than that they offered them jobs, reformers tried to elevate the character of Americans in order to produce a more enlightened kind of politics. The mantle of this tradition of mugwumpery has been passed on to those, like Yale law professor Stephen Carter, who argue that our failure to live up to classical conceptions of the virtuous life has serious spill-over effects that degrade our public life. "We cannot expect our politicians to create a politics better than we are," Carter has written; "people tend to get the politics they deserve." Lying is one of those private vices that has pernicious public consequences. If Americans cut corners with the truth in their daily dealings with one another, they cannot expect that their leaders will treat the truth with reverence and respect. We must cure ourselves before we can cure democracy.

This way of thinking is not very helpful. Our discussions with ordinary Americans suggest that they are not naïve innocents. They understand that the whole point of politics is to get things done that people cannot do by themselves in the course of their daily lives. Say you want to get a school built in your neighborhood, Ben Farrell, the Fall River loan officer, points out. Try all you want, "that is not a decision that one person makes." The whole process is so cumbersome—"so much bureaucratic stuff, too much red tape"—that the only way that school is ever going to get built is by people capable of cutting a few corners. That's why we should not "misconstrue a lack of honesty as someone being a crook." George Washington Plunkitt, the leader of New York's Tammany Hall political machine, once made a distinction between the good graft associated with ordinary, if not always legal, business contracts and the bad graft associated with criminal activities such as blackmail. Mr. Farrell is expressing a simliar idea. Not well informed about politics, holding politicians in low esteem, and not hopeful that politics can accomplish much good, people like Ben Farrell recognize that whatever does get accomplished happens because some people will gain something along the way. That may not be the best of all possible worlds, but given the way the world is, it is not all that bad.

## Business Hopes

The Americans with whom we spoke did not generally believe that business placed a particularly high premium on loyalty. Indeed, as they complain about the lack of loyalty in business, they often sound like recruits for a Ralph Nader campaign against big industry. When the subject turns from loyalty to honesty, however, they begin to sound like Nader's critics, insisting, often vehemently, that honesty is possible in business in a way that it is not in politics. In part this is a reflection of the fact that Americans have usually had more positive feelings toward business than they have had toward politics. But it may also reflect a perceived difference in the nature of these two different realms that yields clues about the way Americans think about honesty in general.

To say that Americans think better of business than of politics does not mean that they think business is beyond moral reproach. Business, we were told by Fall River's Lauren Druze, is about making deals, and that always involves what she calls "positioning people." It bothers Julie Blanc, also of Fall River, that cutthroat types who take advantage of others go further in the business world than honest types. "There's all kinds of games that go on in corporations," according to San Francisco's Richard Banks. People get misled by others all the time and no one wants to take responsibility. Sarah Lloyd, who once worked in public relations, feels that she had to quit because she couldn't stand making products out to be better than she knew them to be. Anyone who values truth, all these people are saying, will not make it far in the world of the modern marketplace.

Fall River's Stephen Turner gets especially annoyed by companies that declare bankruptcy, only to open up again under another name. "But, you know, it's the same guy, and it can be very galling to see that sort of thing happen because you know he stiffed a bunch of people." In the same spirit, San Francisco's Carl Lamb says: "I think there are some parts of business which are accepted to be dishonest from the get-go." He has no problem identifying where to find them: telemarketing, used car dealers, direct mail. (Others add insurance companies, lawyers, salesmen of all kinds, "bait-and-switch" solicitors for telephone service, the gambling industry, and real estate brokers.) Fortunately, he believes, not all firms are like those. But enough of them are to arouse suspicion about whether the aggressive pursuit of profit is compatible with a virtue like honesty.

Despite these examples, the overwhelming majority of our respondents think that honesty has an important role to play in the world of business. You can always find shortcuts if you want to, we were told by San Antonio's Lou Lamkin, citing the case of those who sued McDonald's for serving hot coffee instead of taking responsibility for their own actions. But such tactics go only so far. "A person who deals with the public in an honest fashion, provides a good product for a good price, stands behind his product, and will work with customers that have a dissatisfaction will eventually do much, much better than someone who has less forthrightness in his dealings." Tipton's Dennis Fletcher, the Ayn Rand libertarian, uses nearly identical words to make the same point. So does his neighbor Charleton Marshall, a route supervisor for a wine distributor. Dayton's Gary Radzikowski calls this way of thinking "cash register honesty," by which he means the principle that if someone gives you too much money by mistake, your best response is to give it back. Gloria Lapchik, a Dayton sales representative, adds that good business ethics are often responsible for a company's success rate. "You can be very honest and get ahead in the business world" is how Atherton's Alice Perrone, the executive director of a Silicon Valley community foundation, makes the same point.

As they talked about the role that honesty can and should play in business, our respondents reveal little of the realpolitik (which often passes for cynicism) they find justifiable in politics. There is something odd in this response. Business in America, to a considerable degree, is politics. Not only do many firms benefit from the influence they exercise in Washington and in state and local government, many of the qualities necessary for one activity—workaholism, ambition, the possession of a strategic sense, a willingness to let the ends justify the means—are also necessary for the other. The negative feelings Americans hold toward politicians have been fueled by a series of scandals in which politicians were exposed as liars. But much the same thing could be said about business conduct. It is not just the tobacco industry that has cut corners with the truth: supermarkets, respected news organizations, tire manufacturers, drug companies—the roll call of corporate malfeasance is a long one. How, then, can we explain this persistent sense that honesty is, and ought to be, possible in one realm and not the other?

A great deal depends on what kind of business we are talking about. For instance, Americans seem to have little faith in the heavily industrial manufacturing companies that once dominated the American Midwest, at least according to some of our respondents in a classic Midwestern industrial city, Dayton, Ohio. Henry Muller, the industrial engineer who now teaches engineering, recalls the story of the Ford Pinto, a car built with a tendency to explode during rear-end collisions. Weighing the costs of human life against those of retooling the design of the car, Ford decided that the rational act was to leave the car alone. Mr. Muller is offended on both humanistic and professional grounds. As an engineer, he knows that there are all kinds of ways that cars can be improved so that they will last longer. But the auto companies spurn them, because longer lasting cars mean lower profits. Dayton's Mary Ann Barrows describes the contrast between huge manufacturing companies and what she considers the epitome of the trustworthy company—her family's advertising design firm. Large firms have to assume that everyone is stealing something, since "there's no way they can keep track of inventory." When a firm gets too impersonal, rules of reciprocity and cooperation are replaced by new rules, she believes. One of them is that "whenever you put something over on somebody else, that's a real coup." Another is to make every effort "to get something for nothing."

The views of Mr. Muller and Mrs. Barrows reflect a distrust of impersonal bureaucracies and a preference for those forms of business enterprise that are local in nature. Some of our respondents hope that the anonymity and irresponsibility of large-scale business will also be challenged by the emergence of a "new economy" situated in high technology firms that tend to be smaller and more flexible. Dayton's Thomas Idzal is one of them. Asked whether a person can be honest and still be a success in business, he unhesitatingly replies, "Absolutely." In his view, "business doesn't stay around if they don't treat people fairly." Mr. Idzal is a software developer, successful enough to live in one of the more palatial houses in his expensive suburb. He is quick to note that "over half of our GNP is now service-oriented. We're a manufacturing country. We're an assembly plant country with a lot of services surrounding it." Newer industries are not only more competitive, they place a greater emphasis on the personal qualities of their employees. In those industries, business "is truly a relationship. Like a family. It really is."

The great home of software development in America is in Silicon Valley, and many of the people we talked to there were as enthusiastic in their appreciation of the positive role honesty can play in the business world as Mr. Idzal. Despite the competitive nature of their industry, one which in theory ought to encourage a short-term outlook on the world, they insist that honesty is the only thing that pays in the long term. "If you're dishonest once," says David Wong citing principles he learned from Buddhism, "you may make some profit. The next time around, you're not going to get the business." Theresa Lombardi has seen a lot of people get ahead by cheating, but she attributes her husband's success in business to the fact that others know that his word can be trusted. Jim Crowley has had hands-on experience with the question of honesty in business. Once his company made a bad mistake that resulted in considerable customer anger. Mr. Crowley realized that a forthright apology was needed, but he also knew, from watching President Clinton, that an apology given too quickly will be perceived as insincere. He developed a four-step response to his company's mistake, the first of which was to wait before saying anything in order to convey how seriously the company took the issue. Reflecting on his experience, he tells us that honesty "is not like a light switch" in the sense that either you are honest or you are not. Instead, "honesty is something you've got to work at every day, because the first person you're likely not to be entirely honest with is yourself." Ron Bishop, an eighty-two-year-old retired engineer, was once in charge of eight hundred people at two of his company's locations. "I initiated the program of having quality control four times a year, and I told them everything I knew about what the company was trying to do, whether there might be transfers, whether we were going to get new business, or whether we have to drop out of other businesses." There is no other way to treat modern employees, he insists, than by trying to win their trust, and that can only be done by being honest with them.

On the face of it, the comments of these individuals represent a certain amount of wishful thinking. Business is business, after all, and intense competition usually makes for a certain amount of corner cutting. Nowhere in America has competition been quite so intense as among Internet start-up companies, and it is difficult to believe that firms such as Microsoft or Oracle became leaders in their field by following Marquis of Queensberry rules. That is why it was refreshing to talk with Calvin Lister, the software executive, who acknowledges that "we don't sit there and advertise about all our warts. Why would we do that?" Mr. Lister is fairly realistic in his outlook on the world. He sees Silicon Valley as a place that requires both cooperation, which encourages honesty, and competition, which does not. (Inventive in language as well as technology, Silicon Valley encourages new terms—"coopetition," "comperation"—to describe this world where enemies and friends are not clearly defined.) Under those circumstances, "the notion of honesty becomes pretty diluted. I'm not even sure it fits."

What explains the fact that so few of Mr. Lister's neighbors were as forthright as he was? We hear in the comments made by those in Atherton an attempt to describe not the business world as it is, but as they would like it to be. Much has been made of the transformation of the American economy from one that primarily produces goods to one that primarily offers services. As Francis Fukuyama has emphasized, the new information industries sprouting up around the United States, organized by networks and dependent on human brainpower, distribute tasks sideways rather than through up-and-down chains of command, and are therefore likely to encourage open lines of communication and more egalitarian social relations. By stressing the role that honesty can play in the new industries springing up in California, our other respondents are expressing a hope that the new economy associated with high technology will reward a virtue like honesty more than the heavy industry of yesterday. It is as if an old-fashioned technology like manufacturing is stuck with a kind of postmodern disrespect for the truth, while a postmodern industry like information technology can restore old-fashioned, traditional virtues.

In Silicon Valley, some of the residents we interviewed insist, the whole way one goes about starting a business is different. Charles Young, an engineer and business developer who impressed us as one of the most forthright of our interviewees, asks us to imagine the situation of a person who had a good idea but failed to turn a profit, and who wants to try yet again. He describes how a venture capitalist in Silicon Valley would likely respond:

> Just knowing some of these VCs, there's enough altruism out there to reach a certain distance and say that, you know, I like you. You screwed up once before. Your business has collapsed. But I know you've got some good stuff there. Some good ideas. Let's try again. And the relationship you have with the alliance partners I'm going to line up with are based on win-win kinds of negotiations, not "I'm going to screw you."

"That's one of the most positive aspects of this whole venture capital community," he continues. "It's so small that you can't be dishonest and succeed. Why? Because everybody knows you." It is not only the way money is raised that makes Silicon Valley different, others in the region believed, but also the nature of the products made there. "I think that the technology is making it possible for the playing field to be clean" is how Henry Lo puts it. In the past, he says, it was usually a matter of whom you could bribe to get a particular contract. "You knew the truckers or you could get a certain real estate deal. But now it isn't a question of where your company's located if it is located in cyberspace or even [a question of] knowing certain politicians because they can't tax cyberspace, right?" The only things that matter among Internet start-ups are "Have you really figured out the market? Are you really offering good value?"

These are individuals who are claiming that new ways of doing business carry with them new ways of being honest. Whether this hope is realistic is less important than what it teaches us about honesty itself. For the most important difference our respondents see between old-fashioned manufacturing firms and newer service-sector and technology ones has to do with the role that personal responsibility plays in fostering conditions for virtuous behavior. Old-line manufacturing firms can be viewed in the same way as Americans view government: impersonal, distant, and inefficient. Whenever bureaucracy is responsible for organizing people to work together, no one has personal responsibility for the final product. Under such conditions, there is no reason to be truthful, since the role you play as a small cog in a big machine makes your conduct irrelevant to the company's success or failure. The opposite, many of our respondents want to believe, may be true in newer industries. In the old-line manufacturing firms, says Jay Boylen, the headhunter, "most of the people who get ahead are the ones that have avoided taking any risks." Entrepreneurs, by contrast, because they are so self-confident about their abilities can, so long as they are successful, "voice strong opinions or take a contrary view."

Living in a world in which one manages the truth in daily life, and unwilling to trust politicians with the truth even as they understand why they sometimes have to lie, many of our respondents view the emergence of new forms of industry as one possible place in which personal responsibility will be encouraged. Their hopes may soon be dashed; in terms of monopoly power and aggressive business tactics, Silicon Valley, as the government's attempt to break up Microsoft reminds us, increasingly looks little different from the oil industry when it was transformed by John D. Rockefeller. But the more important point may be that people want to believe that honesty is possible in business because they want to believe that honesty is possible anywhere. Compared with cynicism, naïveté may not be all that bad. At least it leaves open the possibility that somewhere, somehow, one of the virtues we once so admired may come into fashion again.

### Zones of Honesty

Americans think about honesty as a conditional, not an absolute, virtue; it is dependent, as San Antonio's Antonia Gomez puts it, "on the type of life you live." This is a way of thinking that, because it encourages relativism, would not sit well with classical theories of the virtues, but it is widespread nonetheless. Few would put the matter as bluntly as Hartford's Mark Jackson, who says that "cheating is not so much good or bad; it depends on what you're cheating about," but many would understand what he was driving at. Philosophically speaking, Americans are consequentialists: they opt for honesty when the consequences of dishonesty get out of hand. They are also, politically speaking, individualistic: Americans do not pay homage to honesty; honesty is expected to pay homage to them. Unable, when not unwilling, to follow the maxim of being always true to one's word, Americans treat honesty in functional terms. To them honesty is the best policy precisely because it is a policy, something we manage for the sake of getting along somewhat better in the world—and something we can change when circumstances demand a new one.

Even those among our respondents who insist most vociferously on the importance of honesty do so for purposes of what Cheryl Broca of Fall River calls her "self-respect." Ms. Broca, who is thirty-four and divorced, laughingly tells us that, at least according to her mother, she was born in the wrong generation, so strong is her belief in honesty. But it is a belief rooted more in the contemporary language of self-realization than in the classical language of self-denial. "We have to be honest if we want to grow" is how she put it. Even if her honesty resulted in a lower paying job and fewer friends, she would pay the price "because I can look myself in the mirror and say, 'You know what? I feel good about me. I don't have to play their game.'" Truth telling, which can be good for you, can also be good for others. "Telling the truth is not that hard," Greensboro's Whitney Carter, who thinks of herself as a recovering liar, tells us. Sure, there might be bad feelings if you tell the blunt truth to a friend, but if you lie to them, "in the end you are not protecting their feelings. The truth is going to come out sometime." Dayton's Gloria Lapchik recalls learning from the nuns who taught her that if she and her classmates misbehaved, "the holy ghost was going to come down and make us a grease spot." As an adult, she has come to reject much of her strict religious upbringing for the same reason that so many Americans relax older standards of self-discipline: "I don't want to suffer to get my reward." But she still believes in the importance of honesty, even if for more mundane reasons. She tries not to lie because lying gets you into trouble. "To be honest," she says, "is a simple thing." Andres Serrano, an insurance agent and part-time postal truck driver in San Antonio, says that "I'm real hung up on honesty. I just think there is no reason to lie to anybody." His reasons have to do with elementary reciprocity. People need to be able to trust his word and the only way he can live up to their trust is to be honest with them.

Once people get it into their heads that they can determine for themselves when to be honest and when not to be, one can hear adherents to
classical theories of the virtues responding, honesty becomes a mere
convenience, to be disregarded whenever it no longer serves our purpose. No society can survive, they would continue, if people simply
make up their moral rules as they go along. At one level, there is an obvious truth in this response, a truth that hit home to me many times as I
was writing this book. As many of my respondents were quick to notice,
research and writing assume honesty all around. I could not write the
book unless I believed that they were telling me the truth, they could
not offer their cooperation unless they believed that I was as well, and
no one would be interested in reading the book if they did not believe
that all of us were sincere. Like loyalty, the absence of honesty is
keenly felt. We may manage the truth, but there ought always be a truth
to manage.

The Americans with whom we spoke want to take honesty seriously even if they cannot take honesty absolutely. Can they do so? One
way to think about this question is to focus on gay men and lesbians in
San Francisco. For them, the notion of putting one's faith in timeless
moral laws is especially inappropriate because, at least in the Judeo-
Christian tradition, those laws have generally included homosexuality
in the category of forbidden acts. When it comes to decisions about
honesty, gay men and lesbians in San Francisco rely mostly on themselves. "You are constantly weighing all the different things that happen around you at that moment in your life" is how Kenny Miller puts
it. "You make the decision, and it can be right for the moment and it
might not be right two weeks prior or ten weeks hence. So, yeah, you're
constantly weighing and judging as to what is honest and what isn't."

What kind of judgments about honesty do people make when they
rely upon themselves to make them? We have already seen that not all
of the gay men with whom we spoke in San Francisco believe in the
virtue of loyalty; more than a few acknowledge that the image conserv-

atives have of gay promiscuity has considerable basis in truth. Yet their approach to the question of honesty is quite different. So much of the experience of homosexuality, they remind us, once took place in secret. Because one cannot be honest while living in the closet, coming out of the closet represents a painful affirmation of the truth. For all of the efforts of its residents to avoid the language of virtue (and vice), gay San Francisco is a zone of honesty. Nearly all of those who live there do so because they have chosen to be faithful to who they really are.

Such a commitment to honesty is the exception in American life. Most Americans, as we have seen, would rather be kind than be truthful. But this does not apply to a number of our gay respondents, because the announcement of their secret often comes as a hurtful shock to their parents and siblings—yet it is nonetheless an announcement that they must make. Lee Hayes is not a religious person. As his lover was dying of AIDS, he asked Lee where he would go after his death. "Well, Phil, I don't know," Lee recalls replying. "If there is a life after death, you're going to go to the good spot, but if there isn't, you're not going to know the difference." Lee opted for frankness because he doesn't believe in turning away from the truth. "I'm absolutely, impeccably honest. I never cheat anyone. And it isn't for Jesus." His feelings about honesty are no doubt influenced by the way Mr. Hayes came out to his family. He recalls coming home on the day John F. Kennedy was assassinated and finding his parents—wealthy conservative Republicans—celebrating. He chose that moment to announce to them that he was gay. His parents cut him out of their will. It is not just the fact that his brother the criminal was put back into the will and Mr. Hayes was not that fuels his anger many years later. Mr. Hayes still considers the whole matter of how his family treated him as " the most devastating experience I've ever had." The father of two grown children from an earlier marriage, he still wonders why his family did not choose to denounce him but nonetheless to give something—even a token proportion of the millions involved—to his children. If they ever do so, he will forgive them, but for now the pain is too great. Only his sister has tried to keep in touch with him, and he feels that he cannot respond to her because all the others have made it clear that they will never forgive his gayness—and he is not sure he can forgive their antagonism. Being truthful matters a great deal to Mr. Hayes, even when the truth hurts.

Gay men and lesbians have few rules to follow as they consider how and when to be honest about their sexuality. Jack Diamond, who works in marketing, moved to Germany because "I couldn't imagine living on the same continent as my family and being honest with them." In Germany he became more comfortable with his sexuality and eventually decided that he could return home. It was tough. His brother accepted his announcement calmly, but not his sisters and especially not his parents, who, as he put it, suddenly felt that their carefully constructed image of a perfect family had been tarnished. Flo Barnes did not think it would be that difficult to reveal her sexual orientation to her father, she tells us, for she had been giving him clues throughout the years; had his eyes been open, he would have noticed with whom she was spending her time. But when she finally told him directly, he cut her off, for Flo's relationship with another woman not only confronted his homophobia, but also, since her girlfriend was black, his racism. Now her father will not speak with her. She tries to tell herself that it does not matter, but she also does not understand his refusal to offer his love.

Gay men and lesbians in San Francisco lead lives worlds apart from the small-town farmers and committed Christians who live in Tipton, Iowa. Yet Tipton can also be viewed as a zone of honesty, and perhaps for the same reason. For there are villagelike qualities to both kinds of places; whether in small-town America or lifestyle enclaves, people know one another well and reputations can be very local. Tiptonites uphold honesty as a virtue because, as legal secretary Gina Loftus puts it, "what comes around goes around," which to her means that even if someone were to get ahead through dishonesty, the advantages would not last. For San Francisco's gay men, what Mrs. Loftus believed to be metaphorically true in the case of reputation is literally, and tragically, true in the case of AIDS. People are more likely to value and practice honesty when they see themselves personally tied to their communities, and such communities exist, not only in small-town America, but when tragic events bring people to an appreciation of a common fate.

Under conditions in which the truth is one more thing to be managed, Americans hedge injunctions to put honesty first with all kinds of conditions. They recognize the need for politicians to be less than truthful. More favorably disposed toward business than politics, they nonetheless justify the need for honesty in practical, not principled terms. Honesty, they believe, is something we ought to approximate, a virtue that remains important as an ideal, but that always needs to be tempered by reality. Compared with the ideals of an Immanuel Kant or a St. Augustine, the practical, results-oriented way Americans approach age-old questions of truth and falsity may seem disappointing. But in their own way, the Americans with whom we spoke are saying that this is the only way that honesty can be valued in a society that is not always honest when it insists that honesty always comes first.

# V. The Unappreciated Virtue

### Virtue's Gender

Many of the virtues by which Americans are presumed no longer to live, especially those whose origins can be traced back to Greece and Rome, are manly ones. The term itself stems from the Latin word "*vir*," which means "man" and which (like its derivative, "virility") implies strength. Courage, persistence, honor, fortitude—the stuff of Homeric epic poems—are qualities forged in battle. When they came to America, the manly virtues were most likely to flourish in those areas, such as the South, in which military valor was held dear. And if the battle-field was often far away, the playing field, America's true moral equivalent of war, was close by; sport, conquest, and military adventure became so inextricably tied together around manly ideals of virtue that one could rarely tell where one stopped and another began. To this day, when we attempt to demonstrate the importance of such virtues as loyalty, self-discipline, and honesty, we often turn, as a number of our (primarily male) respondents do, to the special exigencies of military situations.

Yet Ancient Greece and Rome are not the only sources of our conceptions of the virtues. From our country's earliest origins until relatively recently, Americans understood themselves to be living in a Christian land. The Bible gave us an appreciation for virtues significantly less manly in character than their classical counterparts: faith, hope, charity, and, most crucial of all, forgiveness. One can find testimonials to forgiveness in both the Old and the New Testament, and ideas of compassion are associated with many of the world's other religions. But it was mainly Jesus who, in asking the Lord to forgive his enemies because they did understand what they were doing, emphasized the centrality of forgiveness to those who followed his teachings. Christianity marked a sharp break with the past for many reasons, but surely one of the most important is its revolutionary attitude toward forgiveness. A people capable of forgiveness are a people who can put behind them endless cycles of bloodshed and revenge, thereby establishing the possibility of peace on earth.

Although forgiveness was a defining—perhaps the defining—quality of Jesus' character, Christian Americans have always been ambivalent about the relevance of forgiveness to their actual lives. Christian virtues stood in such sharp contrast to the classical ones that the pursuit of one seemed to make the realization of the other impossible: forgiveness is not a quality that helps win wars. Even in times of peace, an inclination to forgive could easily be viewed as an invitation to be soft, relaxing the perpetual requirements of self-discipline necessary for the work ethic, sobriety, or sexual restraint. Victorians, so quick to uphold morality's violators as pariahs, were not about to forgive them for their fall into decadence. Victorian morality contained its share of Christian voices urging that we learn the practice of forgiveness, but they were usually drowned out by the Social Darwinist realism of writers like William Graham Sumner (or, in Great Britain, Herbert Spencer). The criminal, Sumner wrote, "has no claims against society." Instead of seeking his rehabilitation in the hopes of forgiving his crime, "society rules him out of its membership, and separates him from its association, by execution or imprisonment, according to the gravity of his offense." Whatever social classes owed one another, at least in Sumner's account, forgiveness was not among them.

To this day, one can hear strains of Sumner's thinking among the diagnosticians of America's moral decline. Judges and juries, James Q. Wilson believes, are too often motivated by a misplaced sympathy when it comes to criminal defendants. Discussing a series of recent trials, Wilson writes that "the stern task of judging the behavior of a defendant, based on a dispassionate review of the objective evidence, has given way to explaining that behavior on the basis of conflicting theories presented by rival expert witnesses speaking psychobabble." Defendants claim that they were not responsible for their actions because of a syndrome—"a psychological condition halfway between insanity and rationality," as Wilson describes it—that excuses away their actions. Wilson reminds us that despite the flowering of very inventive syndromes—ranging from being a battered wife to having a "rotten social background"—juries are not always swayed by these appeals. Still, he has little sympathy with those who would use the "abuse excuse" to argue that, in committing unforgivable acts, they really did not know what they were doing. Wilson, who otherwise does not have much in common with William Graham Sumner, sounds uncomfortably like him when he argues that we should not. "It is the task of the law to raise, not lower, the ante in these circumstances," he writes. "The law is unkind to us when we are weak and especially unkind to those of us who are often weak. It ought to be so."

Debates over the state of America's moral health follow an all-too-predictable pattern. Commenting on the way we live now, conservative or communitarian intellectuals insist that Americans lead morally impoverished lives because the language of virtue is so foreign to them. When it comes to forgiveness, that script can be torn up. It is the intellectuals who often fail to appreciate the need for forgiveness. The more conservative among them, moreover, find fault with the American people because they manifest too much of this virtue rather than too little. Forgiveness offers the opportunity to eavesdrop on unrehearsed comments as Americans ponder when and how—or even whether—they should forgive those who trespass against them.

### For Thy Own Self, Forgive

Forgiveness, especially as it comes to us through Christianity, is a confusing virtue. The questions left unanswered by Jesus' words and deeds have kept theologians preoccupied for twenty centuries. Does only God have the power to forgive? If so, then why does Jesus insist that Peter must forgive his brother, not once, but seventy times seven times? If forgiveness is a quality to which human beings ought to aspire, ought they to forgive evil acts if doing so encourages their perpetrators toward greater evil? Can we be too quick to forgive? Are some ways of forgiving more sincere than others? If we forgive, should we also forget? Do we forgive for ourselves, to overcome our anger and to get on with our lives? Or do we forgive for others, so that they can get on with theirs? If forgiveness is a Christian virtue, should non-Christians be held to its standards? If not, can forgiveness ever become a virtue held in common by a society characterized by religious diversity? Can we forgive ourselves? Indeed, in seeking to forgive others, are we in reality trying to forgive ourselves?

In theory, deliberations about forgiveness ought to be different from those that take place over other virtues such as loyalty, self-discipline, and honesty. Those virtues serve ends that, however noble they sometimes are, also have consequences that can be extremely practical. Americans tell us that such virtues are important to them because no one can run a good business or be a good parent without them. Forgiveness, by contrast, would seem to have little to do with making a profit or enhancing one's status; instead, it brings us closer to God and what he would have us do. "I was taught that Jesus forgives all our sins," we were told by Jack Diamond, one of our gay respondents in San Francisco, "and when I think of the figure of Jesus, I think that is why he was important. Whether he existed or not is irrelevant, but the image and the kind of leadership he showed should be kind of a guideline for people." Even non-Christians and nonreligious people recognize that, in asking us to acknowledge that another person engaged in harmful and destructive acts, but that she is also potentially worthy of redemption, forgiveness demands that we pause from our daily activities and reflect on the nature of right and wrong. Dayton's Gary Radzikowski describes himself as "an agonistic," but goes on to say that "I think forgiveness has some sort of God-like quality." Of all the virtues relevant to the way modern people live, forgiveness comes closest to being a pure one in the sense that the rewards it brings and impositions it imposes are free from any immediate cost-benefit calculation.

Yet there is one way in which forgiveness serves a very practical purpose, and it is not surprising that Americans, a very practical people, respond to it. Jesus did not ask for forgiveness so that he could get on with his life, but many of our Christian respondents do. "I just don't believe in revenge or retribution" is how Atherton's Nancy Watkins, the woman inspired by *Life Is Uncertain…Eat Dessert First*, puts it. Revenge, in her opinion, is a negative and self-destructive emotion, and, when confronted with such feelings, as she was when her first husband left her, one has to let go and say, "That's not part of my life right now." Hers was a fairly common theme among our respondents. Hartford resident Laverne Eaton finally decided to forgive her ex-husband for leaving her, "because when we don't forgive, it holds us back, it eats away at us." Her thoughts were seconded by Margaret Adams of Fall River, who describes herself as a conservative Christian. "Forgiving is good for the forgiver" is how she puts it. She recognizes that there is something wrong with people who pretend that serious transgressions ought to be passed over; a high school English teacher, she regularly assigns *The Great Gatsby* to remind her students how careless and selfish people can be: "They just moved on," she says of Daisy and Tom Buchanan, "and left others to pick up the mess they left behind them." Yet for all that, she also believes that "bitterness destroys," which she takes to mean that at some point people do have to let go. Forgiveness she defines as "a ministry to my own soul as it is to the person who has done whatever it was."

A passion for forgiveness that looks inward to the needs of the forgiver and not outward to the soul of the transgressor would seem to stand in sharp contrast with the way many Christian theologians have understood the lessons of Jesus' life. There is, of course, no one "Christian" approach to forgiveness. Catholics, who emphasize the confession of sins to a priest, are often viewed as more committed to forgiveness than other Christians, and while this image has its stereotypes, it is also true that Catholics put reconciliation and penance—the title of a 1984 apostolic exhortation written by Pope John Paul II—at the heart of the Church. (John Paul II will likely be remembered, among many things, as the pope who forgave his attempted assassin as well as the one who, in the year 2000, asked for forgiveness for the Church's historic sins.) One can find as many Protestant versions of forgiveness as there are Protestant denominations, and not all of them are persuaded that forgiveness is an unalloyed good thing; Stanley Hauerwas and Charles Pinches, for example, find in the Gospel According to Matthew that "rebuke and forgiveness are locked together." Still, there is a general Christian approach to forgiveness, one that suggests that forgiveness is a demanding, not a tension-relieving, exercise. Moments of forgiveness are reflective, not emotional. They are also empathic: a person hurt by the wrongful actions of another forgives by placing himself in the position of the one who has done the hurting so that both can place themselves before God. The purpose of forgiveness is not to move beyond the pain caused by a dreadful act but to use the opportunity presented by that pain to reach a higher understanding of God's purpose. To be sure, only God forgives, but we have to take the first step of inviting God into our lives so that he can forgive. Through forgiveness, we reach transcendence.

Understood this way, therapeutic approaches to forgiveness can sound like a corruption of what was once a noble, even sublime, act of self-sacrifice. Yet, for all its demanding quality, there is nonetheless a therapeutic dimension to Christian understandings of forgiveness. The requirements of forgiveness have in fact launched a major movement in pastoral counseling among conservative Christians in America. It is true that the most literal of American fundamentalists, as the anthropologist Vincent Crapanzano notes, oppose "the marriage of psychological and theological counseling," but such marriages are very common in evangelical circles, where as Crapanzano also points out, one can find Freud's works next to Calvin's. Lewis B. Smedes, an ethicist at Fuller Theological Seminary in Pasadena, California, embodies this marriage as few others do; Fuller, begun by the host of the "Old Fashioned Revival Hour," now boasts a doctoral program in clinical psychology and Smedes—an old Dutch word for Smith—comes out of a Calvinist tradition. He is the author of many works dealing with how Christian ideals can be made relevant to contemporary life, and the best-known of his books deals with forgiveness. *Forgive and Forget: Healing the Hurts We Don't Deserve*, like most self-help manuals, breaks its subject down into stages, in this case four: we hurt, we hate, we heal ourselves, we come together. The last, for Smedes, is in many ways the most important, for it is when we come together that we realize the glory of God. But we cannot neglect the fact that we also forgive to heal ourselves. Indeed, sometimes, when faced with God's mysterious, and often seemingly capricious, powers, we even have to forgive him, "not," Smedes adds, "for his sake. For ours!"

How can we know when a person seeks to forgive another in order to heal a pain inside herself and when she does so in order to achieve some kind of reconciliation with transcendence? The truth is that we cannot. Consider two of those we interviewed whose language suggests that forgiveness for them serves primarily therapeutic purposes. "I used to think there were certain things that could never be forgiven," Kellie Moss, who lives in the northern section of Hartford, tells us, "but now I know that sometimes you have to forgive somebody for certain things that you thought were unforgivable so you can heal the pain inside yourself." San Antonio's Lucy Martin agrees: "If it's better for you to forgive for your own welfare than to hold it against someone, then I think it's good to just forgive them." As it turns out, both of these women tell stories that complicate any effort to conclude that their focus on a person's own needs reeks of excessive narcissism.

Kellie Moss, a sixty-five year old, worked for years as a bank clerk processing checks before retiring a year or two before our session. Widowed once and divorced twice, Mrs. Moss's life has been shaped by two major events: her alcoholism and her efforts, relying on Alcoholics Anonymous, to control it. The first of her husbands was a serious drinker and, when drunk (and not always when drunk), would beat her. She responded by taking to drink herself, and their marriage descended into a hell of mutual distrust and recrimination. After they divorced, their son died when he was ten years old, and Mrs. Moss's former husband came to the funeral. She recalls that he had his work clothes on, which sent her into a rage of anger. "Right in front of everyone else," she recounts, "I said, 'What the hell are you doing here? That's one child you don't have to worry about supporting.'" Shocked by her outburst, her former husband was speechless and allowed himself to be led away from the funeral by Mrs. Moss's brother.

As Mrs. Moss began to lose her own battle with alcoholism, she turned to AA for help. That organization helped her realize that "when you don't forgive someone for something, you have this pain inside of you and you have this bitter anger and that's a luxury alcoholics cannot afford, because that anger and bitterness will get you in a lot of trouble." One day, when she was into the AA program, she encountered her former husband on the street and asked him to forgive her for the way she acted at their son's funeral. Although it was ten years after the event, she could tell how much her comment meant to him, for he had, of course, never forgotten it. Forgiving him was important for Mrs. Moss as well. "I'm so glad I did it," she now tells us. "I feel so good."

Lucy Martin is another of our respondents who emphasized the importance of forgiveness for getting on with one's life. Sixty years old, Hispanic, and raised Catholic, Mrs. Martin, who is also divorced, has three grown children. When we asked her about whether people were generally good or evil, she responded, as did so many of those with whom we spoke, by saying that they are good. Our interviewer then asked if she could nonetheless think of someone who was evil. After a long pause, she came up with the name of Terry Nichols, one of those convicted of the bombing that took more than 168 lives in Oklahoma City. Calm and even-tempered, Mrs. Martin then went on to answer our other questions. When our interviewer finished and turned off the tape recorder, Mrs. Martin told her that Terry Nichols killed her brother, since he was in the Alfred P. Murrah Federal Building when the bomb went off. Mrs. Martin had attended Nichols's trial. Emotional, but not crying, she says that she cannot forgive him for what he did. At the same time, she expresses her hopes that the families of the other victims will not dwell on the tragedy, for if they do, she worries that they will go out of their minds. As for Mrs. Martin, she tries to use her brother's death to serve as a reminder of what a good man he was, something she did not always appreciate when he was alive.

In a very famous, and also very controversial, study, the psychologist Carol Gilligan spoke of female and male differences in moral reasoning; men, she found, were more given to emphasizing abstract principles of justice, while women were more likely to speak in personal and contextual terms. Along similar lines, the linguist George Lakoff draws a distinction between what he calls "strict father morality" and "nurturant parent morality." The former overlaps significantly with what I have been calling conservative and communitarian understandings of American character and emphasizes authority and obedience, while the latter, which Lakoff identifies with liberals, speaks of caring, moral growth, and mutual responsibility. Do men and women forgive in different ways?

Not all women believe it is good thing to pass too quickly over one's own anger. Unlike Kellie Moss who, with the help of Alcoholics Anonymous, moved from the position that some things were unforgivable to an understanding of the need for forgiveness, Carole Yamada of San Francisco found herself traveling in the opposite direction. She once considered herself a forgiving person, but two things altered that. One is that, as a nurse in a city hospital, she came into contact with "people I wouldn't come into contact with normally: street people, really hardened criminals." Some of them can be helped, but some of them, she has also learned, cannot be. Then, Mrs. Yamada had a child. Now, when she hears people talk at a dinner party about the need for forgiveness, she thinks that "if anything ever happened to my son, I would want to exact revenge. I would want to make sure all those people never hurt anybody again."

Betty Mann responded in similar ways. "I used to think of myself as very forgiving," she says, but, like some of the men with whom we spoke, she finds it impossible to forgive her former spouse. "I've been surprised by how much I've clung to my vindictiveness and my hurt and pain and stuff." One reason she began to change her views about forgiveness was her service on a jury trial in a murder case, which tested her liberal beliefs. Rapists ought not to be forgiven, Tammy Hoffman and Shannon Meissner, a lesbian couple in San Francisco's Noe Valley, added. Both made it clear to us that, like many San Franciscans, they were not "law-and-order conservatives." But, added Tammy Hoffman, "rape is such a violating of what it means to be human" that "I've entertained fantasies that all rapists should be immediately castrated." There is a version of feminism that, in sharp contrast to notions about women's special responsibilities for caring, emphasizes such ideas as taking revenge. Clearly, such ways of thinking have reached the more politically engaged women with whom we spoke.

Yet despite these exceptions, forgiveness (and its lack) is associated with gender. Counting couples as well as individuals, we interviewed slightly more women than men. Twenty-four of the 209 people with whom we spoke emphasized forgiveness as a quality that a person needs to develop in order to move beyond or get over personal pain. Of those twenty-four, twenty were women and four were men. Of the four men, only one corresponded to the stereotype of the angry white male, for one was gay, one was black, and one was a former hippie not completely comfortable with bourgeois life.

When we did speak to heterosexual white males, moreover, a small but significant number of them explicitly rejected the idea that forgiveness should be understood as part of a process of personal healing. Forgiveness, these men believe, serves the interest of justice, not of the self. Should people who do awful things like rape be forgiven? we asked Atherton's Bob Ryan. "I forgive them, but I'd rather forgive them while they are being confined or taken care of," was his answer. For Dayton's John Klemm, individuals and God can both forgive, but society cannot, because when a criminal violates the social order, society has to take retributory steps, including capital punishment. Maybe in a thousand years, we can do away with the death penalty, he continues, "but we still have a few unforgivable things that must be dealt with sociologically so that they don't corrupt the society continuously. That's the measure of social justice." Even on interpersonal matters, men were less likely than women to speak of moving beyond pain. A number of the divorced women with whom we spoke talked about the need to come to terms with their anger at their former husbands. They stand in sharp contrast to Dayton's John O'Brian, a superintendent at an automobile factory. His wife took up with another man and moved, with their children, to another state. He has attended divorce classes and received counseling, the lesson of which is that he has to understand the stages involved in the process of reconciling himself to the divorce. Yet he resists. The last stage, he says, is forgiveness, "and I'm not there yet." Mr. O'Brian also supports capital punishment, and for the same reason as John Klemm. Capital punishment has been duly chosen as the appropriate penalty for certain crimes through the democratic process. We therefore need it "because that supports the rule of law."

"The real work of forgiving," writes David Augsburger, a pastoral theologian who also teaches at Fuller Theological Seminary, "is not just the release from hatred, resentment, suspicion, and hostility in the forgiver, it is found in regaining the sister and brother as a full sister, as a true brother." Have those with whom we spoke moved beyond the release of their anger to the reconciliation upon which he insists? For some of our respondents, forgiving was so focused on the needs of the self that such reconciliation is unlikely ever to take place. One of our Fall River respondents, Caroline Bowen, spoke about forgiving "in order to go on with your own life and not dwell on things and drive yourself mentally insane over other people's actions." She took matters one step further, however, when she added that "sometimes I think that the victims want to forgive more than the person that has done wrong." If forgiveness, as she puts it, starts with the offended person in order to bring about "consolation or relief" from a terrible act, there exists no moment of redemption for the person who caused the suffering and hence no opportunity to come together with that person before God. Much of the task of theological inquiry on this subject involves distinguishing true forgiveness from false or insincere versions, and any approach to forgiveness that lacks some kind of dialogue between the offender and the person offended is unlikely to qualify as genuine.

Other approaches consider forgiveness in much the same way that honesty and loyalty are understood: as a guide to good business practice. Atherton's Jim Crowley, the money manager, remembers the time his company had a bad year and its clients, who lost money, were furious. Mr. Crowley could have dismissed their anger as unjustified because everyone knows that investing has its risks. But instead of getting angry at them because of their anger toward him, he learned to cultivate his ability "to let go of anger." Carrying grudges for too long fails to recognize that "anger is a very powerful, emotional force or energy that could either be turned in a positive way or a negative way," and, as far as he is concerned, the definition of maturity involves channeling your anger in the most positive way you can. Sometimes justice—defined as righting a wrong—can be counterproductive. "People who are too much interested in getting justice end up acting out behaviors as humans that aren't entirely constructive."

Yet for all the emphasis that Jim Crowley puts on the personal side of forgiveness, his reasons have little to do with healing, the process that was so important to the women with whom we talked, and much more with the practical side of things. "There is a cliché that says 'Don't get mad, get even,'" he says. "Mine is 'Don't get mad, don't get even, get ahead.'" His neighbor, John Howard, speaks in much the same way. Mr. Howard believes that America is becoming an angrier society; road rage—people taking out guns and shooting at others who collide with their cars—is one example. He sees the same kind of thing in his own mortgage banking business. Sometimes the negotiations get so tense and the lawyers so intransigent that "the pot is continually stirred and it gets to the point where people are so exhausted that they want to resolve whatever it is just to be done with it." Maybe a little more forgiveness on all sides could help people avoid those kinds of counter-productive sessions.

For all the examples one can find of forgiveness serving personal or practical needs, we can also hear in the way some of our respondents talk moments of insight and compassion that have little in common with twelve-step recovery programs. Kellie Moss and Lucy Martin both remind us of the nobility involved in forgiveness. We expect that tragedies like the Oklahoma City bombing would cause moments of serious reflection about the nature of good and evil. But that does not necessarily mean that those who experience them will find the balance between anger and acceptance that Lucy Martin has managed to achieve. As for Kellie Moss, her understanding of forgiveness grew out of an experience with a twelve-step recovery group that speaks addiction language, the kind of therapeutic group often criticized, if not lampooned, by intellectuals of many political persuasions. Yet alcoholism can have devastating consequences for people and families; Kellie Moss was far from alone in talking about uncontrolled drinking and the destructiveness associated with it. In the situation she faced, moving past her anger was exactly what she needed to do. Her willingness to forgive her husband made it possible for her to come to a moment of realization about her duties to others. Forgiveness clearly has its practical side, but when it works to bring Americans into contact with the transcendental ethical ideals that inspired the idea, it is one of the virtues very much alive in America today.

## Forgive, but Don't Forget

For those who believe in the power of forgiveness, the ability to accept another person, even when she has committed a great wrong, is a special gift. Not all of us know individuals who are serving time in prison for murder, but one of our Dayton respondents, Henry Muller, does. A child of very close friends of his killed someone. Because of his personal relationship to her, Mr. Muller cannot believe that she is a bad person. "There were a lot of things going on in her life," he tells us, "and for a very brief instant, something happened. Here was this blip in her life. Somehow she lost control of the situation. We visit her. She is loving. She's sincere. She goes to church. She helps with the mass. All those things." A serious student of Catholic theology in college, Mr. Muller recalls reading about and debating Thomism and existentialism, and what he carries forward from that time is a sense of the possibility of redemption. He does not go far as one of his cousins, an anti-death penalty activist working in Ohio with a group of Catholic priests who has been arrested for her beliefs. But he has been willing to let the prison authorities know that he and his wife would take this person in if she were ever released and help her find a job. Through his willingness to give her another chance, he extends a sense of trust that, he hopes, will be returned if she ever is released. It is, he knows, an act of blind faith, but that is what faith is supposed to be. For Henry Muller, being forgiving, being hopeful, and taking his Catholicism seriously are one and the same.

Americans, we have been told, want to forgive just about everybody and everything. Some clearly have an expansive conception of forgiveness. In primarily Catholic Fall River, we asked people how they felt about priests who abuse their power. Everybody makes mistakes, replied Cheryl Broca. There was no doubt in her mind that priests who do wrong ought to be forgiven because "they're no different than anyone else." The only reason we know about the scandals, she said, was because priests tend to be in the forefront of things. If they were not put on a pedestal to begin with, we would be less insistent on knocking them down. Certainty what they did was wrong, but not forgiving them would also be wrong. "We're all on the same level," she says, which suggests to her that compassion for their trouble, not punishment for their acts, is the appropriate response.

The question of how to respond to wayward priests is neither idle nor abstract for our Fall River respondents. Their community had been the epicenter of a case that tests the limits of forgiveness. Father James R. Porter may hold the record for the number of sexually abused children he left behind. After Porter was first assigned to North Attleboro, Massachusetts in 1960, his behavior was reported to Church authorities who then transferred him to the Sacred Heart Church in Fall River in 1962, where he remained for three years until being transferred again to nearby New Bedford. Porter finally left the Church in 1974, got married, and settled in Minnesota. In 1989, Frank Fitzpatrick of North Attleboro wrote a letter to Bishop Daniel A. Cronin of the Fall River Diocese, in which he recounted the abusive ways Porter had treated him when he was a boy. After various efforts to sweep the matter under the rug, Fitzpatrick's determination resulted in a 1992 *PrimeTime Live* show with Diane Sawyer. The next year, Porter accepted a plea bargain from Bristol County District Attorney Paul Walsh and was given a sentence of eighteen to twenty years in prison.

With the Porter case in the back of people's minds as we conducted our interviews, it is important to emphasize that not all of our respondents there were as forgiving as Ms. Broca. For Paul Richard, childhood sexual abuse is "one of the taboos that you just can't forgive." Lauren Druze thinks that a disgraced priest should no longer be allowed to serve as a priest. Marlene Beaulieu learned that a nun at one of the local Catholic schools, suffering from problem drinking, had been beating children. What was unforgivable in her eyes was that the school authorities knew about it and did not take any action. Yet for each of these individuals, themes of forgiveness remained. For Mrs. Beaulieu, the teacher had clearly "reached her limit," and while she was doing something wrong, she also had a good side. Because no opportunity was ever presented to her to face her own conduct and to admit she was wrong, the opportunity for proper forgiveness was lost. Paul Richard, the fisherman who could never forgive a priest for engaging in child abuse, could forgive a priest who was having a sexual relationship with a woman, because "everybody's human." Mrs. Druze would like to see disgraced priests out of the Church, but the fact that they do wrong does not, in her view, make them terrible people. All of these people are saying that it is not easy to draw a line between acts that can be forgiven and those that cannot be. They want to give people a second chance but also know that they cannot always do so.

For all the talk of how forgiving Americans have become, a considerable number of our respondents would rather see justice done than forgiveness upheld. When asked whether their society forgave too much, some insisted that it forgave too little. Jay Boylen of Atherton finds America's criminal justice system far too lenient. "I think this whole victimization thing is just scary," he says. We are completely "upside down" if we believe that "the O. J. Simpsons of the world have somehow become victims." Stiff punishment is required, even the death penalty, for "there are a lot worse things than someone losing a life." Nan Washington, the Greensboro nurse, was treating a patient dying of breast cancer once and learned that her husband had sexually abused their children. Working in a hospice, she had been taught that her job was to care for the entire family, not just the patient, but jail would be too good for such a man, she thought. "I would have him under the jail, not breathing." Charleton Marshall, the Tipton wine distributor, puts it bluntly: "You kill someone, you should be killed. Rapists, anything violent to another person. I don't see that being forgivable." Dayton's Warren Wilson, one of the more politically knowledgeable among our respondents, was impressed by the ability of Nelson Mandela to forgive those who imprisoned him, even as he was skeptical about whether former Alabama Governor George Wallace atoned enough to deserve forgiveness for his earlier racism. As for himself, he would not extend forgiveness to those who commit ordinary crimes. "If you do not judge, then what?" he asks. "You are required to judge. I don't see any option in the matter. Otherwise, you're back to chaos."

It is not just in the realm of criminal justice that we have become too forgiving for our own good, some of our respondents argued. Tim Crowe of Atherton remembers that when he was in high school, "if you screwed up, you would get whaled on by a football coach with a huge paddle. Well, they don't do that anymore. And so you hear stories of schools that are just totally wild." Dayton's John O'Brian, the man who had a difficult time forgiving his wife for leaving him, expressed his suspicions about those ministers who, in his view, were too quick to forgive President Clinton for his behavior. It is hard to hold people accountable for their actions, he believes, so hard that we will look for ways to avoid that responsibility. One of the ways we have is by forgiving them so that we can get on with our own affairs. As Christian as these individuals may be, they share with some of America's leading moral critics the idea that forgiveness is offered and accepted too easily, and in too many places where it does not properly belong.

Even in liberal San Francisco, some of our respondents expressed unease with the idea of a too-forgiving society. When his family cut him off from his inheritance after he came out, Lee Hayes learned that he had an unforgiving side: "My liberal nature does not forgive everything" is how he puts it. "Being thrown out of your family is a very hard thing to forgive. I've walked away from it and the best thing to do is to forget these people." At a time when gay-bashing episodes, such as the one that resulted in the death of Matthew Shepard in Wyoming, are highly publicized, it ought not to come as too much of a surprise that gay—or straight—men in San Francisco do not feel very forgiving of those who commit such hate crimes. Like so many of the people with whom we spoke in that city, Carl Lamb does not consider himself religious and is uncomfortable using terms he considers moralistic. But he was convinced that there are people in the world whose acts can be forgiven only when they take steps to acknowledge how wrong they were. "I hate to use such cliché phrases," he says, "but repentance or remorse are probably essential in my mind to the notion of redemption." Mr. Lamb, listening to himself speak, becomes surprised at his own words: "Wow. I sound so traditional here. I'm obviously on uncharted territory for me." Just as there are Christians in America who look warily on forgiveness, there are nonreligious people who search for secular alternatives to such Christian ideas as sin and redemption—and cannot always find them.

As contradictory as they may seem, forgiveness and justice are both essential to a good society. Through forgiveness, we remind ourselves that we are not animals acting on the basis of instinct but people who aspire to something more noble. Only the saintly few can accept the hurt done to them with no thought of seeking relief for the pain. But the rest of us can be satisfied with something less than martyrdom, and forgiveness offers us that opportunity. Like the other virtues, including self-discipline, forgiveness demands that we renounce what feels right at this moment or what is popular among our neighbors in favor of what is right in the eyes of a higher authority. By forgiving, we proclaim that we are not governed by our passions but by our reason, rightly understood. Forgiveness brings us together with others, including some of society's outcasts, in a sense of common fellowship. There is something Kantian—even something Rawlsian—about forgiveness. Our respondents do not read much moral philosophy, but they would intuitively understand John Rawls's concept of a veil of ignorance. Rawls asks us to consider how we would distribute society's goods if we could not know where we would be when those goods were distributed. Many of our respondents believe that because we will never know when we might want to be forgiven, we should keep the option of being forgiven open to all.

Yet as essential as forgiveness may be, there are also good reasons to insist that forgiveness be withheld, or at least significantly delayed. A society must retain its capacity to punish bad acts in order to reward good ones, many would insist. Allowing people who wrong others to return too easily into the human community, far from being a virtue, seems like a gratuitous insult to the virtuous, as if all their efforts to live good lives pale by comparison with our need to forgive those who do not. One should not dwell to the point of obsession on the wrongs society has suffered, but the best way to bring closure to those sufferings is often not to forgive the offender but to ensure that the offender has obtained his proper punishment. Even in situations where a serious criminal has repented—and where we have reason, as Mr. Muller does, to believe that the repentance is genuine—we cannot allow a duly convicted individual to go free merely because we trust that she will do better. When people prove themselves capable of heinous acts—such as using positions of trust associated with their church to take advantage of the helpless to satisfy their own lust—we are right to resist any calls for forgiveness they make. Justice may require mercy, but before there can be mercy, there has to be justice.

How can a society forgive and serve justice at the same time? A large number of our respondents had an answer to that difficult question. "I was taught that God gave up his only child to pay for our sins, and who are we to judge?" says Antonia Gomez, the homemaker in San Antonio. "But," she goes on, "if somebody raped and killed my child, could I forgive that person?" Having asked the question, she then answered it. "Forgive . . . I would try," she says, reflecting her deeply held Christian beliefs, even if "I would have a tough time" doing so. But forget? "No, I would never be able to forget." A few interviews later, Christina Rios made the same distinction. She was one of our respondents who believed that we ought to forgive in order to avoid being eaten up inside, but that did not mean that we should also forget. On that point, she believed that when someone harmed you, you were best off not letting go of the memory. Early on in our Tipton interviews, the same theme emerged; Derek Trombley, a retired high school teacher, also believes that forgiveness, but not forgetting, is necessary.

But it was when we came to Greensboro that the distinction between forgiving and forgetting took on a life of its own. So many of the students with whom we talked spoke of forgiving but not forgetting—none of our respondents, anywhere in the country, wanted to forget but not to forgive—that our interviewer was taken somewhat aback. When it comes to the virtues, Americans have their differences, but on the importance of not forgetting, no matter how much you forgive, they seem in remarkable agreement; never in my research for my last two books have I come across a phrase repeated so ubiquitously as the injunction to forgive but never forget. Forgiving, our respondents hold out hope that everyone can be redeemed and that the community of which we are part can be made morally whole. Not forgetting, they remind themselves of the damage done to ourselves and our society by those who transgress the moral order.

Will Thurber was among our Greensboro students who invoked the "forgive, but do not forget" formula. He gave as an example a person who gets drunk, then gets into his car, and driving while intoxicated kills an innocent person. "I think his punishment should be a continued remembrance of the act he committed," he tells us. "I think he should go into counseling, say, every year until he dies, to understand exactly what he did." His comments suggest that remembering is a way of avoiding the very closure that forgiveness offers. Along the same lines, another Greensboro student, Cory Hanson, adds, "Wrongs aren't forgotten. People don't forget things." The comments of these two students suggest that rehabilitation is not enough. We create a prison system to establish a balance in society's moral account: by serving time, the criminal pays off his debt to the society he wronged and is in that sense forgiven. But memory lasts longer than a prison term. By never forgetting a person's wrongful acts, we in effect punish him more than by incarcerating him, for we do not allow him to rejoin society as if he had never done anything wrong. Our individual memories—and, in rare cases, our collective memories—put boundaries around the wrongs a person commits, protecting a space into which that person can never gain access.

While many of our respondents insist that there are certain acts that can never be forgotten, chances are they will eventually be forgotten, if not by them, then by those who come after. In reality, the "forgive, but do not forget" formula expresses a two-stage model of the forgiveness process. We forgive in order to get on with our lives, but, by not forgetting, we hold back some of our forgiveness in order to make a second act of forgiveness, one that offers more complete closure, down the road. "I don't think that forgiveness comes overnight, or even over a few years," Jon Hunter, another Greensboro student, tells us. He echoes the theologian Lewis Smedes, who write that forgiveness ought to take time. Not forgetting is one way of ensuring that it does. Eventually, time dissolves the distinction between forgiving and forgetting. The memory will finally fade, but before it does, the wrongdoer will have had enough time to consider the wrongness of his acts while the rest of us will have had enough time to allow him back into the community. Forgiving but not forgetting is a way of calling for a delay in the redemption proceedings. It reminds all parties to the process that forgiveness should never be given lightly but that it should, at some point, be given.

"I was always taught to forgive," says June Sylvester, a kindly fifty-two-year-old Hartford resident who insisted that our interviewer take home some of the plants and herbs from her garden and to let her know how they were doing. "It might be hard, but I think any act, regardless, should be forgiven. Maybe not forgotten, but forgiven." Like many of her black neighbors in Hartford, Mrs. Sylvester has lived with her share of disappointments. In particular, she remembers the time her aunt passed away and the extended family gathered for the funeral. It was the first time she was ever responsible for organizing a funeral and she learned that her aunt's insurance policy would pay the costs. Because she had to return to Hartford, she left the money with her cousin with specific instructions on how to pay the bill, but her cousin, a drug addict, spent the entire sum on his habit. Should she forgive him? The truth is that she cannot make up her mind. What he did was inexcusable, and in some sense can never be forgiven. On the other hand, he is family, drugs turned him into a man no longer responsible for his own actions, and her minister—Mrs. Sylvester is an active Methodist—tells her the importance of forgiveness. Ultimately she decided that she didn't care whether her cousin ever truly repents. "I have forgiven him," she concludes, "but I can't forget it"—the only way, it seems, that Mrs. Sylvester can make sense of the situation in which she found herself.

### The Case of Karla Faye Tucker

On February 3, 1998, the state of Texas executed Karla Faye Tucker by lethal injection. Fifteen years earlier, Mrs. Tucker, a former teenage prostitute, drug addict, and rock band groupie, had, with her boyfriend, brutally killed two people with a pickax and later talked of the sexual thrill the crime gave her. In the intervening years, she became a born-again Christian, leading many Christian conservatives, including Pat Robertson, to take up her case and to argue against the death penalty for her. Pleas on her behalf were ultimately rejected by the United States Supreme Court and by Texas Governor George W. Bush. She became the second woman executed in the United States since the death penalty was reinstated in 1976 and the first woman executed in Texas since the Civil War.

The Tucker execution presents a test case of America's capacity for forgiveness. Her actions are unlikely to be forgotten soon, especially by the families of her victims, but also by Americans in general; when we brought up her name in our interviews, our respondents, with very few exceptions, knew exactly who she was, and even those exceptions, when reminded of her acts, had opinions about her death. But can her actions be forgiven? With this question in mind, I chose Texas as one of the states in which I would conduct my interviews and I requested that my interviewer there ask about Karla Faye Tucker. Because the case was also in the news around the time our interviews in Iowa were taking place, those respondents also had a great deal to say about the case. I wanted to know whether the "forgive but do not forget" formula would hold where it was tested most severely. By strongly supporting the death penalty, Americans have made it clear that murder is a crime they do not wish to forgive. But as murderers go, Karla Faye Tucker could be viewed as one of the more sympathetic. A woman, a born-again Christian, she would, I thought, be more likely to be forgiven than someone perceived as an unrepentant and dangerous criminal. Support on her behalf from conservative Christians and a plea against imposing the death penalty from the Pope could also provide political "cover" to those prepared to spare her life but worried that they would be labeled soft on crime if they did. Which, then, would it be: the Old Testament or the New? Would Americans demand an eye for an eye or would they extend to her the capacity for forgiveness to which they often aspire?

We found a few people in Texas who thought that Tucker's execution was wrong. Maria Gomez Romero was one of them. Insisting that it was not up to her, or any other person in this world, to forgive Karla Faye Tucker—a crime so hateful could be forgiven only by God—she also said that "I don't think as human beings that we have the right to take a life, just like she did not have the right to take somebody's life." A retired seamstress named Selena Bose agreed; Tucker was on drugs when she committed her crime, she says, and "drugs turn a person crazy" so that "they don't know what they are doing." Therefore, she concludes, "I think they should give her another chance." But these were decidedly minority viewpoints. Lucy Martin, the woman whose brother was killed by Terry Nichols, was in no mood to forgive Ms.

Tucker. She considers herself a forgiving person, but this case involved society. "You have laws and everybody's included. How can you be making exceptions for someone who says, 'I'm sorry' afterward. No, no. You can't say, 'I'm sorry' after the fact. If she was sentenced to die, then she should die." Very similar words were used by most of those with whom we spoke in San Antonio. "If she did something wrong" is how Juan Iglesias puts it, "we should punish her. Not just because she found her religion. We shouldn't forgive her for what she did."

Our Tipton respondents were even more emphatic. "I hate to see that lady killed," says Jason Benning, the lawn-care business owner, "but they did the right thing." The fact that she found Jesus "just doesn't wash with me." As a murderer, adds Dennis Fletcher, she already proved herself an untrustworthy person, so why should we believe her when she says she has found God? "I wouldn't have lost any sleep over it even if I was on the jury," Hugh Heston says, because what she had done was so gruesome. Unlike many of her neighbors, Dominique Mottau thinks that Karla Faye Tucker was "pretty genuine," but, despite Ms. Mottau's own faith in Jesus, she would support her execution. In the best of situations, we would want to sit down with her to find out why she killed, to get her story, so to speak. But she did take two lives, and she will have to ask for Jesus' forgiveness in the next life.

Whatever conflicts and ambiguities exist around forgiveness, they did not exist around the case of Karla Faye Tucker. The question worth asking is why so many Americans plan neither to forgive nor to forget what she did. There is, after all, an aversion to cruelty built in to much of their moral worldview; the limits of both honesty and self-discipline are reached when they bump up against cruelty to others. Support for Karla Faye Tucker's execution also seems to violate America's general sense of nonjudgmentalism, for the death penalty is an ultimate judgment from which there is no turning back. Why do people whose religious views so strongly emphasize the capacity for forgiveness feel so strongly that it is morally permissible—indeed, it is often viewed as a moral duty—to take the life of a person who has taken the lives of others?

Part of the answer involves respect for the law. "We've got trials to determine whether a person is guilty," says San Antonio's Lou Lamkin, one of those who supported Tucker's execution. Lou Anne Mobley, the born-again Christian in San Antonio, believes as strongly in the judicial system as she does in Jesus. "I think society can forgive them," she says of people like Tucker, "but still our justice system has worked well. It has a lot of flaws, but if the death penalty is what we have discerned as the best for those situations, I think they have to pay the price." Dan Forbes, a sheriff's deputy in Tipton, and thus a man responsible for enforcing the law, agrees: "I think that we have to follow the law. If the law found her guilty, then I think execution was probably the right thing for her." One of those who believes that our society is too quick to forgive, Tipton's Chuck Macready thinks that many criminals are let off the hook, all the more reason to insist on the appropriate punishment when one is duly found guilty and sentenced. "She knew what the law was," he says, "and she knew about the death sentence." It is not just the legal system whose verdicts ought to be upheld. Tipton's Elaine York is unwilling to second-guess the decision of the governor in this case. "He had to weigh everything," she says of Governor Bush, "so I can only presume that he knew more than I did."

An additional reason to support Karla Faye Tucker's execution was religious in nature: God has to be the ultimate judge of matters of this sort. Our respondents invoked both testaments in defense of this point of view. "The Bible says an eye for an eye and a tooth for a tooth. And that's the way the world is. If she killed someone, she should be killed. Put to rest peacefully," says Elsa Gonzalez of San Antonio. Her neighbor Rosaria Sanchez invokes Jesus but comes to the same conclusion. Unlike human beings, God loves all his sinners. "I think I would find

God too if I were on death row," she says. If he is really and truly a loving God, he will find a way to forgive her. If she really has found God, she will be better off with him than here on this earth, Tipton's Warren Johnson believes. "What she needed more than anything in the world is forgiveness from the Lord, knowing that she is able to get judged by the Lord, and then having everlasting life with the Lord because he has forgiven a sin." Such is his own relationship with God, Mr. Johnson adds, that he is not afraid of death, and neither should she be.

Respect for the law and respect for God can, in fact, work together, many of our respondents believe, the one strengthening the authority of the other. Lou Lamkin thinks we ought to respect the decisions of juries, but Karla Faye Tucker could not have been surprised by the verdict in her case. "Usually, as a rule," he points out, "most of those people have accepted the fact that they're going to die. They are prepared both mentally and spiritually for it. They are ready to meet their maker, they paid their debt to society, and it's up to God to decide whether they paid their debt to him." Lou Anne Mobley, who thinks that justice was served in the case, is also thankful Karla Faye Tucker "got her heart right with God" before the end. Miguel Aguilera also sees God's authority working together with legal authority. "The only person to redeem is God himself, and we will all meet him one day," he tells us. "And we will all be judged by him on that day. As far as the laws of the land, you commit a heinous crime, you get punished." As for Tucker's conversion, he would say this to her: "I'm glad you found God. At least you'll get to meet him soon enough, and you can discuss it with him."

Opinions like these answer one of the questions that can be raised about the case of Karla Faye Tucker: How can a generally nonjudgmental people support the ultimate judgment? The paradoxical answer is that people extend, rather than make an exception to, their nonjudgmentalism. Calling for the death penalty in a case like this may seem judgmental, because those who do so leave little doubt that such crimes must be punished severely. But in relying on the law or on God to make the final call, they are also saying that the judgment is best left out of their own hands. Rosaria Sanchez, who believes that a truly loving God will find a way to forgive, also knows that she cannot: "I would really leave it up to Jesus Christ," she says. So would Jaime Estefan, a computer technician. "I can't judge," he says of this case. "I can't. Only God knows." Grant Lowell, the Tipton machinist, simply isn't sure that human beings are equipped to make such decisions. Compared with God, we lack the capacity to look into a person's heart. "I'm sure that if you went into all the prisons in this country, you would find a lot of people who said that they found salvation and would never do anything again." But, he adds, "a good percentage of them, if you put them on the street, would either rape, kill, or murder or steal." For him, this leads to an ambivalence about the death penalty, but for others, Tucker's death enabled her, as Tipton's Sharon Rice puts it, to find "the help she needed. I feel that she found the peace she was looking for."

One can understand the reluctance of these Texas and Iowans to pass the ultimate judgment somewhere else, since assuming the responsibility of deciding whether another person should live or die is an awesome task. Still, Americans often insist on the principle that a person has to be responsible for his own acts, even when doing so is difficult. Indeed, they make that judgment with respect to Karla Faye Tucker. Unlike Selena Bose, who believed that drugs drove Tucker to the point of not knowing what she was doing, Sharon Rice does not buy that excuse. "People choose to use drugs," she says, and in so doing they become responsible for what they do when they are on drugs. Defending Tucker's death sentence, Chuck Macready makes much the same point. "People have a choice whether they choose to do right or wrong" is how he puts it, and if they do wrong, we are right to punish them.

If people are to be held responsible for their acts, then shouldn't those who think that Karla Faye Tucker's life can be taken by the state be held responsible for their beliefs? This is a question much on the mind of San Antonio's Christina Rios. She responds to our inquiry about Tucker by immediately supporting her execution. Then she pauses. Her answer, she realizes, is too easy for her to make. After all, she is on the outside, simply expressing her opinion. It would be different if she were on the actual jury "because I would have to live for the rest of my life with the consciousness that I said yes." Doing so would make her an accomplice in the taking of another person's life and she is not comfortable with the thought that "I had something to do with the killing of that person." One admires her honesty, for she is confronting an uncomfortable aspect of this case that many of our other respondents wanted to avoid. But the same point applies even if she, or anyone else, is not on the jury that passes sentence. In a democracy, the actions of government are taken in the name of the people, which makes everyone responsible when government takes a life.

San Antonio's Wayne Thompson was the only person we interviewed in Texas who did not recognize Karla Faye Tucker's name when we brought up her case. "I'm outside the normal curve," he explains to us, because he does not own a television and therefore does not follow highly publicized events. But when reminded of her crime and execution, the case came back to him, and he thinks that "everything worked out for the better, for everybody. The victims, the criminal who was convicted. . . . The governor did what he saw was right, and that worked. I don't have any argument with what happened." Mr. Thompson's words are striking, for they run so counter to the way Americans generally talk about public life. Although they are often critical of the way public affairs are run, when it comes to Karla Faye Tucker, our respondents in Texas express confidence that things run pretty well. Generally suspicious of government, they express their trust in the legal system—and even in politicians like governors. Reluctant to evoke God's name to support one political position or another, they find an important role for God to play in this case. No one should doubt the strength of the conviction on the part of so many of our respondents in Texas and Iowa that Tucker's life was a life worth taking. But it speaks to the seriousness of the issues raised by capital punishment that to reach that conclusion, they had to put aside some of their other convictions, finding trust and reassurance in institutions about which they often express skepticism.

Whether or not one agrees with those who supported Karla Faye Tucker's execution—I do not—one can hardly accuse Americans of being too forgiving on this matter. Tucker is not Mary Magdalene, and the American people are not Jesus Christ. When it comes to forgiving a crime as serious as the one she committed, these residents of Texas and Iowa, all of them Christians and many of them among the most devout Christians with whom we spoke, want to see justice done. Forgiveness, they reserve to another time and place—as well as to another world governed by virtues different from this one.

### Forgetting Forgiveness

Recognizing its necessity but fearing its consequences, Americans often tend to be extremely ambivalent about what forgiveness requires. A decided inability to come down either on the side of Christian charity or on the side of law-and-order strictness was fairly common among those with whom we spoke. Fall River's Caroline Bowen, the woman who believes that victims want to forgive more than perpetrators, could never forgive violence against her own children. Tom Ullman, the gay Mennonite in San Francisco, was one of the few men in our sample who, like Caroline Bowen, emphasized the therapeutic benefits of forgiveness. Yet he is flabbergasted by such events as the bombings in Oklahoma City or at New York's World Trade Center. To forgive people who carry out such acts would be wrong, he believes, if it leads them to conclude that they have been left off the hook of responsibility.

Inside nearly everyone who believes in forgiveness is an acknowledgment of the importance of justice.

By the same token, many of those who put justice first recognize a place for forgiveness second. Daryl Sims, the Hartford computer programmer, like many a conservative, believes that American society is too forgiving. "People who commit horrible acts—horrible, violent acts—should be taken into a square and shot in the head in public," he says, and it bothers him greatly that instead they go to court, delay the sentence that ought to be imposed on them, and have the right to one appeal after another. Yet like most African-American men in this country, Mr. Sims also knows what it means when the criminal justice system makes a mistake. "None of us want to be caught in a situation in which we're the one that was at the wrong place at the wrong time." So maybe, he concludes, it makes sense to be cautious and to err on the side of forgiveness. His comments echo those of Paul Richard. When he was a child, a man murdered his aunt, who was also his godmother. The culprit was arrested and sent to jail, but due to a criminal justice system Mr. Richard considers far too lenient, he served only four years in prison. Burned by that experience, Mr. Richard believes that many acts—priests abusing children, Susan Smith's murder of her two children—can never be forgiven. Yet he also knows that "some people need forgiveness, you know what I mean? No matter what they've done, if they can make amends and try to make things better," they can be forgiven.

One reason that Americans tend to be ambivalent about forgiveness is that this virtue is a particularly demanding one. It is, in fact, so difficult to be forgiving that even those conservative and communitarian commentators who believe that Americans have lost an appreciation for the virtues do not particularly want to see this particular virtue revived. Forgiveness is the forgotten virtue among today's upholders of strict moral codes. Gertrude Himmelfarb, our leading historian of (and advocate for) Victorian morality, recognizes the existence of "caring" virtues that she contrasts to "vigorous" ones, including in the former category trustworthiness, respect, compassion, fairness, and decency— but not forgiveness. For her, as for Marvin Olasky, even the caring virtues need to be applied vigorously. Olasky, who writes out of strong commitments to Christian values, distances himself from William Graham Sumner's indifference to the poor, but his insistence that the compassion we show for them ought not to excuse away any social pathologies developed in the course of their poverty or dependency does not have much in common with the figure of Jesus who appears in the Gospel According to Luke.

The most interesting case of forgiveness forgetting, however, involves William Bennett. Not only does his *The Book of Virtues* have no chapter on forgiveness, it is surprisingly reticent on the subject of Jesus. Evoking manly images through numerous episodes from Greek and Roman epics, Henry V's speech at Agincourt, Theodore Roosevelt's "In Praise of the Strenuous Life," and Tennyson's "Charge of the Light Brigade," *The Book of Virtues,* which retells thirteen stories from the Old Testament, contains only five stories from the New Testament, and only one of those—Jesus' admonition to those without sin about casting the first stone—touches on the virtue of forgiveness. When a man as sincere in his conviction that Americans have lost a sense of virtue as William Bennett can bypass so significantly the man whom Christians consider the most virtuous person who ever lived, we get a sense of how treacherous the virtues can be. Handed-down moral instruction in the right way to live cannot be relied on to tell us how to live in ways that correspond with contemporary political ideologies.

Not only do conservatives tend to forget about forgiveness, they have a way of violating its requirements when they discuss the condition of other people's virtue. Surely they would not be encouraged by the tendency of so many of our respondents to invoke the needs of the self as their reason for wanting to forgive harmful acts. This is taking the therapeutic impulse too far, they would maintain, for if forgiveness means anything, it exists to make oneself right with God, not to smooth over a negotiating session or to ease the pain of divorce in order to marry once again. As true as such observations may be, they tend to be offered in anything but a humble way. "The first rule for mere human beings in the forgiving game," writes Lewis Smedes, "is to remember that we are not God." Because we are not, there will always exist a relationship between forgiveness and humility; we ought not to forgive, as David Augsburger puts it, from a position of moral superiority. Much the same can be said about judging other people's ways of forgiving. Those who find that Americans persistently fail to live up to the standards of virtue conservatives hold out for them, in adopting a tone of moral superiority, invite the question of whether they are practicing the virtues they preach.

Forgetting forgiveness, conservatives find themselves in the position of selecting some virtues as admirable but not others. That is because forgiveness—the odd man out among the virtues—works at cross-purposes to honesty, loyalty, and, especially, self-discipline. To honor the latter, we often must violate the former, for if we are too quick to forgive those who lie, turn their backs on families and friends, or slide into decadence, we send out a message that the virtues really are not virtues at all. At a time of widespread social disorder, when standards of right and wrong are so easily fudged and when deviancy has been defined so far down, conservatives may be right to insist on their priorities. But in so doing, they assume that the more heroic Greek, Roman, and Hebrew virtues continue to be viable while the more caring Christian ones are not. Such an argument is an odd one for any conservative to make, because it implies precisely the kind of moral relativism conservatives are usually quick to denounce. Traditions are traditions and, for better or else, the Christian tradition is built on forgiveness. If conservatives do not like that tradition, they ought to question whether they really want America to become a society that respects its own religious heritage. For if it did, it would also become a society unlikely to continue its support for capital punishment, prison expansion, stricter sentencing, and all those other remedies conservatives believe we need to get our sense of virtue back.

Forgiveness may make conservatives uncomfortable, but liberals and radicals are no quicker to claim it as a virtue of their own. Religious movements in the United States challenging capital punishment talk of forgiveness, as do those conservative Christians who would forgive the sin of homosexuality—if not the sinner who practices it. But the dominant intellectual trend on the left in recent years has been an antihumanistic one that stresses the impersonal power of systems rather than the personal attributes of individuals. If capitalism or modernity are to blame for what ails us, there is no need to forgive people because they never did anything wrong in the first place. That is why one is as unlikely to hear a discussion of forgiveness among radical writers like Michel Foucault as from conservative ones like William Bennett. From a leftist perspective, forgiveness smacks of charity. Those who violate society's laws, they believe, need not charity but rights. We ought not to pity them but to organize them. Forgiveness, precisely because it is such a Christian term, takes us back to premodern ways of thinking about moral obligation, they would argue, when what we require is a postmodern challenge to all such ideas.

If the right manages to be against forgiveness without invoking the term, the left—which can be as selective in its suspicions of the virtues as the right is in its enthusiasm for them—finds a way to be in favor of forgiveness even while not believing in the concept. Liberals and leftists think of American society as so quick to punish wrongdoers that it lacks the capacity to understand why they might be driven to break the law. And even when there is no excuse for the crimes people commit—

as in the case of Karla Faye Tucker—Americans' obsession with capital punishment, from their point of view, symbolizes a society unwilling to give people a second chance. This account of America's unforgiving side is a telling one, but it is a hard case to make if one does not take the idea of virtue seriously. If the left were more willing to acknowledge that virtues such as honesty, loyalty, and self-discipline are more than just rhetorical strategies meant to exclude the marginalized from recognition, it would be in a better position to make the case that a society that practices capital punishment is not as virtuous as it sometimes asserts. People on the left tend to be so convinced that the virtues stand for things they detest that they fail to recognize that a society that honored them more might be one they could find themselves liking.

The importance of forgiveness can be traced back two thousand years to a religion that commanded obedience, yet, of all the virtues, forgiveness is in many ways the most compatible with modern ideas of self-reliance and personal responsibility. A preprogrammed forgiveness, expressed by rote without the involvement of a human heart, is no forgiveness at all; forgiveness must be given voluntarily or its capacity for reconciliation will be lost. "Nobody can make you forgive," writes Lewis Smedes. "Only a free person can choose to live with an uneven score. Only free people can choose to start over with someone who has hurt them. Only a free person can live with accounts unsettled. Only a free person can heal the memory of hurt and hate."

Forgiveness may be the unappreciated virtue among America's cultural commentators, but its resonance with modern notions of individual freedom and responsibility is valued in other quarters. Scientists and politicians, both of whom tend to take a hard-nosed approach to the way the world works, are among those who have rediscovered the value of forgiveness. For physicians and psychologists (including those who have little in common with pastoral counseling and theology), the ability to forgive may be associated with the medical benefits that follow from channeling anger in more constructive directions. For politicians, including South Africa's Nelson Mandela, a willingness to forgive one's opponents has the demonstrable advantage of avoiding endless cycles of revenge and counterrevenge. Despite the myriad of resolved questions raised by forgiveness, there is something to be said for holding on to the idea, surely one of the reasons that so many Americans, no matter how strong their commitments to justice, are determined to do so.

# VI. The Moral Philosophy of the Americans

## *Moral Agreement*

Lamenting the fact that Americans live "after virtue," Alasdair MacIntyre argues that in contemporary society, "all moral judgments are nothing but expressions of preference, expressions of attitude or feeling." Since everyone has feelings, and since one person's feelings are usually different from another's, a society in moral crisis will be characterized by extensive disagreement. Ours is, MacIntyre claims; our arguments about the right and proper way to live are "interminable" and there is no rational way by which people will ever see eye to eye over such issues as abortion, the provision of health care, or the necessity to prepare for war. Liberals would be likely to disagree with MacIntyre's diagnosis but to accept the description. The fact that a wide variety of moral experience exists is, for them, an indication of health. A pluralistic liberal democracy committed to equality and respect for difference ought to appreciate the fact that no one conception of the right and proper way to live has the power to drive out all others.

If our interviews are any indication, there are indeed disagreements over the virtues in contemporary America. One would expect that small-town residents of the farm belt would not see eye to eye with San Franciscans, nor that working-class Catholics in New England would share the same ideas as wealthy entrepreneurs in Silicon Valley. It is not surprising, therefore, that some of those with whom we spoke were quicker to resort to the divorce option than others; some favored capital punishment more decidedly than others; and some were more likely to emphasize forgiveness while others insisted on the priority of justice. Yet we should not confuse differences over how and why the virtues ought to be applied with differences over the underlying moral philosophy that guides people's understanding of the world. For when it comes to fundamental questions about human nature, the formation of character, qualities of good and evil, and the sources of moral authority, our respondents have roughly the same views. There is a common American moral philosophy, and it is broad and inclusive enough to incorporate people whose views of the actual issues of the day are at loggerheads.

## Human Nature

The most famous theory of human nature in American letters is the Calvinistic view of man associated with the Puritans. The eighteenth-century theologian Jonathan Edwards was one who adhered to their tradition. "As all moral qualities, either of virtue or vice, lie in the disposition of the heart," Edwards wrote in one of his treatises, "I shall consider whether we have any evidence, that the heart of man is naturally of a corrupt and evil disposition." Edwards was prompted to this investigation by the doctrine known as Arminianism, which held that one could believe in God's sovereignty without also subscribing to the idea that human beings are inherently wicked and thus at the mercy of God's arbitrary capacity to forgive. Such an idea, Edwards argued at length, runs counter to the notion of God's grace, for, if man were not naturally depraved, he would have no reason to seek God's favor. Edwards's conception of human nature is not a very pleasant one, but it is, he believed, a very necessary one. "How absurd it must be for Christians to object, against the depravity of man's nature, a greater number of innocent and kind actions, than of crimes; and to talk of prevailing innocency, good nature, industry, and cheerfulness of the greater part of mankind?"

Edwards was not a revivalist preacher—that description is more appropriately given to the Englishman George Whitefield—but he was closely associated with the Great Awakening of the 1730s and 1740s, the first and most extended of those periods in which Americans, worried about the shallowness of the practical side of their lives, turned their attention to God and the awesome power of his works. By the time of the Second Great Awakening of the early nineteenth century, as the historian Randall Balmer has written, Arminianism had triumphed over Edwards's Calvinism, and with it came "an alternative Protestant theology which insists that individuals can initiate the salvation process, that they needn't wait for the call of God." American Christianity has never been the same again since. If there is anything as American as apple pie, it is the idea that human beings are not born stained with sin. Of those surveyed by the New York Times on "The Way We Live Now," 73 percent agreed that all people are born inherently good. Americans may be among the most religious people in the world, but they are also among the least theological, and the theology they particularly dislike is one that takes a dim view of human nature.

Although few Americans hold to a Calvinist view, the sociologist Christian Smith found that evangelical Christians were more likely to believe in the inherent sinfulness of people than mainstream Protestants and Catholics. Our study confirms his finding. Of the three respondents with whom we spoke who most strongly agreed that human beings are born bad, two were born-again Christians (both were African-American as well). "The Bible says you are born with a sinful nature because of the way you come into the world," Hartford's Mary Masters says. "So I can't really dispute that. I do believe that's true." As evidence, Mrs. Masters cites the fact that you do not have to teach children how to lie, since it's just part of their nature not to tell the truth. Her neighbor, Lewis Watts, shares the same sentiments. Kids not only lie, he says, they also have an instinct to fight, so you do not need to teach them how to do that either. "You are born with a fallen nature," Mr. Watts believes. "You are born with Adam's sin. There is no way to get around it." Both of these individuals emphasize how difficult it is for human beings to escape from the propensity to do evil. Even born-again Christians can lie, Mrs. Masters observes. "You could be virtuous with the Holy Ghost, with Christ," adds Mr. Watts. "Without Christ, you cannot be. And with Christ, it's hard."

Yet the views of Mrs. Masters and Mr. Watts were in a distinct minority, even among those who considered themselves evangelical in their outlook. San Antonio's Lou Anne Mobley shies away from any view which suggests that human beings are born with certain predispositions that determine how will they act. How could they be if, like Mrs. Mobley, they are born twice? The fact that born-again Christians are more likely than other religious believers to hold to a dark view of human nature does not mean that most evangelicals do; in fact, the evangelical tradition in America emphasizes, in Balmer's words, the role played by "human agency in the salvation process." Because "individuals could choose their spiritual destinies rather than relying on the caprices of a distant God," most born-again Christians are likely to turn away from the gloomily deterministic views of Lewis Watts and Mary Masters. Lou Anne Mobley certainly does. Recalling the times she led a wild life, she says, "I've been on both sides, so I know that the opportunity to do right after you've done wrong exists." The same is true of her husband. He was born into a dysfunctional family, "but he maintained in his heart that he was going to do what's right, so he came out of these horrible circumstances without being a bitter and horrible person." Both Mr. and Mrs. Mobley have given themselves over to Christ as their savior, but that does not mean that they are without any powers of their own. "He made a choice to do what was right," says Lou Anne Mobley of her husband, and the same applies to herself. It also applies to other born-again Christians. Asked whether people are born with or have to acquire their character, Atherton's Julia Fenton without hesitation adopts the view that character is developed. Living virtuously is for her the most important thing human beings can do, but it is they who have to do it. "It's a clear choice of what way you are going to lead your life" is how she puts it.

As alternatives to the idea of human nature as inherently depraved, our respondents, whether evangelical in their religious outlook or not, offer two possibilities. One is to find indispensable what Jonathan Edwards found absurd: the cheerful idea that human beings are born innocent with a predisposition to do good. Because our knowledge of human nature is scanty at best, people tend to project onto human beings the characteristics they want them to have, which means that those who want to believe in the idea of human goodness can find support in the way they think about infants and young children. "Babies are innocent human beings coming into this world. They're blameless" is how Hartford's Denise Turner expresses this point of view. Atherton's Sophie Botzos has four grandchildren, two boys and two girls. "When I see those babies responding to a voice, to a song, to playing, to peekaboo," she says, she knows that if you give kids the love they crave, good things will follow. "No one can teach a baby anything," she points out. "They don't understand words yet." They do have a nature given to them by God, she believes, but she describes that nature as "bare bones." It is up to parents to supply the love to put the flesh on those bones; in that way, they "elicit those beautiful things in their child because there is nothing so heartwarming as a happy baby, giggling with joy."

"Call me an optimist," says Hartford's Donna Teele, "but I really try to see the good in people," even, she adds, "when they're not so good." Optimists about human nature have a ready explanation about why people might, despite being born good, nonetheless go bad: they have learned the wrong lessons from those around them. Do you remember that song from *South Pacific?* we were asked by Dayton's Dorothy Meyer. "They have to be taught, they have to be carefully taught, discrimination and so forth." For her, Oscar Hammerstein's inclusive liberalism defines the right way to think about the human condition. That is why Mrs. Meyer, a devout Catholic, emphasizes not only the importance of the Ten Commandments, but also the relevance of the Eight Beatitudes. In her view, it is an obvious truth that the meek will inherit the earth. "If you don't learn that formula, either at a school setting or a religious setting, and if you don't get it from your parents at home, you're lost, you're at sea, you don't know how to relate to other people and apparently don't have a relationship with the Lord."

A more common way of rejecting the idea that human beings are born bad, however, is not to substitute some Rousseauian notion of their essential goodness, but to adopt John Locke's conception of the mind as a piece of "white paper, void of all characters, without any ideas," onto which experience prints the way we come to understand the world. At the conclusion of our interviews, we administered a brief questionnaire to our respondents in which we asked them to indicate their agreement or disagreement with a few basic propositions. One of them reads: "In my opinion, a person is born either good or bad and there is not much society can do to change that." Thirteen of our 209 respondents agreed with that statement, only 3 of them strongly. By contrast, 192 disagreed, 97 of them strongly.

The students we spoke to in Greensboro—those whose character was, in a sense, still being formed—were the most vehement behind the idea that our character is not innate. "I think people develop their characters," says Glenn Nordstrom, relying on a word—"develop"—that was used over and over again by the Greensboro students. Nan Washington says we should pay particular attention to the developmental years if we are interested in how children will turn out. Todd Quarles, reflecting on the high school students who shot their classmates in Littleton, Colorado, blames the environment in which the kids were raised, not human depravity. And if bad parents can cause children to go bad, good parents can have the opposite effect. Derrik Brown attributes his own sense of religious values to his grandmother, who passed her Christian faith on to him, and he feels a sense of responsibility to pass them on to his children when the time comes. "My feeling is that's something you have to learn," he says about morality. "You don't come into this world immoral—or moral."

In the great debate between nature and nurture, most of our respondents believe in both. Lou Lamkin, the San Antonio computer programmer, grew up in a large family, and while he and one of his sisters turned out to be fairly laid-back, another brother and sister frequently found themselves in trouble with the law. Because they all had the same parents, he leans toward the nature side to explain their differences, but he also recognizes a role for nurture. "There are some genetic predispositions for certain types of behavior, but that can be mitigated by the circumstances that a person grows up in and whether or not they receive a loving, caring environment," he says.

Not all of our respondents reject the notion that biology is destiny. At least three developments in American life have shaken the Lockean premise of the mind as a blank slate. One is the popularity of the language of addiction. A second is the emerging notion that at least one aspect of human behavior, homosexuality, is not chosen but is a product of certain genetic or neurological features of the person. The third involves developments in cognitive science and evolutionary psychology that seem to offer insights into how we became the particular creatures we are. Influenced by these trends, one is most likely to find people holding to the view that human nature is fixed in arenas of life that would generally be considered on the more liberal end of America's political spectrum.

Fall River is one place where people seemed most often to resort to the language of addiction. Not surprisingly, therefore, it is a place that constitutes something of an exception to the overwhelming Lockean consensus in America that the mind is a tabula rasa. Cheryl Broca, a social worker there, is a strong advocate of the idea that destructive behavior has about it an addictive quality, and she consequently believes that Americans ought to pay more attention to the genetic basis of human behavior than they do. Although she holds that character can be learned, she also feels that some people—those who have "a piece missing"—were not raised to be bad but are bad because of a psychological condition over which they have no control. Marlene Beaulieu, who lost two brothers to drug addiction, also thinks that sometimes it does not help us to talk of a person's character because there is "an inborn tendency," something "genetic," that leads a person to do bad things. Greg Sauvage, a school administrator, agrees. Just as we are learning the degree to which alcohol is addictive, we are learning that sometimes people are born with "predispositions" that shape the rest of their lives.

One of the predispositions mentioned by Mr. Sauvage is homosexuality, and when we focus on San Francisco, we find another community in which people tend to be somewhat more skeptical of the idea that the human mind is a blank slate. To be sure, San Franciscans are among those most firmly committed to the idea that because individuals ought to be free to act as they please, they have to be understood as free to make whatever choices they want. "I think smoking is a choice. I think using drugs is a choice. I think drinking alcohol is a choice. I think religion is a choice," we were told by Louise Sullivan, one of our respondents in that city. "Those are the options that you get and you get to choose what you want." Like many of the gay men and women to whom we talked, Ms. Sullivan's identity was closely intertwined with her sexual orientation, and when it comes to a matter so close to her very being, she suddenly shifts direction and says that being gay is not a choice at all. She does not feel qualified to know whether sexual orientation is the result of something genetic or something that is the product of socialization, but she does know, as much as she knows anything, that she did not just wake up one day to consider all the available options with respect to sexuality and pick lesbianism from among them.

Ms. Sullivan's remarks reflect a fairly radical change in the way homosexuality is understood, especially among homosexuals themselves, since the early days of gay liberation. Under the influence of Michel Foucault and other scholars of Western sexuality, gayness had been considered an "invention" or a "social construction," reflecting the arbitrariness of categories that divide people into one orientation or another. In part this was a reaction to the fact that people on the left end of the political spectrum have tended to be wary of identifying any particular characteristics of people—intelligence or criminal aggressiveness, for example—as having a biological, genetic, or neurological basis. Yet on the issue of homosexuality, intellectual positions reversed themselves. Conservatives came to argue that being gay had to be considered a choice because if it were seen as a natural, inborn trait, one could no more call it immoral than a particular hair color or gender. At the same time, gay advocates, reflecting both their own understanding of their sexuality and their opposition to the conservative agenda, increasingly came around to recognizing the possible existence of a "gay gene" that determined their attraction to people of the same sex.

We found a significant number of people willing to accept a role for genetics in fashioning human destiny among our San Francisco respondents. Randy Sullivan, a computer programmer, believes that "you do have some genetic stuff and that there can be good and bad things there." Tom Ullman, bringing Locke up-to-date, asked us to imagine the human mind as an unformatted floppy disk before arguing that, when we are born, there already exists software instructing the disk what to do. "I'm not a scientist," he quickly adds, but it seems obvious to him that some people are just born manic-depressive or psychotic and others are not. Compared with the optimists in our sample who believe that all evil is learned and, because learned, can also be eradicated through good education, Mr. Ullman is something of a genetic pessimist. "I don't know that everyone can be rehabilitated," he says, citing the example of the Unabomber, Theodore Kaczynski: "There are certainly lots of people that society at large would want to lock up because we would just as soon not try to figure out how to fix them." Leslie Hawkins, an advertising production manager, agrees: "You can have something wrong with your brain, something wrong with your physiology that makes you just . . . I don't want to say 'crazy'—I don't know if that's the right word . . . but just different somehow."

Another reason that some of our Californians are reluctant to endorse the Lockean notion of the mind as a blank slate is that a number of them work in the computer industry, and people who do often take the development of information science as a metaphor for the nature of life. Some of them devour books dealing with new findings in biology and the information sciences and find in them ways of thinking about human nature that influence their outlook on the world. Atherton's Tim Crowe is one who believes that "a survival of the species argument probably promotes, after many generations, a positive type of human nature." He also thinks that it is possible that "a divine intervention from God" helps the process along. Doug Reed, the San Francisco medical library manager, tries to keep up as best as he can with the burgeoning literature in cognitive science and evolutionary psychology, from which he has gathered that character is not something a person learns but is given at birth as a result of the way human beings evolve over time. Unlike Mr. Crowe, Mr. Reed does not assign a role for divine intervention in the process, but he is taken with the idea that as we push toward the outer reaches of scientific understanding, we begin to approach the insights of Buddhism and other Eastern religions. There is a wholeness to the world, he believes, a state of perfection that can be achieved, once we realize the miracles of selection that have led us to evolve as we have.

The more one listens to individuals like Mr. Crowe and Mr. Reed, the more obvious it becomes that evolutionary theorists, one of whose leading lights goes out of his way to claim that "much if not all religious behavior could have arisen from evolution by natural selection," are being read by nonscientists as containing quasi-religious explanations of how the world came to be the way it is. Perhaps this ought not to be surprising. The ideas of evolutionary biology would not have been foreign to Jonathan Edwards, who pondered questions of mind and matter at great length. They also speak to the mysteries of human nature and, in their own way, they remind human beings of their insignificance in the face of forces too powerful to control. No wonder that contemporary Christians, both Protestant and Catholic, treat sociobiology as rife with questions of theological significance. If the Lockean consensus concerning the mind's blank slate is ever to be rejected in America, the challenge will come not from premodern forms of Christianity but from postmodern understandings offered by science-based speculation.

No focus on addiction, gay genes, and evolutionary theory should be taken as a sign that the Lockean consensus is about to shatter anytime soon. When it comes to human nature, our respondents know what they think and the overwhelming majority of them think the same way. They believe that people are not born with a predisposition to do evil. Although some are convinced that human beings are innately good, most think that we are shaped both by our environment and that we can be taught to do the right thing. No other way of thinking about human nature is in accord with some of the most deeply ingrained American convictions; like forgiveness, an optimistic view of human nature is appreciated, not for its philosophical depth, but for the functional role it can play in helping people achieve their practical goals. People ought to be viewed as having the freedom to lead their lives as they best see it, our respondents believe, and when things go wrong, and even when they go right, they also ought to be viewed as responsible for the decisions they make.

## Character Formation

If human beings are born to some degree depraved, they need something capable of straightening themselves out. That something is usually called character. "When we were growing up, everyone had to go to church," Quincy Simmons, who does painting and remodeling in Hartford, tells us. "You had no choice. It didn't matter. Every Sunday you had to get ready and go to church." School was not all that different. "During the week, when we went to school, we knew that we could not say anything to the teacher except yes or no or mister or miss or whatever." And then there was home. "This you learn from your mother also, you learn from your parents too: respect." Mr. Simmons is not the only Hartford resident who laments the passing of strong institutions. His neighbor, June Sylvester, grew up in the South, and when she talks about her childhood, it is not the racial segregation she remembers but the structure. She loved her teachers, who were "A-one. They were right there behind you." Regular church attendance taught her the difference between right and wrong. All that is gone these days, she believes. Kids grow up in single-parent families. The schools lack discipline. Television seems to be a substitute for God. She describes the world of today's youth as "a different world," one she barely understands. "Everybody just goes their own way."

This lament for a more authoritative way of life is by no means confined to African-Americans. Judy Wasserman, the Fall River university administrator, who was raised in the Jewish tradition, also misses the structures that shaped her upbringing: "You respected your teacher. You went to some kind of religious meeting every week. You had rituals in your home. You sat down and had dinner together." Now it is all so different. "The kitchen table is sort of gone. The church is sort of gone. The educational system is going through changes. It's no wonder that a lot of people are very insecure." The changes she has witnessed in her life put her into something of an apocalyptic frame of mind. "I think we are really ripe for something happening" is how she puts it. "It almost feels like a quiet before the storm." And the reason for her unease is clear. There is one question our society desperately needs to ask, but no one, it seems, has an answer: "How do you develop character in a situation like this?"

Mrs. Wasserman's question is so powerful because the doctrine of original sin once offered a clear-cut understanding of how character is formed. Whether as an infant, a delinquent, or a recovering addict, one entered the world in a barely civilized state, governed by instinct, incapable of reason. Institutions of moral authority—parents, churches, schools, and, at last resort, a system of criminal justice—took up the civilizing process, instilling character by motivating fear, guiding discipline, organizing habituation, and achieving the internalization of rules. Once character was properly formed, the individual, respectful to and respected by authority, could be set lose to find his way in the world.

Because character formation involved the alchemistic task of making something good (virtue) out of something bad (human nature), it could never be compared to a popularity contest. The process of character formation, premised on individual weakness, always sits uncomfortably in a liberal democratic society. Competencies of character would be impossible to achieve under a regime of perfect equality. For so long as a process of formation is taking place, some will be formed and others will do the forming. Similarly, character formation does not assign an especially high value to personal autonomy. To be sure, taming the instincts makes freedom possible, but the first great task of institutions is to inculcate respect for moral authority.

Once we move away from the idea that human beings, born bad, require strong institutions to make them good, old-fashioned ideas of character formation falter. This does not prevent our respondents from believing in character and having a fairly good idea about what it means; people of good character, they usually say, will be respectful of others, kind, law-abiding, generous, selfless, dedicated to their children, and involved with their communities. Their problem with the concept of character formation is not with the word "character" but with the word "formation." For even if they share a general agreement on what character means, they are no longer sure that character can be fashioned in the traditional way. Highly structured systems of moral authority require that we repress our instincts and needs for the sake of authority. But if we believe ourselves to be inherently good people—or at the very least, neither good nor bad—why can't we trust ourselves more and learn to trust institutions, which are capable of abusing the power they have, less?

San Antonio's Elsa Gonzalez, a nurse, grew up in an environment dominated by the trinity of church, school, and family. Although she considers herself a religious person and constantly invokes religious imagery, Mrs. Gonzalez does not long for the days of old. She was raised Catholic, and, as she talks, she casually remarks, as if the point were too obvious to emphasize, that "the Catholic Church has been outmoded for a long time." Mrs. Gonzalez is divorced, and she has never forgiven the Church for its insistence that even harmful marriages have to be kept intact. "To me, if a wife is beaten up and she is never given a chance, not even to live like a human being, why not divorce? Get him out of there. I mean the kids are watching this, the beating of the wife and the abuse.

Why should they be watching this? So that when they grow up, they're going to do the same thing?" Her divorce was not the only time in her life when Mrs. Gonzalez found herself questioning the moral authority of the institutions around her. She remembers her first trip to New York, at the age of nineteen to attend college, when she met someone who called himself an atheist. Brought up to believe that nonbelievers were sinful, she tried to avoid him, even as he followed her around. It turned out that he had noticed her poverty and wanted to offer her a ride from the Bronx so that she would not arrive late for class. "Sometimes people are born good," she says, reflecting what she learned in New York, and this taught her that, as important as religion may be in shaping character, it is not the only thing. Character formation includes not only what we are told to do, but what we come to understand through our experience.

Another American who wrestles with the problem of character formation is San Francisco's Gina Grossman. Like so many of our San Francisco respondents, she rejects the idea of the mind as a blank slate, even if she also rejects the idea of original sin. "I think some people are born, not with a propensity toward evil, but with certain personality characteristics" is how she puts it. Mrs. Grossman is a therapist, and her experiences treating fairly disturbed people has dispelled any lingering ideas of innate human goodness in all people. Still, as a therapist, she also believes in the importance of character formation. She remembers her days as a single woman, when she tended to be fairly critical of the men she was dating. She talked about it with her own therapist, who asked her what she wanted in a man. "Well," Mrs. Grossman recalls replying, "they have to have a sense of humor, they have to be really smart, they have to like rock 'n' roll," to which her therapist replied that all those things were superficial. "You're leaving out the most important thing," her therapist continued. "They have to be of good character." That lesson stuck. The man she eventually married, a political consultant, engages in his share of negative campaigning, but "there's something at his core," she feels. "He's principled. He's loyal." Focusing on character means you have to ask deeper questions than she once asked about her prospective suitors: "How do you live your life? Do you live it out caring about people around you? If you go past the surface and all the way deep inside, is there this commitment to taking the higher path or doing the right thing?" Mrs. Grossman is not sure of her own good character, but she is of her husband's, "which isn't to say that he does not act like a jerk sometime." She proposes a rather inventive thought experiment through which one can ascertain the possible character of a potential spouse: If the two of them were ever to end their marriage, "he would be a good person to get divorced from. Because he would be fair."

Over the past two decades or so, responding to an emphasis on "values clarification" and other approaches to moral development that appeared to them unwilling to take a stand on the importance of teaching specific virtues, a number of educators began to urge that more attention be paid to the teaching of character in American schools. Many states and school districts responded to their call, either by passing laws emphasizing the need to cultivate character education or by developing specific programs designed to teach those virtues that lay at the heart of the Western tradition. In spite of all this activity, the sociologist James Davison Hunter believes that character is dead in America and that one of the things which killed it is the field in which Gina Grossman specializes: psychology. He believes that even the programs sponsored by conservative and communitarians still rely on the "assumptions, vocabulary, and techniques of secular psychology." So powerful is the moral "regime" of contemporary psychology, Hunter thinks, that no one, not even evangelical Christians, can escape from its way of thinking about the human condition. So long as psychology reigns, people will emphasize obligations to themselves more than duties to others.

Many of our respondents find themselves more comfortable with the language of psychology than they do with the language of sin. But this hardly means that character is dead. As Hunter himself recognizes, conceptions of character have repeatedly been revised throughout American history to take account of the nation's religious and ethnic diversity. These days, the way Americans think about character is being revised to take account of the way they think about human nature. Our respondents are not so much rejecting character as they are asking for new ways to form it that are compatible with a generally positive view of human potential. Knowing more about themselves does not necessarily mean that they will care less about others. On the contrary, they believe that psychology, in giving them a more positive understanding of their own motivations than doctrines of inherent human depravity, makes it possible for them to better understand other people and their needs.

The first step involved in constructing a more positive view of character formation is to move away from a version of discipline that operates on the principle of fear. When we asked Elsa Gonzalez what makes for good character, she immediately responds by saying that people are more likely to be good "if they are churchgoers, if they believe that God is the supreme being and they believe that they have to behave because of the Ten Commandments, not because they are fearful of God but because they are convinced that that is the right way to live." In a similar way, Atherton's Betty Dvorak rejects what she calls "a fear-based approach to being good" as out of step with what leading a virtuous life requires today. Ally Sauvage of Fall River believes that there is no joy "if you're growing up in a situation where you are not allowed to do this and you're not allowed to do that and you have to spend hours in the church and you're supposed to spend hours talking to this God who is not allowing you to do [anything]." The comments of these individuals do not question the importance of character. They instead question what kind of character can emerge when parental and religious authority rely on corporal punishment, images of eternal hell, or excessive guilt-tripping. For Mrs. Sauvage, the only kind of character that can emerge out of a religious experience that is "structured and limiting, all in the name of God" is that of an angry and bitter person, not a mature and well-adjusted one.

None of this means that our respondents tend to be opposed to discipline or think that there is something wrong with upholding absolute standards of right and wrong. It is more about the way messages ought to be delivered than it is about the messages themselves. The experiences of Laura Johnson of Atherton illustrate the fine line that people try to walk. She grew up in both the Roman Catholic and the Russian Orthodox Churches, so she remembers two Easters, two Palm Sundays, and so forth. She also remembers the "heavy guilt" upon which the Catholic side of her family relied, which keeps her from being an active Catholic today. Still, Mrs. Johnson sends her daughter to a Catholic prep school, not so much because of the religious instruction it offers, but because there are fewer students in each class, homework rules are strict, and the school is not afraid of enforcing discipline. As Americans become increasingly unhappy with public schools, they find themselves turning to religious ones as an alternative for their children. Certainly many of our respondents, like Mrs. Johnson, have done exactly that. But rarely do they do so for specifically religious reasons. It is as if they want some of the practice of old-time character formation—especially a greater respect for order and discipline—without the rest of old-time character formation, especially theological instruction and an emphasis on religious obedience.

"Obedience" is the key word here, for old-fashioned versions of character formation assume that human beings, depraved as they naturally are, require firm commands meant to be accepted unthinkingly. As they search for ways to form character that are responsive to more positive conceptions of human nature, our respondents hope that institutions responsible for moral authority will learn to trust people more. Tipton's Sharon Rice comes from a large Catholic family and experienced a strict religious upbringing as a child. She still thinks of herself as a religious person and finds herself turning to the Bible for guidance. When she reflects on her upbringing, she is grateful to her parents for exposing her to the Church's teachings, although not quite in the way her parents expected. That's because the catechism, she believes, does not provide firm answers so much as it offers guidance that an individual is free to accept or reject. Like many Americans, Sharon Rice personalizes religion. "It's an individual guide," she says; once we learn it, "we can choose from there whether we choose to do something right or wrong."

Once religion is personalized, an individual does not have to go to church or belong to a specific denomination to become a good person; true character formation requires a personal relationship with a higher authority. "I'm more into a relationship with Jesus Christ than I am into organized religion," we were told by Flora Bennett, a teacher, and a lay minister, in Hartford. In a similar manner, Julia Fenton, one of the most religious people in our sample, defines a "false religion" as one that "so often functions as keeping people in check and keeping them in this little box that makes life not messy." The born-again Christians in our sample tend to worry that organized religion makes it too easy for people to affirm their relationship with God. They can demonstrate to their neighbors and friends that they are religious simply by showing up in church, but real devotion consists in trying to fashion one's life in accord with Jesus' teachings, whether one accepts membership in a church or not. That is why San Antonio's Lou Anne Mobley does not necessarily think that a person who learns the Bible will be virtuous. It is not being obedient that matters but "the commitment of your heart." You have to be sure in your own mind that you want what God has to offer you.

The distrust of institutions so characteristic of American life puts our respondents in a quandary when it comes to thinking about character formation. On the one hand, the three main formative institutions—family, school, and church—are as important as they ever were if people are to learn what it means to be a moral person. On the other hand, Americans look with suspicion on all of them. When asked who is most responsible for ensuring that people turn out good, our respondents overwhelmingly put parents first—none more so than the students from Greensboro who, because of their age, are closest to their own parents. The problem is that, with the exception of home schoolers who devote themselves to their children, parents are not always sure that they have the time, the skills, and the discipline necessary to form the character of their children. That is why they assign such importance to schools, but they also increasingly wonder whether schools—facing problems of unruly students, lower standards, and less qualified teachers—can be trusted with the job. They may turn to religious schools, but when they do that, they tend to be unsure exactly how much religion their children ought to be exposed to. Our respondents seem to be rejecting old-fashioned ideas of character formation without having well-articulated new ones to put in their place.

Character in America is no longer viewed as preformed, as if it were a quality known in advance, so that, to achieve it, all that is required is internalizing the rules of right conduct. Character, rather, is a base from which children can obtain the confidence from which they discover rules of right conduct that apply best to them. Around such an idea of character formation, it is impossible to hold to the certainties that existed when moral authority could be exercised through a dynamic of command and obedience. Once upon a time, Americans raised families without being able to know whether their children would turn out to be good or bad. Now they raise children uncertain about what good or bad actually are. No wonder our respondents feel a sometimes terrifying sense of insecurity as they consider what it means to lead a good and virtuous life.

But for all the uncertainty our respondents face, they also have some reason to hope. Atherton's Sophie Botzos, who is in her seventies, remembers the time her daughter came home and informed her parents that she was going to choose her own religion. This was something Mr. and Mrs. Botzos could barely understand, but in reality, they had little choice in the matter. Now that their daughter has turned forty, they realize that everything came out okay. "I think in the end she's come to realize that most of what she believes is already there" is how Mrs. Bot-zos puts it. "She is used to being able to think on her own. It's all right." Her experience was only one of many recounted by parents who feared the fact that their children were raised without the stricter forms of religious authority they experienced as children, yet who found that their children were capable of discovering meaningful values by which they ought to lead their lives.

## Far Beyond Good and Evil

What does it mean for a person to be evil? we asked our respondents. Some of them came up with fairly definitive answers. An evil person "is just malicious and they just do harm to people every chance they get, and there's not one ounce of good in them," says Caryn O'Toole, a Fall River bank teller. "They have no good qualities. They wake up with bad thoughts. They go to bed with bad thoughts. All they want to do is hurt everyone they meet, and that's how they live on a day-to-day basis." Atherton's Julia Fenton also offers an interesting definition. For her, Christ's goodness is manifested in his great love, and so an evil person "is one that redefines 'love.' For example, when someone who is trying to control you or shame you" calls what she is doing love, that would be an example of evil. "Evil works through confusion and through chaos,"

Mrs. Fenton adds, and nowhere are its consequences more pernicious than when God's greatest gift is manipulated. A final example comes from Dayton's Warren Wilson, whose own character was formed through his experience in the military. He remembers discovering that one of his subordinates was sexually harassing the women who worked for him. He was a dangerous man who got his way by being intimidating and threatening and, when accused, lied at every stage of the process. "I would classify that type of person as evil," Mr. Wilson says. "That's the closest I've come to meeting somebody in that category."

Although some of our respondents were prepared to define evil, a far greater number did not find the term helpful. "I think that the word 'evil' is losing its value," we were told by San Francisco's Stephen Richardson, a retired engineer. "It's too commonly applied to things that are distasteful, things that are tragic." Mr. Richardson quickly adds that his views are shaped by the fact that he does not believe in God, which means that he also does not believe in the devil. His views are somewhat atypical, because more than half of the Americans surveyed (53 percent) believe in the existence of hell. But a far larger proportion of Americans (77 percent) believe in heaven, which suggests, that when it comes to religion, Americans want the good things but not necessarily the bad. And even those who believe in hell do not think of it as a place where evil people are sent to atone for their sins; the New York Times survey, for example, found that only 7 percent of its respondents ever prayed for something bad to happen to someone. Most Americans, if surveys are to be trusted, share Mr. Richardson's sense that there is little to be gained by calling people evil.

"Evil," that's a strong word, we were told by one respondent—and then another, and then another. "Evil in my mind has this sort of like really religious, Satan-inspired [aspect], like somehow this person has been preordained or here's a curse or something like that," one of the Greensboro students, Cory Hanson, says. "I definitely think there are bad people. Certainly that's a horrible thing. Certainly that person is definitely wrong. I don't know if 'evil' is a word I would use." He was not alone. Tipton's Elaine York came close to arguing that evil is an impossibility, for even the nastiest of people cannot "be nasty all the time. Sometimes they slip." Mrs. York believes that all human beings have hearts and minds and that evil comes from their minds, perhaps because they lack a sense of self-worth. Ultimately, however, the human heart will win out. "Deep in their heart they know they have something good about them. Sooner or later they are going to do something good."

Our respondents were prepared to name historical figures they would consider evil. Adolf Hitler was mentioned often, as were Saddam Hussein, Pol Pot, Josef Stalin, Idi Amin, Slobodan Milosevic, and the Ayatollah Khomeini. Among figures in the news, mass murderers—Jeffrey Dahmer, David Berkowitz (the Son of Sam), Ted Bundy, Charles Manson—were frequently mentioned, as were Theodore Kaczynski (the Unabomber) and Susan Smith, the South Carolina woman who drowned her children in a lake. Respondents in Texas brought up David Koresh. One of the Greensboro students mentioned Eric Rudolph, the alleged abortion clinic and Atlanta Olympic bomber, and another included rock star Marilyn Manson. Rupert Murdoch was cited by one self-described radical lesbian in San Francisco and one of our Tipton residents mentioned Newt Gingrich. Despite their distaste for the concept of evil, our respondents, as long as they do not know them personally, can find plenty of examples of people who embody it.

Among those they do know personally, our respondents tend to deny finding anyone evil. Of course this was not true of everyone; one of our Fall River respondents, who calls himself "streetwise," knew someone involved in a series of gruesome robberies and was pleased to report that the man's body was recently found in the Maine woods, the evident victim of a mob retaliation. Others who said that they knew someone they could consider evil rendered the concept essentially meaningless by conflating it with someone who hurt them: an ex-spouse, a former boss, a person who took away the respondent's virginity, or an occasionally cruel grandmother. But most of them found it unlikely that an evil person might exist in their immediate neighborhood, family, or workplace. To the degree that the concept of evil exists in the imagination of our respondents, it does so as an abstraction.

William Blake once said that in Milton's *Paradise Lost*, Satan has all the good lines, and whether true or not, it is undoubtedly the case that in *Othello* or *Macbeth* the characters who cause the most harm to others utter the greatest speeches. The human imagination seems to require a larger than life sense of evil to make sense out of the good. Yet nevertheless reluctant to find much evil in the world around them, our respondents are not sure that they want to find much good either. Like evil, saintliness is something of an abstraction to them, applicable to heroic figures of the historical or religious imagination. (Mother Teresa, Albert Schweitzer, Pope John Paul II, and, to my surprise, Sammy Sosa were people often referred to as saintly). To be sure, some of our respondents were in awe of parents who took care of children with Down's syndrome or people who work altruistically to help the disadvantaged or acted out of a strong Christian belief in faith, hope, and charity. But most thought of saintliness as something of a not-in-my-backyard phenomenon. Some of them even felt that way about relatively benign forms of saintliness. "If you mean would I like to live next door to somebody who is so 'saintly' that they take in every stray dog and cat, or start a soup kitchen out of their own house, no, I wouldn't," says Atherton's Sophie Botzos. "I like living where I can be peaceful and enjoying what we've worked for."

Obvious dangers abound when people are reluctant to acknowledge the possibility and ubiquity of good and evil. San Francisco's Flo Barnes did not think that Jeffrey Dahmer, the Milwaukee serial killer, was evil. "I just thought he was very sick, and I felt sorry for him. I don't think I heard anyone else say that they felt sorry for him, but I did." (She felt less sorry for someone who killed puppy dogs and was sentenced to four years in jail; she would have sentenced him to fifty). In Fall River we talked to Karim Abdullah, who thinks that Jeffrey Dahmer was evil, but not Adolf Hitler. Taking the view that people who deal in a personal way with others ought to be held to a higher moral standard than impersonal forces, he says that Dahmer directly cut people up and ate them, while Hitler just sat in his office and gave orders. To some degree Mr. Abdullah's opinions may be due to the fact that, as an immigrant from an Arab country, he identifies with Palestinians and does not want to accept claims made by Jews that the greatest evil of our times was directed against them. But his views, as well as those of Flo Barnes, seem to give credence to those who would argue that without a strong sense that evil exists in the world, we will come to accept a cultural relativism in which we can no longer distinguish between degrees of cruelty.

Seeing good in people can turn out to be a bad thing to do. For a conservative critic like the political philosopher Allan Bloom, a people who live beyond good and evil are a people who talk about values rather than virtues. "The term 'value,'" he wrote, "meaning the radical subjectivity of all belief about good and evil, serves the easygoing quest for comfortable self-preservation." Indeed, most of those with whom we spoke could be considered comfortable, if not always economically, than at least in their outlook on the world, and self-preservation was very much at the center of their concerns. Bloom also writes that the use of a nonnegotiable term like "evil"—for example, in Ronald Reagan's speech calling the Soviet Union an "evil empire"—closes off discussion, making those who want to see the good in people uneasy. When you pronounce someone evil, you are in fact ostracizing them from your community, and Americans, with some exceptions, are reluctant to engage in dramatic stigmatization.

Should Satan disappear, he will be missed; writers as diverse as Andrew Delbanco and Elaine Pagels have explored how central ideas of evil have been to Western tradition, and how much is sacrificed when they atrophy. Yet it may be that Americans see little evil around them because there really is so little evil close at hand. The twentieth century was one in which figures of unprecedented evil made an appearance. It was also a century in which Americans began to take seriously the evils that had existed in their own society, including the deliberate extermination of Native Americans, the internment of Japanese-Americans, and the slavery imposed on African-Americans. But America has not welcomed dictators and has taken steps to correct the abuses of its past. There is something odd about Bloom's discomfort with the reigning niceness he found so ubiquitous among his students. People who lack a radical sense of evil may not be capable of grasping the full complexity of the human condition; they may be ill prepared for evil when it shows its face and they may even, in rare cases, be unable to recognize the evil existing inside themselves. Yet compared with radical evil, radical niceness is worth appreciating. The lack of a tragic vision of life among our respondents may not just represent a failure of nerve, an unwillingness to look into the darkness of the human soul. It may also represent a fairly realistic assessment of what it takes to make a society function smoothly.

### The Emergence of Moral Freedom

"I wanted to do it because I wanted you to know that there are still some people out there who have morals." Michaela Summers, an eighteen-year-old Southern Baptist who is majoring in elementary education at the University of North Carolina, Greensboro, is speaking about the reasons she agreed to participate in our study. "You don't get a lot of people who are Christians voicing their opinion," she says, which is why Ms. Summers, an active member of the university's Inter-Varsity

Christian Fellowship, is so willing to express her views. As she does, they reveal a person of serious and sober disposition. Ms. Summers is a devoted daughter who puts her mother "right up there with Mother Teresa." Her parents—"I love [them] to death"—have been married for twenty-three years, and while they have the usual disagreements about money, they make it a point never to argue in front of their children. Michaela does not have a boyfriend, at least in part because she is against divorce and is therefore a bit scared of the kinds of commitment a real and lasting marriage would entail. She thinks that smoking is sinful and drinking immoral, and nothing, in her view, justifies narcissistic, self-indulgent behavior. For her, the Bible furnishes a set of rules by which people ought to live, and, for all her modesty, when she considers that "somebody that was perfect and did nothing wrong" like Jesus would nonetheless die on the cross to take "every single person in this world's sins," she feels that she is selfish by comparison.

I am also glad that Ms. Summers agreed to be interviewed, because what stands out is how unusual her comments are. This is not because of her religiosity; many of our respondents are Christian and take their faith in Jesus as devoutly as she does. But the dominant trends among religious believers in America are toward more individualized forms of faith in which personal autonomy—switching congregations, deciding when and how to pray, emphasizing individual piety or social involvement, having a born-again experience—plays a significant role. One can see aspects of that autonomy among the strongest religious believers in our sample—such as Lou Anne Mobley, Warren Wilson, and Julia Fenton—for, when they spoke to us, they stressed either the importance of individual choice or the way their faith worked miracles in their own lives. In contrast, Michaela Summers's beliefs evoke images of a time when Americans thought of themselves as born into a particular religion that gave them firm instruction in how to live and to which they would remain committed the rest of their lives.

Yet when all is said and done, not many among our respondents think about what it means to lead a moral life in ways similar to Michaela Summers. The least religious among them, as one might expect, can be found among San Franciscans, one of whom describes Mother Teresa, whom Michaela Summers so admires, as a "bitch on wheels." But it is not necessary to dwell in the Castro district or Noe Valley to get a grasp on the degree to which Americans resist taking instruction from unquestioned sources of moral authority. Just down the peninsula from the Castro is Atherton—a community as suburban as San Francisco is urban and as Republican and conservative as San Francisco is Democratic and liberal. One of its residents, Jim Crowley, appreciates the role that religion can play in emphasizing respect for the virtues, but, he adds, "religions to me are kind of totalitarian in the sense that it is an externally imposed discipline as opposed to internally imposed." Bob Ryan, who is seventy-six years old and still active as chairman of a construction company, also does not want religious people telling him what to do. People's choices have to be respected, he tells us, even if people engage in self-destructive acts like smoking or drinking. "I don't like laws" is how Paula Gordon, a florist, makes the same point. "I don't even like the helmet law or seat belt law or the smoking law."

When people believe that individuals are born with a blank slate and are unlikely to be radically evil or radically good, it is a short step to believing that the best place to turn for moral guidance is to themselves. "Somebody can't make you do something you don't want to do," San Antonio's Lucy Martin, tells us. "You know, you draw your own guidelines." Whitney Carter, another University of North Carolina student, puts the point as simply as possible: "I hate to be told what to do." Tipton's Dominique Mottau is a twenty-six-year-old single mother who works with victims of substance abuse and violence. The only way to change another person's behavior, she insists, is to communicate with that person and find out what is on her mind, because "the answer really is in each individual." Mark Lilla, a political philosopher, once observed that "the cultural and Reagan revolutions took place within a single generation, and have proved to be complementary, not contradictory, events." The responses we heard in all parts of America confirm his observation. Americans borrow from the left its emphasis on the need to respect individual rights but shun its emphasis on government intervention, while they take from the right its belief in freedom and ignore its calls for a moral revival. The old adage that America is a free country has, at last, come true, for Americans have come to accept the relevance of individual freedom, not only in their economic and political life, but in their moral life as well.

The defining characteristic of the moral philosophy of the Americans can therefore be described as the principle of moral freedom. Moral freedom means that individuals should determine for themselves what it means to lead a good and virtuous life. Contemporary Americans find answers to the perennial questions asked by theologians and moral philosophers, not by conforming to strictures handed down by God or nature, but by considering who they are, what others require, and what consequences follow from acting one way rather than another. Some of our respondents adopt moral freedom as a creative challenge. For them, the collapse of traditional institutions of moral authority is something worth celebrating. Schooled in the language of self-fulfillment and convinced that words like "maturity" and "growth" are preferable to words like "sin," they find themselves quite comfortable with the idea that a good society is one that allows each individual maximum scope for making his or her own moral choices.

Not all Americans are quite so sunny in their views of human nature and character formation, but even those who lament the passing of a more traditional moral order—at first glance, the enemies of moral freedom—have been touched by its appeals. The way the born-again Christians among our respondents describe how they were once sinners but now have come to see the light of Jesus suggests a voyage of personal discovery. For all her appeals to tradition, Lou Anne Mobley has chosen to home-school her children, and by doing so, she has joined a trend by which those who seek to transmit the lessons of authority do so in ways contingent upon the freedom of choice available to them. The parents of most of the students we interviewed at the University of North Carolina at Greensboro experienced the 1960s, and their children want to use their own moral freedom to avoid the marital breakups their parents went through. There is no necessary opposition between moral freedom and moral authority. Under some circumstances, moral freedom can even be the latter's friend, for when a traditional way of life is the product of a person's own decision, it is likely to be held on to with greater tenacity and appreciation than when it is inherited unthinkingly. Strict, hierarchical, and authoritative moral institutions often produce as many radical antagonists as they do unwavering adherents. The strongest ties are sometimes those we bind ourselves.

Moral freedom is anything but an all-or-nothing affair. As they decide for themselves the best way to live, people can and do consult traditional sources of moral wisdom. Our respondents mentioned in passing not only popular television programs and self-help books, but also the example of Jesus Christ; philosophers, from Plato and Aristotle to Kant and William James; novelists, such as F. Scott Fitzgerald, Jane Austen, and Alexander Solzhenitsyn; theologians, including Teilhard de Chardin and the Rabbi Hillel; historical figures, from Winston Churchill to Dorothy Day; and films, ranging the gamut from *Saving Private Ryan* to *The Thin Blue Line*. Some of them sought pastoral guidance from ministers, priests, and rabbis, while others relied on counselors and therapists. Many appreciated the wisdom of their elders and told of being inspired by great teachers. But for nearly all of them, when a moral decision has to be made, they look into themselves—at their own interests, desires, needs, sensibilities, identities, and inclinations—before they choose the right course of action.

Americans have become comfortable with the idea of moral freedom because its optimistic theory of human nature makes more sense to them than the one it replaced. Earlier worldviews in America, from the Puritans' to the Victorians', argued that a strong God, like a strong state, was required by the failings of a weak people. Many of our respondents do not think of themselves as weak. Nor do most other Americans; reflecting the same high level of confidence in their abilities, the *New York Times* poll found that 85 percent of those surveyed believed they could pretty much be anything they wanted to be. Americans do not have a sense that the world would be a better place if they lost some of that confidence—and its corresponding theory of human nature, emphasizing both the inherent goodness of people and their capacity to alter their inborn nature. Theories of human nature are usually meant to be normative as well as descriptive. When we posit that human beings are born depraved, we give them a reason to act as if they were. Americans would rather assume that human beings are born good, thereby giving them a standard to which they can aspire.

Their common moral philosophy inoculates Americans against those who preach to them that they ought to live in some other way than they do. Leftists learned this lesson when they failed to convince Americans to stop their love affair with capitalism, only to discover that Americans like the economic freedom capitalism promises. Conservatives are now learning this lesson as they fail to persuade Americans to return to the norms, traditions, beliefs, and practices of yesterday, for they are discovering the reluctance of Americans to give up the moral freedom they are acquiring. There is a moral majority in America. It just happens to be one that wants to make up its own mind.

# VII. The Strange Idea of Moral Freedom

## The Impossibility of Moral Freedom

Like many African-Americans, Hartford computer programmer Daryl Sims considers himself a religious person, although he is somewhat dubious about organized religion. Along with his faith in a higher power, however, comes a strong commitment to the kind of moral freedom characteristic of so many of those with whom we spoke: "People believe that things are predestined. Well, I don't believe that. I mean, we were given free will to make our choices. The choices we make create the twists and turns in the road." His views overlap significantly with those of Kevin Gilmore, an all-American-looking graduate student in biophysics at the University of California, San Francisco. Mr. Gilmore points out that "you can teach morality like you teach to a computer: here's the Bible, here, read it, do what it tells you" or "you can teach people to think about what's right and what's good and what's bad and not see things as black and white." Because we are so vulnerable to advertisers intent on selling us products we might not want, it is especially important, in Mr. Gilmore's opinion, to teach children to think for themselves. "I don't think you can teach a kid to follow orders, and to follow what you say is right," he tell us. "You can try to convince the child that that's right, but if we don't let the child think for themselves and make their own decisions, you're leaving them, as an adult, vulnerable to these ad campaigns where they're told what to think."

These respondents, like the many others who spoke in similar ways, casually take for granted something quite revolutionary: never have so many people been so free of moral constraint as contemporary Americans. Most people, throughout most of the world, have lived under conditions in which their morality was defined for them. Now, for the first time in human history, significant numbers of individuals believe that people should play a role in defining their own morality as they contemplate their proper relationship to God, to one another, and to themselves.

The nineteenth century witnessed the triumph of economic freedom. Brilliantly formulated by Adam Smith, whose *The Wealth of Nations* was published in 1776, the principles of economic freedom ultimately destroyed the mercantile economies of Europe and North America. Those principles were instrumental in creating a society in which the right to own property, to hire workers, and to manufacture and dispose of goods was accepted as the most productive way for that society to create and distribute its wealth. The twentieth century was the century of political freedom. When it began, women did not possess the right to vote, nor, in practice, did most African-Americans in the South. Yet once the principle of political freedom was extended to some, there was nothing to stop it from being extended to all. By century's end, the idea that people had a right to vote and to run for office—and that such a right could not be denied them on the basis of their ownership of property, their race, or their gender—had become so widely accepted that no Western society could be considered a good society unless its political system was organized along democratic lines.

The twenty-first century will be the century of moral freedom.

Moral freedom has become so ubiquitous in America that we sometimes forget how pathbreaking it is. We simply no longer live in a world in which women are encouraged to stay home and raise their children, government's word is to be trusted, teachers can discipline as well as instruct, the police enforce laws against what is considered immoral conduct, and religious leaders are quick to offer—and their parishioners are quick to accept—unambiguous prescriptions for proper Christian conduct. Now women will want for themselves a greater say in how they ought to live, employees will look for jobs that give them some say in the work they do, churchgoers will ask questions and not just receive answers, young people will manage their own sexuality, and political leaders will take moral instruction from the voters rather than the other way around.

Although political freedoms are enormously important, they are restricted to one sphere of human activity: obtaining and exercising political power. The same is true of economic freedom, which, by definition, is limited to such essential (but essentially mundane) matters such as the buying and selling of commodities. Moral freedom involves the sacred as well as the profane; it is freedom over the things that matter most. The ultimate implication of the idea of moral freedom is not that people are created in the image of a higher authority. It is instead that any form of higher authority has to tailor its commandments to the needs of real people.

Moral freedom is so radical an idea, so disturbing in its implications, that it has never had much currency among any but a few of the West's great moral theorists. Even those who made passionate arguments in defense of freedom in general did not extend their argument to moral freedom. Indeed, the common position among most Western thinkers has been to argue the necessity for moral constraint as a precondition for freedom in all other aspects of life.

It has long been recognized that economic freedom assumes a preexisting moral consensus. For if there are no binding moral rules—if individuals are as free to drop or add their moral beliefs with the same alacrity with which they can buy or sell stocks—then all social relations, including those of free exchange, will be threatened. What, in the absence of binding moral rules, would prevent me from deciding, after you had given me possession of the car I agreed to buy from you, that I ought to keep my money after all? As the philosopher David Hume pointed out, exchange premised upon the notion of a contract requires prior agreement to a moral ideal—in this case, the existence of a promise—that cannot itself be treated contractually.

Theorists of economic freedom sometimes argue that capitalist social relations are "natural"—that, for example, the desire to own property is hard-wired into human beings and hence universal in nature. If that were true, we would not necessarily require moral constraint in order to have economic freedom, since all we would need is the space to act on our most natural instincts. But such a way of posing the issue seems patently untrue, because some societies have a highly cultivated appreciation for private property while others do not. It seems far more realistic to say that laissez-faire requires an elaborate set of rules before it can be expected to work properly. Friedrich Hayek, the twentieth century's greatest theorist of economic freedom, spent as much time justifying the need for constraining rules as he did arguing for the primacy of self-interest. A free society, Hayek wrote, requires "submission to undesigned rules and conventions whose significance and importance we largely do not understand." Citing such authorities as Hume, Edmund Burke, James Madison, and Alexis de Tocqueville, Hayek reiterated (and brought up-to-date) the classically liberal idea that voluntary economic exchange can exist only when morality is treated in a nonvoluntary fashion. Our capacity to act rationally is dependent upon a morality that evolves outside our cognitive control.

It is not just with respect to economic freedom that we have learned

201

to appreciate the importance of moral restraint. Immanuel Kant was one of the great theorists of freedom in the Western tradition. In no other thinker can one find such powerful efforts to secure a grounding for the proposition that the greatest value to human beings lies in their capacity for autonomy. But we can be autonomous, according to Kant, only to the degree that we act in accord with timeless moral precepts not chosen by us. Moral action, in his view, was the exact opposite of a do-as-you-please affair. We must imagine what would happen if all other people act as we are tempted to do, a thought experiment that makes immediately clear why acting selfishly or shortsightedly would be wrong. Should I nonetheless decide to act in ways contrary to the categorical imperative—should I, for example, conclude that under the circumstances in which I find myself at the moment I would be best off lying or being unfaithful to my spouse or refusing to forgive someone who deserved forgiveness—I would not be morally free but the opposite. That is because if everyone else had made the same decision as I did, the result would be a form of anarchy in which nothing, including autonomy, would be possible.

Religious freedom is yet another realm of liberty that is not the same as moral freedom; indeed, it generally requires the definite absence of moral freedom to come into existence. John Locke's *Letter Concerning Toleration*, a classic text in the history of religious freedom, does not extend tolerance to all, for, in grounding the concept of toleration in Christian teachings, it leaves Jews to the mercy of their own conceptions of justice and excludes entirely those "who deny the Being of a God." By the time the idea of religious toleration came to the United States, its basis was broader than Locke's. But for America's eighteenth-century theorists, religious freedom was still freedom for religions and only incidentally freedom for believers—or, even more improbably, nonbelievers. The freedom to hold and act upon one's religious beliefs is not the same thing as the freedom to decide for oneself what and how to believe. The free exercise clause of the United States Constitution countered the idea of an established church. It imagined a world in which Baptists and Catholics would have the same right to practice their religion as Congregationalists. It did not contemplate a world like that of our respondents, in which people consider a wide range of options from orthodoxy to nonbelief and then decide which one suits them best.

And how could it? The idea of people having the freedom to choose their own way of believing—a little more this week than last, a little bit of Protestantism this month and Catholicism the next—assumes that the individual is in charge of his own destiny. Such an idea was foreign to eighteenth-century conceptions of religious freedom, which assumed that God was in charge of a person's destiny. The reason to keep the state out of religion was because there was a power higher than the state to which a person owed his obedience. In his "Memorial and Remonstrance Against Religious Assessments" of 1785, James Madison defended the idea that "it is the duty of every man to render to the Creator such homage and such only as he believes acceptable to him," but he also wrote that "what is here a right towards men, is a duty towards the Creator." The idea of religious freedom stakes out a position independent of the state's authority only to clear the way for God's authority. Freedom of conscience presumes that we have a conscience, that we are already predisposed to say no to our instincts and desire for immediate gratification.

It was not just with respect to religious belief that America's eighteenth-century theorists of freedom assumed the existence of a prior moral world in which freedom would be valued and protected. Students of the classical world, influenced by European writers from Machiavelli to Montesquieu, they were, to one degree or another, adherents of a conception of republican virtue which emphasized that freedom was possible only when individuals restrained their self-interest for the sake of the public good. Stern, proper, respectful—such virtuous people could hardly be described as morally free. They did not consider all possible actions before deciding which one to take. Instead, they were more likely to consider those few things that might be permissible within a larger sphere of all the things that could not be done. So censorious are such republican conceptions of virtue that the generation of historians who first called attention to them concluded that republicanism was inevitably hostile to an emphasis on liberty. That interpretation has been more recently challenged, yet even if eighteenth-century republicans were to some degree liberals, they were anything but libertarians. Theirs was a world of restraint, not a world of possibility.

It is not surprising that the enemies of freedom over the past two centuries were also opponents of moral freedom: Conservatives since at least Edmund Burke have believed that because "duty and will are . . . contradictory terms," our moral obligations "are such as were never the results of our option." But we realize just how radical the idea of moral freedom is when we recognize how little support the idea has received from freedom's greatest friends. To be sure, not all friends of liberty were enemies of moral freedom; not only does John Stuart Mill's *On Liberty* defend the idea that people should be free to determine for themselves the plan of their lives, he also extended the realm of liberty to new terrain when he wrote that "over himself, over his own body and mind, the individual is sovereign." Still, nearly all the great liberal thinkers—even Mill in some of his writings—presupposed the existence of common moral ideals within which liberty would be exercised. The one freedom forbidden to us was the freedom to choose all the arenas in which to be free. Some things were too important to be left to the whims of caprice and self-interest. And nothing was more important than assuring that the moral rules that shaped society's other rules were secured by something transcendental, impervious to the passions of the moment, and filled with symbolic grandeur.

Summing up this entire tradition of Western thought, the late-nineteenth-century sociologist Emile Durkheim argued that society could not exist without morality; indeed, he wrote, society *was* morality. Durkheim called the moral rules that delineate what is deemed permissible and what is considered out-of-bounds the "collective conscience." According to theorists of republican virtue, both order and liberty were possible because humans listened to their conscience instead of following their desires. In the modern world, where social interactions are far more voluminous and impersonal, society becomes possible only to the degree to which the "no" that the conscience speaks to the individual becomes generalized to society as a whole. Ideally, the collective conscience would act in an almost mystical way; we would imbibe its teachings in ways that would never make us quite realize how coercive society can be. But if that failed, there was always the state—an institution sometimes painted by Durkheim in magisterial colors—to back morality up.

If there was anything of a consensus in an area of thought as disputatious as moral theory, it was the notion that moral freedom was an impossible idea. For any one of a number of representative thinkers, a term like "moral freedom" would have seemed an oxymoron. Timeless, transcendental, absolute—morality stood in the sharpest possible contrast to the realm of freedom, which was transient, inconsistent, and dependent upon mere circumstance. Even when Friedrich Nietzsche launched his attack on morality's claims for privileged status, he hardly did so in the name of moral freedom (although many of his twentieth-century disciples would nonetheless interpret him that way). Thinkers might disagree on the extent to which people ought to be free, with conservatives preferring less and liberals advocating more. But almost no one, conservative or liberal, disagreed with the proposition that some ways of life could never be free. At the dawn of the twentieth century, moral freedom remained as strange an idea as it had been since freedom first became an object of modern longing.

## *Moral Freedom Comes to America*

Although Americans pride themselves on their commitment to freedom in general, they have been as reluctant to embrace moral freedom as any other modern people. It is true that out there at the margins of respectability, where it is often difficult to distinguish the genuinely innovative idea from the decidedly kooky, there have always been individuals in this country advocating one form or another of moral freedom. A society that relied on a revolution for its establishment, and that was dominated by empty spaces for the adventurous to fill, could hardly avoid finding some in its midst whose advocacy of liberty spilled over into advocacy of the proposition that people ought to be able to lead their own lives as they, and they alone, best see fit. One can see early hints of the idea of moral freedom among deists who challenged traditional conceptions of an all-knowing God, among utopians searching for communities in which cooperative ideals could be enshrined, and among people inspired by the writings of a Ralph Waldo Emerson, a Henry David Thoreau, or a Walt Whitman. America has never lacked for dissenters, including dissenters from an idea as widely accepted as the idea that moral restraint was necessary to make other forms of freedom possible.

No other group of Americans is as responsible for introducing notions of moral freedom into American discourse than some of those who spoke in the name of women. Not all who did so, of course, considered moral freedom a blessing. In the early days of the republic, many women, influenced by the idea of republican virtue, saw themselves as playing a special role in moral instruction, a role that would be undermined by too great an involvement in politics. Few were the women who were willing to take on directly such deeply entrenched nineteenth-century ideals as the family or Victorian sexual codes; and even when women began to do so, for example in the form of offering advice about birth control, they often did so in extremely conventional lan-guage. Feminism was as much about the opposition to easy divorce on the part of Lucy Stone or the Woman's Christian Temperance Union as it was about confronting bourgeois morality. Among many, if not most, feminists, the idea of moral freedom was anathema.

Yet while the idea of moral freedom could have emerged anywhere, it did so most vividly in the most unsettling area of human life: sex. For women, questions about freedom quickly became questions about the right to control their own bodies. It was radical feminists like Victoria Woodhull who first began to agitate on behalf of the proposition that freedom could not be said to exist so long as laws existed that denied women control, not only over their own property, but also over their sexuality. "This thing we call Freedom," she wrote in 1871, "is a large word, implying a good deal more than people have been able to recog-nize." As the historian Eric Foner argues, Woodhull insisted on free-dom's unity, "resting on individual sovereignty in all areas of life." Nothing if not literal, she took her views to their logical conclusion, arguing in favor of free love. In so doing, Woodhull anticipated the direc-tion that arguments for moral freedom would take a century after she penned her words.

But Woodhull was as much a symbol of moral freedom's delayed arrival as she was a prophet of its eventual success. The net effect of her campaign for the freedom to control one's own sexuality was to unleash the far more powerful forces of public morality in America. When Woodhull was arrested for publicizing the Reverend Henry Ward Beecher's affair with Elizabeth Tilton, it was the man who arrested her, Anthony Comstock, whose name came to symbolize the moral atmos-phere of the late nineteenth century. It is true, as the historian Rochelle Gurstein demonstrates, that the idea of "reticence" in American culture would eventually be repealed, but, as her documentation reveals, it is also true that the forces in favor of imposing reticence were, for a considerable period of time, quite powerful indeed. Victoria Woodhull's intellectual descendants would live on, giving rise to the occasional cult or utopian experiment in living, the flapper decade of the 1920s, the development of bohemia in Greenwich Village, the public exploits of figures like Mabel Dodge Luhan, frequent journeys to Europe in search of less oppressive climes, and eventually the beatniks. But the institutions and practices against which such movements railed—marriage, church, sobriety, schools, conventional opinion—managed to survive. To the degree that Americans were given a choice in the matter, they time and again voted to uphold moral restraint.

There are at least two reasons that it took so long for the idea of moral freedom to become a powerful force in American life. One is that many forms of freedom also took a long time to come to fruition. A significant number of Americans, so long as there was slavery, had no freedom at all, and even after their emancipation, many African-Americans were denied the most elementary forms of freedom until halfway through the twentieth century. The first great statement from the U.S. Supreme Court defending free speech was made in 1925, and that was made in dissent. The first decision protecting the religious freedom of unpopular religious groups like the Jehovah's Witnesses did not come until 1940, a time when the court had in front of it the horrors of societies that denied basic liberties to their citizens. And when the Supreme Court finally spoke about sex—"a great and mysterious force in human life," which was "a subject of absorbing interest" and "one of the vital problems of human interest," as the court put it—it did so in the context of upholding a conviction for violating obscenity laws. A society that for the first century and a half of its existence had barely gotten used to the idea that people ought to be free to express their beliefs, practice their faith, vote, demonstrate for their rights, and read what they wanted was far from ready to accord people the freedom to construct their lives as best as they saw fit.

A second reason that moral freedom came so late is the absence of a political constituency in favor of the idea. Conservatives in American history had spoken on behalf of authority, not freedom, and when the subject was moral authority, their defense of established institutions and practices was even more vehement. More important, the left—which sees itself as in the forefront of social change—has historically been as uncomfortable with the idea of moral freedom as the right. Groups denied freedom by American customs and practices were, like conventional feminists, less interested in challenging what freedom meant than they were in obtaining it in its political form. Movements to free the slaves, and later on movements to secure equality for the descendants of slaves, generally based themselves on the most conservative of moral sources: the dignity of work, faith in God, respect for human dignity, the autonomy guaranteed by property. Leaders of America's labor movement had little sympathy for Marxism, but they shared with Marxism its contempt for libertinism, which they associated with bourgeois decadence; one could hardly find a morally more respectable rebel than Samuel Gompers, the founder of the American Federation of Labor. To the degree that American progressivism had a moral vision, it had much in common with sterner forms of Protestant restraint. The New Deal may or may not have been economically radical—historians are still debating that question—but there is no doubt that it was morally conventional. When Franklin Roosevelt in 1941 announced the four freedoms—of speech, of worship, from want, from fear—moral freedom was not among them. Moral freedom could not take root in American life because so few significant constituencies were willing to advocate on its behalf.

It was the challenge presented to the United States by nations with no commitments to freedom at all that ironically proved the value of a certain skepticism toward moral freedom. How, one wonders, could the Nazis in Germany—and later the Communists in the Soviet Union—

ever have been stopped if we had allowed every individual to decide for himself or herself whether anti-Semitism was truly evil or whether communism was the wave of the future? World War II and the Cold War illustrate the wisdom of Durkheim's emphasis on the importance of coordinating our actions. What greater proof does one need for the proposition that achieving collective moral ends—economic security for citizens at home, respect for all regardless of religion and race, resistance in the face of totalitarian aggression, and the preservation of world peace—can be ensured only by people who are not free to choose their moral ends however they so desire?

When the generation that survived the Depression and fought World War II finally witnessed a more normal world, it puts its faith not in a vision of individuals as free choosers of their own moral beliefs, but in miracles of social cooperation: a national highway system, the continuance of Social Security, modified economic planning, and a large military establishment mobilized in the hopes of preserving the peace. Security, not freedom, was the watchword of this generation. That its conformity became something of a cliché does not detract from the fact that, morally speaking, this was a generation that longed for the tried-and-true: the Pledge of Allegiance, the suburban home, the picket fence, the gray flannel suit, Boy Scouts and Girl Scouts, prayer in school, the stay-at-home mom.

The postwar generation was probably the last generation to act as if moral freedom was an unthinkable idea. These were people who may not have read Kant and Durkheim and may not have known much about the history of republican virtue, but the lessons taught by those thinkers were second nature to them. No one had to instruct them in the fact that liberty and restraint were dependent on each other. The principles that told them the proper way to act stressed the importance of delayed gratification, binding vows, sexual fidelity, faith in God, sobriety, loyalty to country, duty to others. We know, of course, because the novels and social criticism of the 1950s told us so, that not everyone lived up to those ideals. But we also know that even moral codes honored in the breach are still moral codes. If in eighteenth- and nineteenth-century European philosophy moral freedom was an idea rarely thought, in the first half of twentieth-century America moral freedom was an idea rarely practiced. Had you asked most Americans in 1950 whether they lived in a free country, they would have quickly answered in the positive. And had you asked them whether this meant that they could pretty much live in any manner that best seemed to fit their inclinations—that they could join or quit any church at will, enter into divorce as frequently as they entered into marriage, join or not join the armed forces as they saw fit, and pick the school that, in their opinion, would best educate their children—they would not have understood the question.

## Enter the 1960s

All this changed in the 1960s and—as the journalist David Frum has recently pointed out—the 1970s. For the first time in American history a number of thinkers began to take the idea of moral freedom seriously, and enough people paid them attention to launch a significant challenge against moral authority. The result was a radical transformation in the moral and theological framework of American society. Reviewing the entire history of religion in America since the first Spanish and French settlements, the historian Sidney Ahlstrom concluded that "only in the 1960s would it become apparent that the Great Puritan Epoch in American history had come to an end." If nothing is so powerful as an idea whose time has come, then the idea of moral freedom, when it finally came, was powerful enough, at least for a time, to sweep all before it.

Sheer, unapologetic, fulsome praise of moral freedom characterized the writings of Norman O. Brown, Wilhelm Reich, Herbert Marcuse, Charles Reich, and other theorists of 1960s cultural liberation. What had once appeared to earlier theorists of freedom as the necessary restraint that made all other freedoms possible appeared to them as repression pure and simple. Marcuse's *Eros and Civilization* (1955) and Brown's *Life Against Death* (1959) were quintessential expressions of this point of view. Freud was for both men a weapon to be aimed against all those thinkers for whom a preexisting moral order was held to be a requirement of human freedom. In Brown's account, Kant's rationality is "really the necessary schemata of repression," Durkheim's division of labor "does not promote the happiness of the individual," and those Protestant notions of ethical conduct that formed the basis of republican virtue became the ingredients of the anal personality: "orderliness, parsimony, and obstinacy."

Marcuse also attacked any notion that freedom could ever be dependent on repression. Relying on Freud's insight that civilization progresses by sublimating pleasurable instincts, Marcuse argued that contemporary societies were overgoverned by the "reality principle." Generating more repression than they needed to impose order and discipline, they desexualized libidinal instincts, transforming our erotic capacities into means of oppression against us. From Marcuse's perspective, freedom demanded a lifting of all attempts to sublimate Eros. True morality could be found in what Marcuse called "libidinal morality":

> No longer employed as instruments for retaining men in alienated performances, the barriers against absolute gratification would become elements of human freedom; they would protect that other alienation in which pleasure originates—man's alienation not from himself but from mere nature: his free self-realization. Men would really exist as individuals, each shaping his own life; they would face each other with truly different needs and truly different modes of satisfaction—with their own refusals and their own selections.

Behind the oppression of contemporary capitalism, Marcuse caught a glimpse of what he considered to be genuine moral freedom: "sensuous rationality," he wrote, "contains its own moral laws."

If the classic thinkers in the liberal tradition held that economic or religious freedom was dependent upon moral constraint, Marcuse and Brown argued the exact opposite: without full moral freedom, all other freedoms were illusory. Stripped of the erotic aspects of our nature, Marcuse held, we cannot be free, no matter how free we think we may be in our work, our politics—or even, oddly, our sex lives (for Marcuse had his own doubts about the libertinism of the times). In a 1961 preface to *Eros and Civilization*, Marcuse not only stressed that "the rights and liberties of the individual" had not yet been created, he warned that personal efforts at liberation could turn "into a vehicle of stabilization and even conformity." In a similar manner, Brown claimed that without moral freedom no other form of freedom was possible. Liberalism had not given us freedom, Brown argued in *Love's Body*, but loneliness and alienation: "The Western legal fiction, with its fetishism (personification) of property, its reification of persons, eliminates the facts more completely, by eliminating the moment of truth, the interregnum, the search for new incarnations."

Such uninhibited notions of moral freedom as found in Brown and Marcuse did not, at first, directly influence the New Left movements that blossomed in the 1960s. Those movements, in fact, seemed to have much in common with the earlier cultural conservatism of movements for racial justice, domestic versions of feminism, and the labor movement. Students for a Democratic Society emerged out of the distinctly culturally conservative League for Industrial Democracy, an "old left" organization if there ever was one. The first significant declaration of the New Left, the Port Huron Statement, spoke in an old-fashioned language of moral rectitude. "We are used to moral leadership being exercised and moral dimensions being clarified by our elders," the document stated, before going on to blame those elders, not for their moralizing, but for their failure to be true to their own moral values. (The first substantive section of the Port Huron Statement was called, in fact, "Values.") Although the Port Huron Statement argued that "the goal of man and society should be . . . finding a meaning in life that is personally authentic," its very use of the term "morality" conveyed a language closer to Kant or theorists of republican virtue than to Marcuse. Bad faith, not bad intentions—that was the problem with America. The Port Huron Statement looked back to existentialism more than it looked forward to the movements of personal liberation that would follow it. In that sense, the Port Huron Statement reflected the concerns of the radical sociologist C. Wright Mills, whose influential book *The Power Elite*, for all the attention it paid to political institutions, was tone-deaf to emerging forces of cultural and psychological liberation that exploded into popular consciousness after the book appeared.

It was not long before Marcuse would replace Mills as the New Left's primary guru. Freedom was no longer to be understood as the right to vote or to practice one's religious beliefs or to say what one thought; indeed, Marcuse taught that such earlier forms of freedom were themselves repressive. Freedom had become "liberation," a term borrowed from movements against colonialism in the Third World, but which could easily be applied to the personal as well as the political. "In the contemporary period," Marcuse wrote in 1961, "psychological categories become political categories," one of the earliest expressions of the idea that the personal and the political were one and the same. No longer did we have to imagine our inner selves as anchored for our external selves to move about. On the contrary, our inner selves were part of the action; unless and until we challenged our very assumptions about who and what we were, unless we broke through all convention to dig down into our psyche, we could not call ourselves free at all.

This was moral freedom in its most radical form. Movements on behalf of freedom often find themselves linked to academic disciplines. Economic freedom, obviously, finds its justification in the science of economics; from Adam Smith to the present, it is often hard to tell when economic analysis ends and when free market advocacy begins.

Theorists of political freedom, in urging that the suffrage be taken out of the hands of the few and extended to the many, relied on the state to extend political rights to all, and with the state came political science and public administration. But as Marcuse rightly understood, neither economics nor political science would do when the scope of freedom expanded to morality; psychology became instead the proper academic grounding. Freedom was a function of happiness, and happiness, in turn, required intensive self-examination. One had to know who one was—who one *really* was—before one could know what was right.

As the experience of Victoria Woodhull anticipated, women were among the first to insist on psychological dimensions of the freedom they were demanding. Not all of the radical feminists of the 1960s were in favor of "consciousness-raising," the effort on the part of women to talk about the oppressions they were discovering in their own lives. But enough of them were to mark the way the movement understood the implications of what freedom would mean. One early feminist activist, Jean Tepperman, wrote, "The women's movement seemed to offer opportunities to accept one's own needs as legitimate." Consciousness-raising, suggested Pam Allen in a widely read 1970 article, created a "nonjudgmental space" for women to explore their identity. "Discussion was intense because we were speaking about subjects formerly whispered or entirely suppressed," recalled Roz Baxandall of her experiences with consciousness-raising. "Orgasms: do we fake them? what gives us pleasure? Housework: who does the dishes and the laundry? . . . We began to put our energy into understanding women, and therefore understood ourselves."

The women's movement of the 1960s and 1970s broke away from male-dominated groups like Students for a Democratic Society, but within a few years, its emphasis on psychological liberation became the dominant feature of all radical organizations except the Marxist sectarians and black nationalists. Even as the more politically engaged activists in the New Left tried to keep the focus on such conventionally political issues as racial injustice or the war in Vietnam, the movement turned to experiments with drugs, lifestyles, music, personal relationships, and sexual promiscuity. At their worst, such experiments were little more than pure self-indulgence; unprecedented affluence made it seem to the young that they could, without serious consequences to themselves, reject entirely the repressive morality of their parents. When offered opportunities for promiscuity, substances that offered glimpses into nirvana, promises of genuine authenticity, alternatives to work and career, and collective living rather than loneliness, how many twentysomethings could resist? Besides, given the size of the baby-boom generation, everyone else was doing it. During the 1960s lifestyles once dreamed of by fringe groups at the outer edges of society became the order of the day.

Not everyone wanted to take these experiments at their worst, however, and when justification for them was sought, it was found in works that popularized and domesticated the moral freedom urged by theorists like Brown and Marcuse. Typical of these was Charles Reich's best-selling book, *The Greening of America*, which argued that those who dropped out of society in favor of alternative lifestyles embodied a new consciousness, sententiously identified as Consciousness III. Reich wrote,

> The foundation of Consciousness III is liberation. It comes into being the moment the individual frees himself from automatic acceptance of the imperatives of self from automatic acceptance of the imperatives of society and the false consciousness which society imposes.... The meaning of liberation is that the individual is free to build his own philosophy and values, his own life-style, and his own culture from a new beginning.

This was Durkheim stood on his head. No longer was society the conscience—not consciousness—that constrained the individual; now the individual was all and society the obstruction.

The moment moral freedom emerged out of the turmoil of the 1960s, there also developed a sustained reiteration of all those ideas central to the Western tradition that emphasized the absurdity of the idea. "Every culture," wrote Philip Rieff, a University of Pennsylvania sociologist shocked by the 1960s, "is so constituted that there are actions one cannot perform; more precisely, would dread to perform." To attack culture was to attack all those constraints on human instincts that made civilization—and, with it, freedom in any meaningful sense—possible. This was the same point made, if from the opposite perspective, by Norman O. Brown, which may help explain why neoconservatives such as Irving Kristol and Norman Podhoretz, who became significant opponents of the 1960s and everything for which they stood, nonetheless admired Brown's writings. "One of the reasons I respect them so deeply," Kristol announced in 1971, "is that Mr. Brown is a serious thinker who is unafraid to face up to the radical consequences of his radical theories." And nothing was more radical than Brown's insistence that "for his kind of salvation to be achieved, humanity must annul the civilization it has created." The stakes involved in Brown's writings, and in the actions of those inspired by him, were high: "civilization and humanity, nothing less," as Kristol dramatically put it.

If Marcuse and Brown made Eros the moving spirit of liberation, conservatives like Kristol made sex—not quite the same thing—the symbol of moral decadence. In his 1971 essay Kristol pointed out that liberals urged us not to take pornography, which they viewed as a fringe issue, seriously, while radicals, for whom pornography was a symbol of freedom from constraint, urged us to take it very seriously indeed. "I believe that the radicals . . . are right and the liberals are wrong," he concluded, even adding that he had "a sneaking sympathy" for those radicals who criticized democracy for not paying serious attention to versions of the good life as well. Since the issue posed by the 1960s was moral freedom on one side and moral authority on the other, both sides could agree, much as Victoria Woodhull had done, that all questions of moral freedom finally come down to questions of sex.

One way to define the legacy of the 1960s is to argue that if you do not have freedom over sex, you do not have freedom over anything. That is certainly how the leading cultural radicals of that decade understood what was at stake. "The affirmation of love's body against the life-denying brutality of 'traditional values,'" journalist Ellen Willis wrote in 1989, also invoking the spirit of Norman O. Brown, "was at the heart of what made me a feminist." Anything but an apologist for unrestricted freedom—Willis was too much the "old left" radical for that—she nonetheless glimpsed in her opposition to conventional morality new possibilities: "For me, the ability to get high (I don't mean only on drugs) flourished in the atmosphere of abandon that defined the '60s—that pervasive cultural invitation to leap boundaries, challenge limits, try anything, want everything, overload the senses, let go." The same sensibility applied to sex as well: "While I rejected monogamy as a moral obligation, it was mostly the sense of freedom I wanted, the right (after the years of not enough) to feel open to the world's possibilities, without prior censorship." Writing many years later, and understanding full well the limits of those moments induced by sex and drugs, Willis nonetheless longed for their sense of ecstasy: "This is what freedom is like, this is what love could be, this is what happens when the boundaries are gone."

Conservatives understand the legacy of the 1960s in exactly the opposite fashion from writers like Willis: if moral authority cannot be asserted over the sexual, it cannot be asserted anywhere. And they have few doubts that, as a result of the 1960s, sexuality—and therefore moral freedom—is out of control in America at the turn of a new century. Indeed, Irving Kristol's 1971 musings on pornography do have about them something old-fashioned when compared with the arguments for sexual liberation that would follow. One direct result of the 1960s was that sex was brought out from the hidden places associated with the pornographic and made instead a visible, everyday, reality. People may have stopped reading Brown and Marcuse, but their message—or at least what both radical students and conservative critics took to be their message—was everywhere. No longer constrained by musty notions of virtue and self-control, freed of consequences through birth-control technology, unregulated by taboos against abortion, and crossing the line between the genders, unrestrained sexuality really did seem to be the longest lasting legacy of the 1960s.

The consequences of this unleashing of moral freedom, conservative writers agreed, had to be bad. Sexual liberation, as Harvard's Harvey Mansfield would put it, was "at once the most and the least successful" of the legacies of the 1960s. "It was the most successful because it was the most avidly adopted and has had the most consequences." And it was the least successful because those consequences were uniformly negative. Contemporary conservatives view sexuality as a true state of nature, the place in which both genders, but especially males, act on the basis of biological urges that, if not curtailed, would reduce human beings to their most animal-like features. Just as the political philosophers of the seventeenth and eighteenth century understood the state or the social contract as a requirement for taming the state of nature, conservatives believe that institutions like the family and religion ensure that no one is permitted to enslave himself or herself to the passions in the mistaken belief that such enslavement is really a form of freedom. Those institutions were the very institutions against which the cultural radicals of the 1960s led their attack. The legacy of that era is not human happiness, as so many of its prophets promised, but, in Richard John Neuhaus's rather idiosyncratic inventory, "drugs, cults, mass murderers, the explosion in divorce, teen-age pregnancies, and abortion." For conservatives, and for a significant number of former radicals as well, the lesson of the 1960s was clear: Western thinkers were right to hold that in the absence of moral constraint, no other form of freedom was possible.

## *"Second Opinion" Morality*

Before the 1960s, social critics emphasized the degree to which Americans, in the words of Erich Fromm, had escaped from freedom. This was the era of organization men in gray flannel suits, housewives seduced by the feminine mystique, children growing up absurd and rebelling without a cause, and other-directed people mindlessly forming lonely crowds. Book after book told Americans that they were manipulated by hidden persuaders, ruled by a power elite, sexually repressed compared with adolescents in Samoa, and herded into a nation of sheep. Whether the accounts of these critics were actually true is less important than the conclusions to which they pointed. Unless they broke out of the chains of conformity in which their institutions imprisoned them, Americans were said to face a future not unlike the totalitarian regimes against which democracy was being forced to compete.

Whatever the faults of contemporary Americans, excessive conformity is not one of them. After the 1960s, social critics reversed the diagnoses of those who wrote half a century ago. Now Americans are said to bowl alone, not in crowds lonely or otherwise. Kids grow up more ambitious than absurd. Overworked and overspent, they dare their organizations and all-too-visible persuaders to keep up with their changing tastes. Far from other-directed, they are too inner-directed for their own good, resisting authority whenever and wherever they can. Anything but sheeplike, every American seems to have an opinion on truths that were once considered self-evident. Liberated from the very organizations that once defined their way of life, they are attracted to a culture of narcissism, tempted by expressive individualism, and inclined to assert their rights and ignore their responsibilities. Americans cannot be shallow, selfish, and secular, as so many of our contemporary critics find them, and be submissive at the same time, for the very individualism bemoaned by the critics testifies to a refusal on the part of Americans to have their morality defined for them.

So broad is the current complaint against moral freedom in America that it is no longer the sole property of theological and political conservatives. Whether expressed in the data-driven language of social science, through the nostalgic lens of the historian, or in the message of communitarianism, there is a widespread feeling that the legacy of the 1960s is corrosive of the American social fabric. True, the excesses of the 1960s, especially its rampant drug culture and free-floating sexuality, have been somewhat tamed, but the underlying message of putting one's own needs first has survived. Disrespectful of established authority, cut off from tradition, unwilling to focus on the long term, Americans, we have been told by a cacophony of different voices, live with moral freedom and experience, in a lack of close attachments to family and faith, the painful results.

Two recent commentaries on American life express well the argument against moral freedom. One is "A Call to Civil Society," a document issued by the Council on Civil Society, a joint product of the New York–based Institute for American Values and the Divinity School of the University of Chicago. Signed by a number of prominent writers, including John DiIulio, Jean Bethke Elshtain, Glenn C. Loury, Cornel West, and James Q. Wilson, the "Call" asked its readers to look back to the religious and civic traditions that shaped American's founding and provided the inspiration for great leaders from Abraham Lincoln to Martin Luther King Jr. When the Founding Fathers spoke of "laws of nature and of nature's God" and when King made reference to a "higher law," they were expressing the sense that "democracy depends upon moral truths." Moral truths take on their importance because, timeless and transcendental as they are, they have their origin in forces—such as nature on the one hand or the realm of the supernatural on the other—that are outside the control of human beings. "Our moral truths under-write our social well being primarily because they teach us to govern our appetites and to transcend selfishness," the "Call" claimed. Those who refuse to have their appetites held in check—the children, so to speak, of Herbert Marcuse—thus live under a moral lie. They fail to realize that freedom does not mean "immunity from restraint." Instead freedom must be understood as "an ethical condition," as "the morally defined mean between license and slavery." Human beings, the "Call" concluded, are "not autonomous creatures who are the source of their own meaning and perfection." We are rather "intrinsically social beings" who require "connectedness" in order to "approach authentic self-realization."

The second high-level effort to speak to the state of America's moral soul was initiated by the National Commission on Civil Renewal, chaired by former Senator Sam Nunn and William Bennett. "Compared with previous generations," the commission stated, "Americans today place less value on what we owe others as a matter of moral obligation and common citizenship; less value on personal sacrifice as a moral good; less value on the social importance of respectability and observ-ing the rules; less value on restraint in matters of pleasure and sexual-ity; and correspondingly greater value on self-expression, self-realization, and personal choice." The commission further argued that the ultimate cause of America's social decline lay in the emergence of new, and dis-turbing, conceptions of freedom:

> We must ask ourselves some hard questions about this new understanding of individual liberty. Dare we continue to place adult self-gratification above the well being of our children? Can we relentlessly pursue individual choice at the

*expense of mutual obligation without corroding vital social bonds? Will we remain secure in the enjoyment of our individual rights if we fail to accept and discharge our responsibilities? Is there a civic invisible hand that will preserve our democratic institutions in the absence of informed and engaged citizens?*

To most of these questions the implicit answer offered by the commission was no.

Listening to the way our respondents talk gives a certain amount of credibility to those who argue that contemporary Americans have too much freedom for their own good. When they decide whether to tell or shade the truth, to stay with their job or family or leave, to discipline their instincts for the sake of long-term reward, and to forgive but not to forget, our respondents are guided by subjective feelings more than they are by appeals to rational, intellectual, and objective conceptions of right and wrong. It is not standards of excellence to which they turn, but what seems best capable of avoiding hurt to others. They do not think that virtue consists in subsuming their needs and desires to the authority of tradition. Indeed, some of them are not even sure that virtuous is what they want to be. Without firm moral instruction, Americans approach the virtues gingerly. They recognize their importance, but since they are wary of treating moral principles as absolutes, they reinvent their meaning to make sense of the situations in which they find themselves. One can never know whether the 1960s were cause or effect of these transformations. But America, like the other liberal democracies of North America and Western Europe, is, morally speaking, a new society. Were Immanuel Kant or Emile Durkheim to appear in America today, he would find as little support for the categorical imperative or the collective conscience among our respondents in Texas and Iowa as in California and Massachusetts. What so many philosophers and theologians for so long considered an impossible idea has become the everyday reality in which modern Americans live.

But just because Americans may be living after virtue does not mean that they are living before vice. Both conservatives distressed by the moral condition of contemporary America and those liberals, feminists, and gay rights activists who find America more tolerant see a direct link between the 1960s and now. From the point of view of those aghast at what the 1960s has bequeathed us, one mistake—the wrong drug or, later, the wrong sex partner—and life itself could be threatened. From the point of view of those influenced by the social changes of that time, by contrast, one too many concessions to established institutions of authority and freedom itself could be sacrificed. But for the people with whom we spoke, the 1960s—understood as a political movement designed to challenge the status quo in favor of revolutionary transformations in lifestyle—barely exist. Even in San Francisco, despite the fact that we asked people questions about the most morally contentious issues of the day, only a couple of our respondents reflected on what the tumultuous events of those years meant for them and for their country.

The debate over the 1960s and its legacy confuses two different phenomena. One is the freedom to choose how to live. The other is the freedom to consider oneself unbound by moral rules. The Americans with whom we have spoken make a distinction between them. The former, they usually insist, is something worth having. And the latter, most of them feel, is something worth avoiding. Moral freedom is not perceived by our respondents as a victory for one way of life stressing liberation over another way of life stressing oppression. Nor is moral freedom something Marcuse-like for which people fought and celebrate once they have. It much more resembles a condition that to some degree has been imposed on people in ways over which they have little control and to which they have little choice but to adapt. When Americans think of the kind of moral anarchy and irresponsibility that conservatives associate with the excesses of the 1960s, they do not think about their own lives but about the models held up by the media, the free agent manipulations of celebrities and sports figures, the self-regarding actions of corporations, and the dishonesty exhibited by politicians. Americans do not think of themselves as escaping from society's obligations as much as they feel that society's institutions have escaped from them.

Moderate in economics and politics, our respondents are moderate in morality. The great bulk of them no longer adhere to traditional ideas about virtue and vice, but neither do they live as moral libertines. They do not take their marriage vows as binding under all circumstances and for all time, but they often approach the question of divorce in a morally serious way, reserving it as an option when the price of excessive loyalty is unwanted cruelty. They are not as loyal as they once were in the workplace, but only after being provoked into that position by extensive, and often ruthless, disloyalty on the part of their employers. They know that one cannot always be honest, but instead of concluding that one can never tell the truth, they try to create informal rules that govern when truth is required and when it is not. No longer committed to the Protestant ethic in its stricter forms, they are open to self-indulgence, but often to reinforce—rather than to challenge—the discipline they know their way of life demands. In their effort to find balance in all things, they forgive to get on with life but do not forget so that evil will not be lightly passed over.

True, our respondents do not speak about virtue the way the Greeks and Romans, the early Christians, the founders of the United States, Abraham Lincoln, or the characters in George Eliot novels did. Yet their views also contain a sense of proportion; if few of our respondents would demonstrate the power of loyalty by waiting as patiently as Penelope did for her husband, Odysseus, to come home, even fewer would lie with the malevolence that Iago showed toward Othello. The Americans with whom we spoke do not discard the importance of loyalty, self-discipline, honesty, and forgiveness. Indeed a case could be made that they are doing their best to try to make them work under social and economic conditions far different than those in which these ideas of virtue were first formulated.

Our respondents are not saying, with Dostoevski's Grand Inquisitor, that in the absence of God, anything goes. They are instead expressing a desire to have a conversation with God, or with any other source of moral authority, in which they will not just listen but also be free to express their own views. The concept of moral freedom corresponds to a deeply held populist suspicion of authority and a corresponding belief that people know their own best interest. Historically, populistic impulses expressed themselves in politics; Americans distrusted elites, especially those whose power appeared to rest on breeding and connections, in favor of appeals to the common man. Now that same populistic sensibility extends to all kinds of institutions; if Americans have learned to obtain a second opinion concerning their medical condition, they are also likely to seek additional opinions concerning their moral condition. As radical an idea as this may seem to those once issued commands and expected them to be obeyed, "second opinion" morality seeks to work with, not against, the institutions that make social life possible.

In an age of moral freedom, moral authority has to justify its claims to special insight. Religion offers the best window into the ways such justifications are likely to take place. In April 2000, *The Wall Street Journal* published a story focusing on the way Americans are "redefining God" to suit their own tastes and inclinations. Featured were Christian ministers who drew upon the Jewish tradition, reformed Jews seeking gender-inclusive language, and Americans of all faiths who borrow from every religion and none simultaneously. Like many of those we interviewed, these were individuals who, reluctant to accept something as right or true just because authority and tradition have proclaimed them right and true, are determined to play a role in creating the morality by which they will be guided. "I've started to think of God more as a lover than as a father," one person said. If his comment is representative, the autonomy so many Americans crave does not stop with awe at the threshold of the Judeo-Christian tradition.

Readers were quick to suggest that the whole idea of redefining God was absurd. One letter writer to *The Wall Street Journal* suggested that human beings had no power to alter who God is since it was God who created us, not the other way around. Another suggested that however convenient people find the process of tailoring their religious convictions to fit their lifestyles, only God has the power to define who he is. A third pointed out the dangerous consequences of believing that human beings are in charge of their own destiny, for down that road lies a subjective understanding of morality, not firm moral truths.

The letter writers to *The Wall Street Journal*, arguing against the proposition that people ought to be free to pick and choose their religion as they best see fit, have behind them some two thousand years of tradition. Neither the Calvinism of the Puritans, the Catholicism brought to America by European immigrants, the fundamentalist Protestantism that emerged in the first decades of the twentieth century, nor Jewish respect for Talmudic law looked upon freedom of moral choice as a capacity to be encouraged. Whatever emerges from the efforts on the part of so many Americans to redefine their faith, it is unlikely to resemble Jonathan Edwards's Northampton, the urban parishes of 1950s Catholicism, the revival meetings of Billy Sunday, or synagogue life on the Lower East Side.

Yet the desire of so many Americans to have a greater say in the moral choices they make is anything but a bitter renunciation of religion. It is more likely to take the form of a prayer that someone in a position of religious authority will take them seriously as individuals with minds and desires of their own. Searching for a moral voice that speaks in yesterday's language, critics of America's moral condition fail to hear those voices seeking ways of believing appropriate to conditions of moral freedom. The social critic Wendy Kaminer is correct when she points out the degree to which presumably secular America remains dominated by a religious culture. Far from a land populated by secular humanists, Americans want faith and freedom simultaneously. That would seem like an odd combination to Europeans, for whom faith has often meant dogma and freedom has often meant dissent. But it suggests that in America, religious institutions will not break under the weight of moral freedom but bend, as many of them have bent already, to accommodate themselves to the freedom of moral choice to which Americans have increasingly grown accustomed.

What is true of religious institutions applies to other institutions such as schools, if from the opposite direction. In the spirit of the 1960s, educational reformers began to advocate radical changes in their institutions, proposing that schools should stop disciplining students, encourage free-form expression and individual creativity, deemphasize honor classes and tracking, and find new ways to teach such subjects as math and history. In extreme versions of educational reform, moral anarchy rather than moral freedom seemed to be the operating principle, as if schooling itself ought to be abolished. So powerful were the forces behind educational reform that in most established school districts, one version or another of educational reform produced schools that no longer resembled the strict, segregated, vocational, and prayer-infused institutions of the 1950s.

Americans today want second opinions about both what and how their children learn in schools. Resisting the influence of liberal school administrators with as much determination as they resist the messages of conservative religious moralists, those who support greater school choice through vouchers and charter schools see freedom of choice as a way of encouraging greater institutional responsibility. Those who continue to support public schooling often express a desire for higher standards and an insistence on the value of teaching character. If American schools move in a more "conservative" direction toward discipline, it will be for the same reasons that churches move in a more "liberal" direction of therapeutic inclusion. After anarchy, moral freedom can be a requirement for reestablishing authority.

Finding the balance between institutional authority and moral freedom will never be easy. Critics point out that some institutions, such as the United States military, may not be able to carry out their most important functions if they become too sensitive to the demands of women for greater equality and autonomy. One can only wonder whether individuals dedicated to moral freedom can find the resources to stick with the not always pleasurable tasks of raising children and committing oneself to a spouse. Individuals intent on finding a sympathetic physician may ignore the advice of someone who knows best what makes them sick. Like alcohol, too much moral freedom can be a dangerous thing.

Yet in a time of moral freedom, no institution will be able to stick its head in the sand and pretend that the people who approach it for advice and guidance can be treated as supplicants. Morality has long been treated as if it were a fixed star, sitting there far removed from the earthly concerns of real people, meant to guide them to the true and the beautiful. In the contemporary world, however, people experience in their own lives many situations for which traditional conceptions of morality offer little guidance: What do you do when the pursuit of one virtue, say honesty, conflicts with another, such as avoiding cruelty? Does the zealous application of any virtue, by the mere fact of its zealousness, become a vice? How do you apply moral precepts to situations unforeseen by those religious and philosophical traditions developed for another time and place? Can seemingly unambiguous moral principles be capable of multifaceted interpretations? No matter how strong their religious and moral beliefs, nearly all people will encounter situations in which they feel the need to participate in interpreting, apply-ing, and sometimes redefining the rules meant to guide them. Are they somehow less moral if they do? Telling them that they are will cut no ice with a gay couple determined to legalize their union in an era of het-erosexual divorce; women who find that an early marriage stultifies their desire to become more autonomous later in life; or religious believ-ers who find that the best way to express one's faith in God is to reject traditional denominations.

Because we can never know what freedom will bring in its wake, defenders of social order have never, at least at first, been comfortable with any of the forms taken by freedom in the modern world. Economic freedom did not create a hoped-for society of independent yeoman but a regime of mass consumption. Political freedom did not result in active and enlightened civic participation but in voter apathy and disinterest. In a similar way, moral freedom is highly unlikely to produce a nation of individuals exercising their autonomy with the serious and dispassion-ate judgment of an Immanuel Kant. Yet moral freedom is as inevitable as it is impossible. Once people are free to choose their cars and their candidates, they will not for long be satisfied with letting others deter-mine for them the best way to live. As correct as critics of America's moral condition are to insist on the need for shared understandings of the moral life, it is better, given moral freedom's inevitability, to think of it as a challenge to be met rather than as a condition to be cured.

"I should have loved freedom, I believe, at all times, but in the times in which we live I am ready to worship it," wrote Alexis de Tocqueville at the end of *Democracy in America*. Those times were despotic ones, and Tocqueville's great fear was that the establishment of a government committed to equality under such conditions would "not only oppress men, but would eventually strip each of them of several of their highest qualities of humanity." Despite his misgivings, Tocqueville never became an enemy of democracy, because democracy, he knew, was a force that could not be stopped. "I am persuaded that all those who attempt in the ages upon which we are entering, to base freedom upon aristocratic privilege will fail; that all who attempt to draw and to retain authority within a single class will fail." Like democracy, the arrival of moral freedom is bound to have consequences we will regret. But if we appreciate political and economic freedom, we will have to find a way to appreciate the moral freedom that cannot help but accompany it.

# Notes

## Introduction

1 "Do you ever read . . .": Anthony Trollope, *The Way We Live Now* (Oxford and New York: Oxford University Press, 1982), 1:209.

1 "The country is changing . . .": Ibid., 2:45.

1 "Mid-Victorian England . . .": Gertrude Himmelfarb, *Marriage and Morals Among the Victorians* (New York: Vintage Books, 1987), 21.

3 The results, published in a special issue: Alan Wolfe, "The Pursuit of Autonomy," *The New York Times Magazine*, May 7, 2000, 53–56.

## I. Varieties of Moral Experience

8 resembles Michael Tolliver: Armistead Maupin, *28 Barbary Lane: A Tale of the City Omnibus* (New York: HarperCollins, 1990).

9 San Francisco is the kind of place: Robert H. Bork, *Slouching Toward Gomorrah: Modern Liberalism and American Decline* (New York: ReganBooks HarperCollins, 1996); William J. Bennett, *The Death of Outrage: Bill Clinton and the Assault on American Ideals* (New York: Free Press, 1998); Gertrude Himmelfarb, *One Nation, Two Cultures* (New York: Knopf, 1999); Jerry Falwell, *Listen America* (Garden City, N.Y.: Doubleday, 1980); and Paul Weyrich, "An Open Letter to Conservatives," at www.freecongress.org.

11 Fundamentalist Christians: Vincent Crapanzano, *Serving the Word: Literalism in America from the Pulpit to the Bench* (New York: New Press, 2000).

11 Sectarian in outlook: "Freedom Network Page," at www.aclu.org; *A Right Wing and a Prayer: The Religious Right and Your Public Schools* (New York: People for the American Way, n.d.).

11 Conservative Christians are not moved: For arguments along these lines, see Sara Diamond, *Not by Politics Alone: The Enduring Influence of the Christian Right* (New York: Guilford Press, 1999); and Didi Herman, *The Antigay Agenda: Orthodox Vision and the Christian Right* (Chicago: University of Chicago Press, 1997).

16 For conservative critics of America's moral condition: William J. Bennett, *The Book of Virtues: A Treasury of Great Moral Stories* (New York: Simon and Schuster, 1993).

16 "The whole point . . .": Laurence Tribe, *Abortion: The Clash of Absolutes* (New York: Norton, 1990), 80.

17 Ronald Dworkin has argued: Ronald Dworkin, *A Matter of Principle* (Cambridge, Mass.: Harvard University Press, 1985), 197.

17 "In the actual world . . .": Alasdair MacIntyre, *After Virtue: A Study in Moral Theory*, 2d ed. (Notre Dame, Ind.: University of Notre Dame Press, 1984), 2.

18 "... For how can a people profess ...": Michael Novak, "The Cultural Roots of Virtue and Character," in *The Content of America's Character: Recovering Civic Virtue*, ed. Don E. Eberly (Lanham, Md.: Madison Books, 1995), 59.

21 The virtues have come to America: For a treatment of some of the different origins of the virtues, see Donald N. McCloskey, "Bourgeois Virtue," *The American Scholar*, Spring 1994, 177–91.

22 "would be something like ...": William James, *The Varieties of Religious Experience: A Study in Human Nature* (1902; reprint, New York: Mentor Books, 1958), 412.

## II. Til Circumstances Do Us Part

23 "Thanks to the decline ... hierachy of values": Christopher Lasch, *The Revolt of the Elite and the Betrayal of Democracy* (New York: Norton, 1995), 5–6.

23 William Bennett's *The Book of Virtues*: William J. Bennett, *The Book of Virtues: A Treasury of Great Moral Stories* (New York: Simon and Schuster, 1993), 663–737.

23 We are, writes the social critic Barbara Dafoe Whitehead: Barbara Dafoe Whitehead, *The Divorce Culture* (New York: Knopf, 1997).

24 The problem with our politics: Alan Ehrenhalt, *The United States of Ambition: Politicians, Power, and the Pursuit of Office* (New York: Times Books, 1991).

24 By focusing too much on the bottom line: Frederick Reichheld, *The Loyalty Effect: The Hidden Force Behind Growth, Profits, and Lasting Value* (Boston: Harvard Business School Press, 1996).

24 The British conservative Roger Scruton writes: Roger Scruton, "On Loyalty," *National Review*, April 5, 1999, 46.

24 "the central duty amongst all duties": Josiah Royce, *The Philosophy of Loyalty* (1908; reprint, Nashville: Vanderbilt University Press, 1995), xxiv.

27 what sociologists call "urban villagers": Herbert Gans, *The Urban Villagers: Group and Class in the Life of Italian-Americans* (New York: Free Press, 1962).

30 why companies allowed themselves the luxury: Mathew B. Krepps and Amy Bertin Candell, *Industrial Inefficiency and Downsizing: A Study of Layoffs and Plant Closures* (New York: Garland, 1997).

32 "'no long term' ...": Richard Sennett, *The Corrosion of Character: The Personal Consequences of Work in the New Capitalism* (New York: Norton, 1998), 24.

32 "I make my own ...": Ibid., p. 29.

32 "a somewhat fatalistic ...": Ibid.

33 These days, workers and companies both: One study found that "free agent" managers tend to be more loyal in their new jobs than those who stayed behind. See Linda K. Stroh and Anne H. Reilly, "Loyalty in an Age of Downsizing," *Sloan Management Review* 38 (Summer 1997): 83–90.

38 One of oldest ideas involving loyalty: Edward Banfield, *The Moral Basis of a Backward Society* (New York: Free Press, 1958).

39 Intellectual copyright law gives firms: For some of the issues involved, see Lawrence Lessig, *Code: And Other Laws of Cyberspace* (New York: Basic Books, 1999).

41 Yet in practice, divorce rates: The National Marriage Project, *The State of Our Unions, 1999: The Social Health of Marriage in America* (New Brunswick, N.J.: Rutgers University 1999), 21.

45 "become more acutely conscious . . .": Whitehead, *Divorce Culture*, 4.

48 "economic stress may exact . . .": Rand D. Conger, Xiao-Jia Gee, and Frederick O. Lorenz, "Economic Stress and Marital Relations," in *Families in Troubled Times: Adapting to Change in Rural America*, ed. Rand D. Conger and Glen H. Elder Jr. (New York: Aldine de Gruyter, 1994), 203.

53 But we do know that the divorce rate peaked: National Marriage Project, *State of Our Unions*, 20–21.

53 There is also evidence from surveys: Ibid., 29–31.

60 "We must assume that divorce . . .": Whitehead, *Divorce Culture*, 188.

60 "loyalty provides the unifying framework . . .": Reichheld, *Loyalty Effect*, 3.

61 ". . . a rubber stamp . . .": Bennett, *Book of Virtues*, 665.

62 America's philosopher of loyalty: Royce, *Philosophy of Loyalty*, 48–69.

62 "harbors an insouciant faith . . .": George P. Fletcher, *Loyalty: An Essay on the Morality of Relationships* (New York: Oxford University Press, 1993), 153.

62 "We can win back something . . .": Royce, *Philosophy of Loyalty*, 104.

## III. Eat Dessert First

65 Following the historian Peter N. Stearns: Peter N. Stearns, *Battleground of Desire: The Struggle for Self-Control in Modern America* (New York: New York University Press, 1999).

66 "Work, thrift . . .": Gertrude Himmelfarb, *One Nation, Two Cultures* (New York: Knopf, 1999), 5.

66 "the Victorian ethos . . .": Ibid., 8.

66 "To repress a harsh answer . . .": Charlotte Gilman, *Reflections of a Southern Matron*, as cited in Sterns, *Battleground*, 87.

68 Institutions once designed to instill: A characteristic example of this way of thinking is Charles L. Sykes, *A Nation of Victims: The Decay of the American Character* (New York: St. Martin's, 1992).

68 A therapeutic mentality dominates: Philip Rieff, *The Triumph of the Therapeutic* (Chicago: University of Chicago Press, 1966); and James L. Nolan Jr., *The Therapeutic State: Justifying Government at Century's End* (New York: New York University Press, 1998).

69 As much as Americans are instructed: All of which helps explain the emergence of a new Victorianism among some social critics; see, for example, Rene Denfeld, *The New Victorians: A Young Woman's Challenge to the Old Feminist Order* (New York: Warner Books, 1995); and Wendy Shalit, *A Return to Modesty: Discovering the Lost Virtue* (New York: Free Press, 1999).

70 Self-indulgence and self-restraint: Max Weber, *The Protestant Ethic and the Spirit of Capitalism* (1920; reprint, London: George Allen and Unwin, 1976).

70 Capitalism, in Weber's view: For a review of the literature spawned by Weber's

hypothesis, see Harold B. Jones, "The Protestant Ethic: Weber's Model and the Empirical Literature," *Human Relations* 50 (1997): 757–78.

70 Bell called the resulting tensions: Daniel Bell, *The Cultural Contradictions of Capitalism* (New York: Basic Books, 1976).

70 America's upper class: David Brooks, *Bobos in Paradise: The New Upper Class and How They Got There* (New York: Simon and Schuster, 2000).

71 Riesman wrote about a society: David Riesman, in collaboration with Reuel Denney and Nathan Glazer, *The Lonely Crowd: A Study of the Changing American Character* (New Haven: Yale University Press, 1950), 55.

72 Of course the references are different: David Riesman, *Faces in the Crowd: Individual Studies in Character and Politics* (New Haven: Yale University Press, 1952), 339, 365, 477, 511.

73 catch-as-catch-can entrepreneurial spirit: Michael Lewis, *The New New Thing* (New York: Norton, 1999).

77 "Don't be too quick . . .": Sol Gordon and Harold Brecher, *Life Is Uncertain . . . Eat Dessert First: Finding the Joy You Deserve* (New York: Delacorte, 1990), 33.

78 ". . . signifies a reaffirmation . . .": Himmelfarb, *One Nation, Two Cultures*, 65.

79 In defining deviancy down: Daniel Patrick Moynihan, "Defining Deviancy Down," *The American Scholar,* Winter 1993, 17–30.

79 Reporting on the state of middle-class morality: Alan Wolfe, *One Nation, After All: What Middle-Class Americans Really Think About God, Country, Family, Racism, Welfare, Immigration, Homosexuality, Work, the Right, the Left, and Each Other* (New York: Viking, 1998).

82 the Victorians were not as confident: Karen Halttunen, *Confidence Men and Painted Women: A Study of Middle-Class Culture in America, 1830–1870* (New Haven: Yale University Press, 1982).

84 Dworkin argues strongly: See, for example, Ronald Dworkin, *Life's Dominion: An Argument About Abortion, Euthanasia, and Individual Freedom* (New York: Vintage, 1994).

85 "Where demeaning, degrading, or destructive . . .": Robert George, *Making Men Moral: Civil Liberties and Public Morality* (Oxford: Clarendon Press, 1993), 96.

86 People were said to be addicted to: For examples, see Aviel Goodman, *Sexual Addiction: An Integrated Approach* (Madison, Conn.: International Universities Press, 1998); Jerome D. Levin, *The Clinton Syndrome: The President and the Self-Destructive Nature of Sexual Addiction* (Rocklin, Calif.: Prima Publishing, 1998); Carla G. Surratt, *Netaholics: The Creation of a Pathology* (Commack, N.Y.: Nova Science Publishers, 1999); Ronald M. Pavalko, "Problem Gambling: The Hidden Addiction," *National Forum* 79 (Fall 1999): 28–32; Commission on Behavioral and Social Sciences and Education, National Research Council, *Pathological Gambling: A Critical Review* (Washington, D.C.: National Academy Press, 1999); Barbara Killinger, *Workaholics: The Respectable Addicts* (New York: Simon and Schuster, 1992); Leo Booth, *When God Becomes a Drug: Breaking the Chains of Religious Addiction and Abuse* (Los Angeles: Tarcher, 1991); Michael H. Crosby, *The Dysfunctional Church: Addic-*

*tion and Codependency in the Family of Catholicism* (Notre Dame, Ind.: Ave Maria Press, 1991); and Anne Wilson Schaef, *When Society Becomes an Addict* (San Francisco: Harper and Row, 1987).

86 Encouraged by authors seeking best-seller status: For a scholarly treatment of the issue, see John Steadman Rice, *A Disease of One's Own: Psychotherapy, Addiction, and the Emergence of Co-Dependency* (New Brunswick, N.J.: Transaction Publishers, 1996); for an engaging critique, see Wendy Kaminer, *I'm Dysfunctional, You're Dysfunctional: The Recovery Movement and Other Self-Help Fashions* (Reading, Mass.: Addison-Wesley, 1992).

86 The most common complaint: Jeffrey Schaler, *Addiction Is a Choice* (Chicago: Open Court, 2000). For a review of some of the philosophical issues involved, see Jon Elster, *Strong Feelings: Emotion, Addiction, and Human Behavior* (Cambridge, Mass.: MIT Press, 1999).

86 Despite the fact that Americans believe: Herbert Fingarette, *Heavy Drinking: The Myth of Alcoholism as a Disease* (Berkeley and Los Angeles: University of California Press, 1988).

88 old-fashioned Victorian morality: Richard Klein, *Cigarettes Are Sublime* (Durham, N.C.: Duke University Press, 1993).

89 A 1997 Gallup Poll indicated that: Lydia Saad, "More Americans Fear Risk of Second-Hand Smoke," *The Gallup Poll Monthly* 382 (July 1997): 19.

94 And stoic conceptions of self-discipline often work: For various treatments of these issues, see Katherine S. Newman, *No Shame in My Game: The Working Poor in the Inner City* (New York: Knopf, 1999); George C. Bear, "School Discipline in the United States: Prevention, Correction, and Long-Term Social Development," *School Psychology Review* 27 (1988): 14–32; and Nadine Van Stone, J. Ron Nelson, and Joan Niemann, "Poor Single-Mother College Students' Views on the Effect of Some Primary Sociological and Psychological Belief Factors on Their Academic Success," *Journal of Higher Education* 65 (September–October 1994): 571–84.

## IV. Honesty, to a Point

97 The great St. Augustine: St. Augustine, "Against Lying," in *Treatises on Various Subjects* (New York: Fathers of the Church, 1952), 125–79.

97 "to be truthful . . .": Immanuel Kant, "On a Supposed Right to Lie Because of Philanthropic Concerns," in *Groundings for the Metaphysics of Morals*, trans. James W. Ellington (Indianapolis: Hackett, 1981), 65.

98 The philosopher Sissela Bok: Sissela Bok, *Lying: Moral Choice in Public and Private Life* (New York: Vintage, 1989).

98 Even economists and sociobiologists: Edwin A. Locke and Jaana Woiceshyn, "Why Businessmen Should be Honest: The Argument from Rational Egoism," *Journal of Organizational Behavior* 16 (September 1995): 405–14; Dwight B. Lee and Richard B. McKenzie, "How the Marketplace Fosters Business Honesty," *Business and Society Review* 92 (Winter 1995): 5–9; Craig T. Palmer, "When to Bear

False Witness: An Evolutionary Approach to the Social Context of Honesty and Deceit Among Commercial Fisherman," *Zygon* 4 (December 1993): 455–68; and Rufus A. Johnstone, "Signaling of Need, Sibling Competition, and the Cost of Honesty," *Proceedings of the National Academy of Sciences* 96 (October 26, 1999): 12644–49.

99   As the political philosopher Ruth Grant: Ruth W. Grant, *Hypocrisy and Integrity: Machiavelli, Rousseau, and the Ethics of Politics* (Chicago: University of Chicago Press, 1997).

99   Borrowing metaphors from the world of the theater: Erving Goffman, *The Presentation of Self in Everyday Life* (Garden City, N.Y.: Doubleday, 1959), 13.

100  "unwilling to influence . . .": Alasdair MacIntyre, *After Virtue: A Study in Moral Theory*, 2d ed. (Notre Dame, Ind.: University of Notre Dame Press, 1984), 32–35.

100  Duplicity, some critics charge: See, for example, Carl Hausman, *Lies We Live By: Double-Talk and Deception in Advertising* (New York: Routledge, 2000).

109  Once relatively trustful toward government: One of the first studies of this phenomenon is Seymour Martin Lipset and William Schneider, *The Confidence Gap: Business, Labor, and Government in the Public Mind* (New York: Free Press, 1983). More recent evidence is summarized and analyzed in Mark E. Warren, ed., *Democracy and Trust* (Cambridge: Cambridge University Press, 1999).

109  That gap is as high: David Whitman, *The Optimism Gap: The I'm Ok—They're Not Syndrome and the Myth of American Decline* (New York: Walker, 1998).

111  Bob Woodward: Bob Woodward, *Shadow: Five Presidents and the Legacy of Watergate* (New York: Simon and Schuster, 1999).

111  "No permanence, no perserverance . . .": Hannah Arendt, "Truth and Politics," in *Between Past and Future: Six Exercises in Political Thought* (New York: Viking Compass, 1968), 229, 253, 256.

112  ". . . the existing order of things": Jeffrey C. Goldfarb, *The Cynical Society: The Culture of Politics and the Politics of Culture in American Life* (Chicago: University of Chicago Press, 1991), 30.

116  "We cannot expect . . .": Stephen L. Carter, *Integrity* (New York: Basic Books, 1996), 226–27.

117  George Washington Plunkitt: William L. Riordain, *Plunkitt of Tammany Hall* (New York: Dutton, 1963), 3.

118  In part this is a reflection: Lipset and Schneider, *Confidence Gap*, 29.

123  As Francis Fukuyama has emphasized: Francis Fukuyama, *The Great Disruption: Human Nature and the Reconstitution of Social Order* (New York: Free Press, 1999).

## V. The Unappreciated Virtue

131  And if the battlefield: On this general subject, see Kim Townsend, *Manhood at Harvard: William James and Others* (New York: Norton, 1996).

133  ". . . the gravity of his offense": William Graham Sumner, *What Social Classes Owe to Each Other* (Caldwell, Idaho: Caxton Printers, 1963), 120.

133 "the stern task of judging . . .": James Q. Wilson, *Moral Judgment: Does the Abuse Excuse Threaten Our Legal System?* (New York: Basic Books, 1997), 2, 23.

133 Wilson reminds us: On the battered woman defense, see Donald Alexander Downs, *More than Victims: Battered Women, The Syndrome Society, and the Law* (Chicago: University of Chicago Press, 1996); on rotten conditions of life, see Richard Delgado, " 'Rotten Social Background': Should the Criminal Law Recognize a Defense of Severe Environmental Deprivation?" *Law and Inequality Journal* 3 (1985): 9, cited in Wilson, *Moral Judgment*, 23.

133 Still, he has little sympathy: See Alan Dershowitz, *The Abuse Excuse* (Boston: Little Brown, 1994).

133 "It is the task . . .": Wilson, *Moral Judgment*, 27.

136 John Paul II: Pope John Paul II, *Reconciliation and Penance* (Hales Corners, Wis.: Priests and Brothers of the Sacred Heart, 1984). Documents dealing with Catholic understandings of this issue are contained in Liturgy Documentary Series 7, *Penance and Reconciliation in the Church* (Washington, D.C.: United States Catholic Conference, 1986). For excerpts from the Pope's Homily asking for forgiveness for the historic sins of the Catholic Church, see Alessanda Stanley, "Pope Asks Forgiveness of Errors of the Church over 2000 Years," *The New York Times*, March 13, 2000, p. A1.

136 "rebuke and forgiveness are locked together": Stanley Hauerwas and Charles Pinches, *Christians Among the Virtues: Theological Conversations with Ancient and Modern Ethics* (Notre Dame, Ind.: University of Notre Dame Press, 1997), 108.

137 Through forgiveness, we reach transcendence: My understanding of Christian forgiveness is based on two Catholic sources: Joan Mueller, *Is Forgiveness Possible?* (Collegeville, Minn.: Liturgical Press, 1989), 60–84; and Richard M. Gula, S.S., *To Walk Together Again: The Sacrament of Reconciliation* (New York: Paulist Press, 1984); as well as two Protestant sources, one evangelical and one mainstream: Miroslav Volf, *Exclusion and Embrace: A Theological Exploration of Identity, Otherness, and Reconciliation* (Nashville: Abingdon Press, 1996); and Donald W. Shriver, *An Ethic For Enemies: Forgiveness in Politics* (New York: Oxford University Press, 1995).

137 "the marriage of psychological and theological counseling": Vincent Crapanzano, *Serving the Word: Literalism in America from the Pulpit to the Bench* (New York: New Press, 2000), 156.

137 Fuller Theological Seminary: For a fascinating account of Fuller Theological Seminary, see George Marsden, *Reforming Fundamentalism: Fuller Seminary and The New Evangelicalism* (Grand Rapids, Mich.: Eerdmans, 1987).

137 Indeed, sometimes, when faced with God's mysterious: Lewis B. Smedes, *Forgive and Forget: Healing the Hurts We Don't Deserve* (New York: Harper and Row, 1984), 89.

139 In a very famous, and also very controversial, study: Carol Gilligan, *In a Different Voice: Psychological Theory and Women's Development* (Cambridge, Mass.: Harvard University Press, 1982).

140　The former overlaps significantly: George Lakoff, *Moral Politics: What Conservatives Know That Liberals Don't* (Chicago: University of Chicago Press, 1996), 65–140.

141　There is a version of feminism: For arguments about women's special ethics, see Nel Noddings, *Caring: A Feminine Approach to Ethics and Moral Education* (Berkeley: University of California Press, 1984); and Joan C. Tronto, *Moral Boundaries: A Political Argument for an Ethic of Care* (New York: Routledge, 1993). For a quite different approach emphasizing feminist anger, see Andrea Dworkin, *Intercourse* (New York: Free Press, 1987).

142　"The real work of forgiving . . .": David Augsburger, *Caring Enough to Forgive: True Forgiveness* (Ventura, Calif.: Regal Books, 1981), 32, cited in Mueller, *Is Forgiveness Possible?* 61.

145　Americans, we have been told,: Dennis Prager, "The Sin of Forgiveness," *The Wall Street Journal*, December 15, 1997, p. A22.

162　"caring" virtues: Gertrude Himmelfarb, *One Nation, Two Cultures* (New York: Knopf, 1999), 81.

162　Olasky, who writes out of strong commitments: Gertrude Himmelfarb, *Poverty and Compassion: The Moral Imagination of the Late Victorians* (New York: Knopf, 1991); and Marvin N. Olasky, *The Tragedy of American Compassion* (Washington, D.C.: Regnery Gateway, 1992).

162　Evoking manly images through numerous episodes: William J. Bennett, *The Book of Virtues: A Treasury of Great Moral Stories* (New York: Simon and Schuster, 1993), 103, 205, 206, 296, 299, 447, 555, 615, 684, 745, 749, 756, 758 (for Old Testament stories), 141, 386, 642, 695, and 759 (for New Testament stories).

163　"The first rule for mere human beings . . .": Smedes, *Forgive and Forget*, 113.

163　Because we are not: Augsburger, *Caring Enough to Forgive*, 8, cited in Mueller, *Is Forgiveness Possible?* 63.

165　"Nobody can make . . .": Smedes, *Forgive and Forget*, 142–43.

165　For physicians and psychologists: See, for example, E. D. Scobie and G. E. W. Scobie, "Damaging Events: The Perceived Need for Forgiveness," *Journal for the Theory of Social Behavior* 28 (December 1998): 373–401; Griffin Doyle, "Forgiveness as an Intrapsychic Process," *Psychotherapy* 36 (Summer 1999): 190–98; Robert D. Enright and Joanna North, eds., *Exploring Forgiveness* (Madison, Wis.: University of Wisconsin Press, 1988); and Everett L. Worthington, ed., *Dimensions of Forgiveness: Psychological Research and Theological Perspectives* (Radnor, Pa.: Templeton Foundation, 1999).

166　For politicians, including South Africa's Nelson Mandela: Martha Minow, *Between Vengeance and Forgiveness: Facing History After Genocide and Mass Violence* (Boston: Beacon Press, 1999); and Peter Digeser, "Forgiveness and Politics: Dirty Hands and Imperfect Procedures," *Political Theory* 26 (October 1988): 700–724.

## VI. The Moral Philosophy of the Americans

167  "all moral judgments . . .": Alasdair MacIntyre, *After Virtue: A Study in Moral Theory*, 2d ed. (Notre Dame, Ind.: University of Notre Dame Press, 1984), 6, 12.

168  "As all moral qualities . . .": Jonathan Edwards, "The Great Christian Doctrine of Original Sin Defended," in *A Jonathan Edwards Reader*, ed. John E. Smith, Harry S. Stout, and Kenneth P. Minkema (New Haven: Yale University Press, 1995), 225, 227.

169  By the time of the Second Great Awakening: Randall Balmer, *Blessed Assurance: A History of Evangelicalism in America* (Boston: Beacon Press, 1999), 9. See also Nathan Hatch, *The Democratization of American Christianity* (New Haven: Yale University Press, 1989), 174, 180.

169  Although few Americans: Christian Smith, *American Evangelicalism: Embattled and Thriving* (Chicago: University of Chicago Press, 1998), 23.

170  "individuals could choose their spiritual destinies . . .": Balmer, *Blessed Assurance*, 9.

172  "white paper, void of . . .": John Locke, *An Essay Concerning Human Understanding* (1690; reprint, Amherst, N.Y.: Prometheus Books, 1995), 59.

175  Under the influence of Michel Foucault: Michel Foucault, *The History of Sexuality*, trans. Robert Hurley (New York: Pantheon, 1978). See also David F. Greenberg, *The Construction of Homosexuality* (Chicago: University of Chicago Press, 1988).

175  At the same time, gay advocates,: Simon LeVay, *The Sexual Brain* (Cambridge, Mass.: MIT Press, 1993).

177  "much if not all religious behavior . . .": Edward O. Wilson, *Consilience: The Unity of Knowledge* (New York: Knopf, 1998), 258.

177  No wonder that contemporary Christians: From a Catholic perspective, see Stephen J. Pope, "Sociobiology and Human Nature: A Perspective from Catholic Theology," *Zygon* 33 (June 1998): 275–91; from a Protestant perspective, see Warren S. Brown, Nancey Murphy, and H. Newton Malony, *Whatever Happened to the Soul?: Scientific and Theological Portraits of Human Nature* (Minneapolis: Fortress, 1998).

178  No other way of thinking: For evidence that our respondents may be correct in their beliefs, see Christopher Peterson, "The Future of Optimism," *American Psychologist* 55 (January 2000): 44–55.

182  Over the past two decades or so: William Kilpatrick, *Why Johnny Can't Tell Right from Wrong* (New York: Simon and Schuster, 1992); and Thomas Lickona, *Educating for Character: How Our Schools Can Teach Respect and Responsibility* (New York: Bantam, 1991).

182  "assumptions, vocabulary, and techniques . . .": James Davison Hunter, *The Death of Character: Moral Education After the Death of God* (New York: Basic Books, 2000), 127.

188  But a far larger proportion of Americans: www.norc.uchicago.edu, "Heaven,

Hell," survey. For similar findings, see George Gallup Jr. and D. Michael Lindsay, *Surveying the Religious Landscape: Trends in U.S. Beliefs* (Harrisburg, Pa.: Morehouse Publishing, 1999), 30.

190 William Blake once said: Cited in C. Fred Alford, *What Evil Means to Us* (Ithaca, N.Y.: Cornell University Press, 1997), 99.

191 "The term 'value,' . . .": Allan Bloom, *The Closing of the American Mind* (New York: Simon and Schuster, 1987), 142.

192 Should Satan disappear: Andrew Delbanco, *The Death of Satan: How Americans Have Lost the Sense of Evil* (New York: Farrar, Straus and Giroux, 1995); and Elaine H. Pagels, *The Origin of Satan* (New York: Random House, 1995).

193 But the dominant trends among religious believers: For background on these points, see Phillip E. Hammond, *Religion and Personal Autonomy: The Third Disestablishment in America* (Columbia, S.C.: University of South Carolina Press, 1992); Wade Clark Roof, *Spiritual Marketplace: Baby Boomers and the Remaking of American Religion* (Princeton: Princeton University Press, 1999); Robert Wuthnow, *Sharing the Journey: Support Groups and America's New Quest for Community* (New York: Free Press, 1994); Robert Wuthnow, "Mobilizing Civic Engagement: The Changing Impact of Religious Involvement," in *Civic Engagement in American Democracy*, ed. Theda Skocpol and Morris P. Fiorina (Washington, D.C.: Brookings Institution, 1999), 331–63; Kimon Howland Sargeant, *Seeker Churches: Promoting Traditional Religion in a Nontraditional Way* (New Brunswick, N.J.: Rutgers University Press, 2000); and Robert D. Putnam, *Bowling Alone: The Collapse and Revival of American Community* (New York: Simon and Schuster, 2000), 65–79.

195 "the cultural and Reagan revolutions . . .": Mark Lilla, "A Tale of Two Reactions," *New York Review of Books*, May 14, 1998, p. 7.

## VII. The Strange Idea of Moral Freedom

201 As the philosopher David Hume: David Hume, "An Inquiry Concerning Human Understanding," in *Essays: Moral, Political, Literary*, ed. T. H. Greene and T. H. Gorse (London: Longmans Green, 1875), 2:72–73.

201 Theorists of economic freedom sometimes argue: Richard Pipes, *Property and Freedom* (New York: Knopf, 1999), 65–66.

201 "submission to undesigned rules . . .": F. A. Hayek, *The Constitution of Liberty* (Chicago: University of Chicago Press, 1960), 62–63.

202 if everyone else had made the same decision: Immanuel Kant, *Grounding for the Metaphysics of Morals*, trans. James W. Ellington (Indianapolis: Hackett, 1981).

202 "who deny the Being of a God": John Locke, *A Letter Concerning Toleration* (Indianapolis: Hackett, 1983), 51.

203 It imagined a world: John T. Noonan Jr., *The Lustre of Our Country: The American Experience with Religious Freedom* (Berkeley and Los Angeles: University of California Press, 1998).

203 "it is the duty . . .": James Madison, "Memorial and Remonstrance Against Reli-

gious Assessments," in *The Complete Madison: His Basic Writings*, ed. Saul K. Padover (New York: Harper and Brothers, 1953), 300.

204 So censorious are such republican conceptions: Gordon Wood, *The Creation of the American Republic, 1776–1781* (New York: Norton, 1972), 46–90; and J. G. A. Pocock, *The Machiavellian Moment: Florentine Political Thought and the Atlantic Republican Tradition* (Princeton, N.J.: Princeton University Press, 1975), 506–52.

204 That interpretation has been more recently challenged: James T. Kloppenberg, *The Virtues of Liberalism* (New York: Oxford University Press, 1998), 59–70.

204 "duty and will . . .": Edmund Burke, "An Appeal from the New to the Old Whigs," in *The Portable Edmund Burke*, ed. Isaac Kramnick (New York: Penguin, 1999), 491.

204 ". . . the individual is sovereign": John Stuart Mill, *On Liberty* (1859; reprint, Indianapolis: Hackett, 1978), 9.

204 Still, nearly all the great liberal thinkers: This point is emphasized in Peter Berkowitz, *Virtue and the Making of Modern Liberalism* (Princeton, N.J.: Princeton University Press, 1999).

205 But if that failed: For a helpful overview of Durkheim's writings in this area, see Robert N. Bellah, ed., *Emile Durkheim on Morality and Society* (Chicago: University of Chicago Press, 1973).

206 In the early days of the republic: Linda K. Kerber, *Women of the Republic: Intellect and Ideology in Revolutionary America* (Chapel Hill, N.C.: University of North Carolina Press, 1980), 200.

206 Few were the women: Carl Degler, *At Odds: Women and the Family in America from the Revolution to the Present* (New York: Oxford University Press, 1980), 249.

206 offering advice about birth control: Constance M. Chen, *"The Sex Side of Life": Mary Ware Dennett's Pioneering Battle for Birth Control and Sex Education* (New York: New Press, 1996).

207 Victoria Woodhull: Barbara Goldsmith, *Other Powers: The Age of Suffrage, Spiritualism, and the Scandalous Victoria Woodhull* (New York: Knopf, 1998), 274.

207 "This thing we call . . .": Cited in Eric Foner, *The Story of American Freedom* (New York: Norton, 1998), 109.

207 "resting on individual sovereignty . . .": Ibid.

207 When Woodhull was arrested: Nicola Beisel, *Imperiled Innocents: Anthony Comstock and Family Reproduction in Victorian America* (Princeton, N.J.: Princeton University Press, 1997), 86.

207 the idea of "reticence": Rochelle Gurstein, *The Repeal of Reticence: A History of America's Cultural and Legal Struggles over Free Speech, Obscenity, Sexual Liberation, and Modern Art* (New York: Hill and Wang, 1996).

208 The first great statement: *Gitlow v. New York*, 268 U.S. 652 (1925).

208 decision protecting the religious freedom: *Cantwell v. Connecticut*, 310 U.S. 296 (1940).

208 "a great and mysterious force . . .": *Roth v. U.S.*, 354 U.S. 476 (1957).

209 American progressivism: Robert Crundun, *Ministers of Reform: The Progressive's Achievement in American Civilization, 1889–1920* (New York: Basic Books, 1982).

209 The New Deal: For a treatment of the question of how economically radical the New Deal was, see Alan Brinkley, *Liberalism and Its Discontents* (Cambridge, Mass.: Harvard University Press, 1998).

211 the 1970s: David Frum, *How We Got Here: The 70's, The Decade That Brought You Modern Life—for Better or Worse* (New York: Basic Books, 2000).

211 "only in the 1960s . . .": Sidney E. Ahlstrom, *A Religious History of the American People* (New Haven: Yale University Press, 1972), 8.

212 "really the necessary schemata . . .": Norman O. Brown, *Life Against Death: The Psychoanalytic Meaning of History* (Middletown, Conn.: Wesleyan University Press, 1985), 203, 260, 275.

212 "No longer employed . . .": Herbert Marcuse, *Eros and Civilization: A Philosophical Inquiry into Freud* (1955; reprint, Boston: Beacon Press, 1961), 227–28.

212 "sensuous rationality . . . moral laws": Ibid., 228.

213 "the rights and liberties . . .": Ibid., viii–ix.

213 "The Western legal fiction . . .": Norman O. Brown, *Love's Body* (1966; reprint, Berkeley and Los Angeles: University of California Press, 1990), 102.

213 "We are used to . . .": "The Port Huron Statement," in Massimo Teodori, *The New Left: A Documentary History* (Indianapolis: Bobbs Merrill, 1969), 165–66.

215 "The women's movement . . .": As quoted in Alice Nichols, *Daring to Be Bad: Radical Feminism in America, 1967–1975* (Minneapolis: University of Minnesota Press, 1989), 86. See also Sara Evans, *Personal Politics: The Roots of Women's Liberation in the Civil Rights Movement and New Left* (New York: Knopf, 1979).

215 "nonjudgmental space": As quoted in Nichols, *Daring to Be Bad*, 88.

215 "Discussion was intense . . .": Rosalyn Fraad Baxandall, "Catching the Fire," in *The Feminist Memoir Project: Voices from Women's Liberation* (New York: Three Rivers Press, 1998), 211.

216 "The foundation of Consciousness III . . .": Charles Reich, *The Greening of America* (New York: Crown, 1995), 241.

217 "Every culture . . .": Philip Rieff, *The Feeling Intellect: Selected Writings*, ed. Jonathan Imber (Chicago: University of Chicago Press, 1990), 223.

217 "One of the reasons . . .": Irving Kristol, "Pornography, Obscenity, and the Case for Censorship," in *Conservatism: An Anthology of Social and Political Thought from David Hume to the Present*, ed. Jerry Z. Muller (Princeton, N.J.: Princeton University Press, 1997), 366. See also Norman Podhoretz, *Ex-Friends* (New York: Simon and Schuster, 1999), 198–99.

217 "I believe that the radicals . . .": Kristol, "Pornography," 367–68.

218 "The affirmation . . . prior censorship": Ellen Willis, "Coming Down Again," in *No More Nice Girls: Countercultural Essays* (Middletown, Conn.; Wesleyan University Press, 1992), 261–62.

218 "This is what freedom . . .": Ellen Willis, "Introduction: Identity Crisis," in ibid., xxii.

219 "... the least successful ...": Harvey C. Mansfield, "The Legacy of the Late Six-ties," in *Reassessing the Sixties: Debating the Political and Cultural Legacy*, ed. Stephen Macedo (New York: Norton, 1997), 24.

219 "drugs, cults ...": Richard John Neuhaus, *The Naked Public Square: Religion and Democracy in America* (Grand Rapids, Mich.: Eerdmans, 1986), 140.

220 Book after book told Americans: Erich Fromm, *Escape from Freedom* (New York, Rinehart, 1941); William J. Lederer, *A Nation of Sheep* (New York, Norton, 1961); Betty Friedan, *The Feminine Mystique* (New York, Norton, 1963); Paul Goodman, *Growing Up Absurd; Problems of Youth in the Organized System* (New York, Random House, 1960); David Riesman, in collaboration with Reuel Denney and Nathan Glazer, *The Lonely Crowd: A Study of the Changing American Character* (New Haven, Yale University Press, 1950); C. Wright Mills, *The Power Elite* (New York: Oxford University Press, 1956); Margaret Mead, *Coming of Age in Samoa: A Psychological Study of Primitive Youth for Western Civilization* (New York: Blue Ribbon Books, 1928); Vance Packard, *The Hidden Persuaders* (New York: David McKay, 1957); Sloan Wilson, *The Man in the Gray Flannel Suit* (New York: Simon and Schuster, 1955); and William H. Whyte, *The Organization Man* (New York: Simon and Schuster, 1956).

220 Liberated from the very organizations: Robert D. Putnam, *Bowling Alone: The Collapse and Revival of American Community* (New York: Simon and Schuster, 2000); Juliet Schor, *The Overworked American: The Unexpected Decline of Leisure* (New York: Basic Books, 1991); Robert N. Bellah et al., *Habits of the Heart: Indi-vidualism and Commitment in American Life* (Berkeley: University of California Press, 1985); Christopher Lasch, *The Culture of Narcissism: American Life in an Age of Diminishing Expectations* (New York: Norton, 1978); Amitai Etzioni, *The Spirit of Community: Rights, Responsibilities, and the Communitarian Agenda* (New York: Crown, 1993).

221 Whether expressed in the data-driven language: For various examples of nos-talgic treatments of this issue, see Ray Oldenburg, *The Great Good Place: Cafés, Coffee Shops, Community Centers, Beauty Parlors, General Stores, Bars, Hangouts, and How They Get You Through the Day* (New York: Paragon House, 1989); James Howard Kunstler, *The Geography of Nowhere: The Rise and Decline of America's Man-Made Land-scape* (New York: Simon and Schuster, 1993); Stephen L. Carter, *Civility: Manners, Morals, and the Etiquette of Democracy* (New York: Basic Books, 1998); Stephen L. Carter, *Integrity* (New York: Basic Books, 1996); Deborah Tannen, *The Argument Culture: Moving from Debate to Dialogue* (New York: Random House, 1998); Alan Ehrenhalt, *The Lost City: Discovering the Forgotten Virtues of Community in the Chicago of the 1950s* (New York: Basic Books, 1995); and Ray Suarez, *The Old Neighborhood: What We Lost in the Great Suburban Migration, 1966–1999* (New York: Free Press, 1999).

221 "A Call to Civil Society": Institute for American Values, "A Call to Civil Society: Why Democracy Needs Moral Truths" (New York: Institute for American Val-ues, 1998).

222 "We must ask ourselves . . .": National Commission on Civic Renewal, "Final Report," at www.puaf.umd.edu.

226 *The Wall Street Journal* published a story: Lisa Miller, "Redefining God," *The Wall Street Journal*, April 21, 2000, p. W1.

227 The letter writers: *The Wall Street Journal*, May 3, 2000, A27.

228 The social critic Wendy Kaminer: Wendy Kaminer, *Sleeping with Extra-Terrestrials: The Rise of Irrationalism and Perils of Piety* (New York: Pantheon, 1999).

228 educational reformers: The school reform literature is enormous. For example, see Alexander Sutherland Neill, *Summerhill: A Radical Approach to Child Rearing* (New York: Hart, 1960); Jonathan Kozol, *Free Schools* (Boston: Houghton Mifflin, 1972); and Alfie Kohn, *No Contest: The Case Against Competition* (Boston: Houghton Mifflin, 1986).

228 In extreme versions of educational reform: Ivan Illich, *Deschooling Society* (New York: Harper and Row, 1971).

229 Critics point out that some institutions: Stephanie Gutmann, *The Kinder, Gentler Military: Can America's Gender-Neutral Fighting Force Still Win Wars?* (New York: Scribners, 2000).

231 "I am persuaded . . .": Alexis de Tocqueville, *Democracy in America*, ed. Phillips Bradley (New York: Knopf, 1966), 2:322.

# Acknowledgments

I want to thank Pam Solo at the Institute for Civil Society and to Craig Dysktra at the Lilly Endowment for their confidence in me. With the funding they generously provided, I was able to hire eight people to carry out interviews around the United States. My gratitude to all of them is deep: Julie Plaut Mahoney (Fall River), Susan Schantz (Hartford), Steven Dandaneau (Dayton), Jim Crawford (Greensboro), Bill Bryant (Tipton), Jasmine Ferrier (San Antonio), Amy Schalet (San Francisco), and Marianne Cooper (Atherton). In addition, two other graduate students played an essential role coordinating the results of the interviews and helping me with the transcription and the coding: thanks to Stephen Hodin (Boston University) for getting the project up and running and to Kim Kosman (Boston College) for her unflagging enthusiasm and energy. Elizabeth Weston and Susan Schulten offered helpful comments on Chapter VII. My administrative assistant at the Boisi Center for Religion and American Public Life at Boston College, Susan Richard, was indispensable to the completion of this book.

Alane Mason, my editor at Norton, was the book's toughest critic and I thank her for the shrewdness of her commentary. As they have done so many times, my family stood behind me throughout the whole process.

# Index